AF726092

TAX Cafe®

Taxcafe.co.uk Tax Guides

How to Save Property Tax

By Carl Bayley BSc FCA

Important Legal Notices:

Taxcafe®
TAX GUIDE – "How to Save Property Tax"

Published by:
Taxcafe UK Limited
2.4 West Bridge Mill
Kirkcaldy
KY1 1TE
United Kingdom

Email: team@taxcafe.co.uk

Thirty-second edition, January 2026

ISBN 978-1-917392-08-2

Copyright
Copyright © Carl Bayley 2002-2026. All rights reserved.

No part of this publication may be reproduced or transmitted in any form or by any means (electronically or mechanically, including photocopying, recording or storing it in any medium by electronic means) without the prior permission in writing of the publisher except in accordance with the provisions of the Copyright, Designs and Patents Act 1988 or under the terms of a licence issued by the Copyright Licensing Agency Ltd, Saffron House, 6-10 Kirby Street, London EC1N 8TS.

<u>Warning:</u> Any unauthorised reproduction or transmission of any part of this Tax Guide may result in criminal prosecution and a civil claim for damages.

Trademarks
Taxcafe® is a registered trademark of Taxcafe UK Limited. All other trademarks, names and logos in this Tax Guide may be trademarks of their respective owners.

Disclaimer
Before reading or relying on the content of this Tax Guide, please read the disclaimer.

Disclaimer

1. Please note that this publication is intended as general guidance only and does NOT constitute accountancy, tax, financial or other professional advice. The author and Taxcafe UK Limited make no representations or warranties with respect to the accuracy or completeness of the contents of this publication and cannot accept any responsibility for any liability, loss or risk, personal or otherwise, which may arise, directly or indirectly, from reliance on information contained in this publication.

2. Please note that tax legislation, the law and practices of government and regulatory authorities (e.g. HM Revenue and Customs) are constantly changing. Furthermore, your personal circumstances may vary from the general information contained in this tax guide which may not be suitable for your situation. We therefore recommend that for accountancy, tax, financial or other professional advice, you consult a suitably qualified accountant, tax specialist, independent financial adviser, or other professional adviser who will be able to provide specific advice based on your personal circumstances.

3. This guide covers UK taxation only and any references to 'tax' or 'taxation', unless the contrary is expressly stated, refer to UK taxation only. Please note that references to the 'UK' do not include the Channel Islands or the Isle of Man. Foreign tax implications are beyond the scope of this guide.

4. While in an effort to be helpful this tax guide may refer to general guidance on matters other than UK taxation, Taxcafe UK Limited and the author are not expert in these matters and do not accept any responsibility or liability for loss which may arise from reliance on such information contained in this guide.

5. Please note that Taxcafe UK Limited has relied wholly on the expertise of the author in the preparation of the content of this tax guide. The author is not an employee of Taxcafe UK Limited but has been selected by Taxcafe UK Limited using reasonable care and skill.

6. The views expressed in this publication are the author's own personal views and do not necessarily reflect the views of any organisation he may represent.

Dedication & Thanks

For the Past,
To Diana, the memory of your love warms me still. Thank you for bringing me into the light and making it all possible. To Arthur, your wise words still come back to guide me; and to my loving grandmothers, Doris and Winifred. Between you, you left me with nothing I could spend, but everything I need.

To Sarah, still with us forever in our hearts, it was truly a privilege to know you.

Also, to my beloved friends: Mac, William, Edward, Rusty, Dawson, Morgan, and the world's oldest puppy, Ollie: always in our hearts. Thank you for all those happy miles, I still miss you all.

For the Present,
To the lovely lady Linda, bless you, my princess, I'm so proud of you. Thank you for bringing the sunshine back into my life, for opening my ears, and putting the song back into my heart. I owe you more than you will ever know.

For the Future,
To James, a true twenty-first century gentleman and one of the nicest guys I have ever met. To Robert, the 'chip off the old block', who is both cursed and blessed to have inherited a lot of my character; luckily for him, there is a lot of his mother in him too! I am so very proud of you both and I can only hope I, in turn, will be able to leave each of you with everything you need.

Thanks are due to:
The Taxcafe team, past and present, especially Gordon: for their help in making these books more successful than I could ever have dreamed; my old friend and mentor, Peter Rayney, for his inspiration and for showing me tax and humour can mix; Rebecca, Paul, and David for taking me into the fold at the Tax Faculty, and for their fantastic support at our practical tax conference over many years; and Gregor for the brain-storming sessions, and giving me a chance to see theory put into practice.

And last, but far from least, thanks to Nick for giving me the push!

C.B., Roxburghshire, January 2026

About the Author

Carl Bayley is the author of a series of 'Plain English' tax guides designed specifically for the layperson and the non-specialist. His aim is to help landlords, other business owners, and families understand the taxes they face and make savings through sensible planning and by having the confidence to know what they can claim. Carl's speciality is his ability to take the weird, complex world of taxation and set it out in the kind of clear, straightforward language taxpayers can understand. As he often says, "My job is to translate 'tax' into English."

Carl enjoys his role as a tax author, as he explains, "Writing these guides gives me the opportunity to use the skills and knowledge learned over more than forty years in the tax profession for the benefit of a wider audience. The most satisfying part of my success as an author is the chance to give the average person the same standard of information as the 'big guys' at a price everyone can afford."

He takes the same approach when speaking on taxation, a role he undertakes with great enthusiasm, including his highly acclaimed annual 'Budget Breakfast' for the Institute of Chartered Accountants. In addition to being a recognised author and speaker, Carl has spoken on taxation on radio and television, including the BBC's 'It's Your Money' programme and BBC Radio 2's Jeremy Vine Show.

Beginning his career as a Chartered Accountant in 1983 with one of the 'Big 4' accountancy firms, Carl qualified as a double prize-winner then began specialising in taxation. He worked for several major international firms until beginning the new millennium by launching his own practice, through which he provided advice on a wide variety of taxation issues; especially property taxation, inheritance tax, and tax planning for small and medium-sized businesses, for twenty years, before deciding to focus exclusively on his favourite role as author and presenter.

Carl is a past Chairman of the Tax Faculty of the Institute of Chartered Accountants in England and Wales; President of ICAEW Scotland; and member of the ICAEW Board. In June 2023, he stepped down after almost twenty years on the Institute's governing Council. He co-organised the annual Practical Tax Conference from 2002 to 2019.

Aside from his tax books, Carl is an avid creative writer. His first novel, *Trinity of Souls*, was published in 2024, with *Destiny of Souls* following in 2025, and *Journey of Souls* coming out in spring 2026. When he isn't working, he takes on the equally taxing challenges of hill walking and horse riding: his Munro tally is now 106 and, while he remains a novice rider, his progress is cantering along nicely. Carl lives in the Scottish Borders, where he enjoys spending time with his partner, Linda.

Contents

Introduction **1**
Scope of this Guide **5**

Chapter 1 - What is Property Tax? **10**
1.1 Knowing Your Enemy 10
1.2 What Taxes Face a Property Investor? 10
1.3 Which Taxes Are Most Important? 11
1.4 Property Stamp Taxes 11

Chapter 2 - What Kind of Property Investor Are You? **12**
2.1 Overview 12
2.2 Does it Matter What Kind of Property You Invest In? 15
2.3 Property Businesses & Terminology 16
2.4 Do You Even Have a Business? 20
2.5 Deemed Trading 20
2.6 Tax Treatment of Property Disposals 22
2.7 Changes of Intention 26
2.8 The Boundary Between Investment and Trading 27
2.9 Joint Ownership & Property Partnerships 31
2.10 Non-Residents 34

Chapter 3 - How to Save Income Tax **36**
3.1 Introduction to Income Tax 36
3.2 Income Tax Principles 37
3.3 Income Tax Rates 39
3.4 Calculating the Income Tax Due 40
3.5 Tax Returns Under Self-Assessment 42
3.6 Making Tax Digital 45
3.7 Amending Prior Years' Tax Returns 49
3.8 Claims and Elections Deadlines 51
3.9 Registering a New Property Business 51
3.10 Marginal Tax Rates Explained 52
3.11 Accounting Methods: Accruals versus Cash 54
3.12 Claiming Tax Deductions 56
3.13 Administrative Expenses 59
3.14 Use of Home & Other Premises Costs 59
3.15 Motor Expenses 62
3.16 Travel and Subsistence 64
3.17 Training and Research 65
3.18 Other Allowable Costs 66
3.19 The Tax Relief Cap 67
3.20 Scottish Income Tax Rates 67

Chapter 4 - Saving Income Tax on a Property Business **72**
4.1 The Taxation of Rental Income 72
4.2 Tax Deductions 73
4.3 When is a Property a Rental Property? 75
4.4 Legal and Professional Fees 76

4.5 Interest Relief: What is Allowable? 78
4.6 Finance Costs 83
4.7 Interest Relief Restrictions (Section 24) 86
4.8 Repairs and Maintenance 95
4.9 Replacing Furniture, Furnishings & Equipment 103
4.10 Capital Allowances for Landlords 104
4.11 Plant and Machinery Allowances 110
4.12 Capital Allowances on Motor Vehicles 112
4.13 Further Points on Capital Allowances 114
4.14 The Structures and Buildings Allowance 116
4.15 Rent Arrears 120
4.16 Rent-a-Room Relief 123
4.17 The Property Income Allowance 124
4.18 Rental Losses on UK Property 126
4.19 Overseas Lettings 128
4.20 Non-Commercial Lettings 129
4.21 Other Receipts from Property 130
4.22 The Cash Basis for Landlords 131
4.23 Capital Expenditure Under the Cash Basis 139

Chapter 5 - How to Save Capital Gains Tax 143
5.1 The Importance of Capital Gains Tax 143
5.2 Capital Gains Tax Rates 144
5.3 What is a Capital Gain? 146
5.4 When Does a Capital Gain Arise? 146
5.5 Spouses and Civil Partners 147
5.6 The Amount of the Gain 147
5.7 Base Cost 150
5.8 Capital Gains Tax Reliefs 153
5.9 Private Residence Relief (PRR) 154
5.10 Private Letting Relief (PLR) 155
5.11 Gardens, Grounds, and Outbuildings 156
5.12 Delays in Occupying a New Home 157
5.13 What is a Residence? 158
5.14 Private Residence Restrictions 160
5.15 Second Homes 161
5.16 Homes Abroad 165
5.17 Job-Related Accommodation 167
5.18 What if Part of Your Home is Not Private? 168
5.19 The Annual Exemption 170
5.20 When is Capital Gains Tax Payable? 170
5.21 What Must I Report to HMRC and When? 172
5.22 Jointly Held Property 175
5.23 Capital Losses 175

Chapter 6 – How to Save Stamp Taxes 177
6.1 Stamp Duty Land Tax (England and Northern Ireland) 177
6.2 Residential Property 177
6.3 Higher Charges on Residential Property 179
6.4 The Non-Resident Surcharge 182
6.5 Non-Residential Property 182

6.6	Market Value and Mortgages	184
6.7	Multiple Purchases	184
6.8	Leases	186
6.9	Fixtures and Fittings	187
6.10	Land and Buildings Transaction Tax (Scotland)	187
6.11	Additional Dwelling Supplement (Scotland)	188
6.12	Key Differences (Scotland)	190
6.13	Land Transaction Tax (Wales)	192
Chapter 7 – How to Save VAT and Other Property Taxes		**194**
7.1	VAT Principles	194
7.2	VAT on Residential Property	195
7.3	VAT on Commercial Property	197
7.4	Interaction between VAT and Other Taxes	198
7.5	National Insurance for Property Investors	199
7.6	Visitor Levy	200
7.7	Mansion Tax	200
Chapter 8 – Other Property-Based Businesses		**202**
8.1	Trading Income	202
8.2	Property-Based Trades	204
8.3	Residential Mobile Home Parks	205
8.4	Casual Income	206
Chapter 9 - Advanced Tax Planning		**208**
9.1	Introduction to Tax Planning	208
9.2	The Benefits of Joint Ownership	208
9.3	Using Your Spouse to Save Capital Gains Tax	210
9.4	Saving More Tax with Transfers to Spouses	211
9.5	What if You Are Already Joint Owners?	215
9.6	Have Your Cake and Eat It	216
9.7	Marriage and Civil Partnerships	217
9.8	Separation and Divorce	218
9.9	Planning with Other Joint Owners	219
9.10	Inherited Property	220
9.11	Till Death Do Us Part	222
9.12	Securing Private Residence Relief	222
9.13	General Elections	223
9.14	Developing Your Home	224
9.15	Something in the Garden	228
9.16	Getting a Slice of the Action	230
9.17	Student Loans	231
9.18	Properties Held in Trust	232
9.19	Tax-Free Property Transfers	235
9.20	Using a Trust to Get Extra Private Residence Relief	236
9.21	Temporary Periods of Absence	237
9.22	Planning with Absence Periods	239
9.23	Furnished Holiday Lets: The Aftermath	240
9.24	Business Asset Disposal Relief	246
9.25	Business Premises Owners	248
9.26	Rollover Relief	250

9.27 Part Disposals 252
9.28 Lease Premiums 253
9.29 The Benefits and Pitfalls of Re-Mortgaging 255
9.30 Using Your Basic Rate Band to Save CGT 256
9.31 Avoiding the Child Benefit Charge 258
9.32 Getting Extra Tax Relief for Rent Arrears 259
9.33 Partnership Problems and Opportunities 261
9.34 Limited Liability Partnerships 265
9.35 Emigrating to Save Capital Gains Tax 265
9.36 New Arrivals 267

Appendices 269

Introduction

Welcome to this thirty-second edition of *How to Save Property Tax*, fully updated for all the changes in property taxation that have taken place since our last edition, including the November 2025 Budget and other announcements up to the date of publication.

Thirty-two editions on, it is astonishing to think it is over twenty years since we first published this guide, and it is immensely satisfying to see the demand for good quality information on property taxation, coupled with sensible, practical, guidance on simple tax saving measures, continues unabated.

People in the UK have invested in property for centuries, but recent decades have seen property investment become a hugely important area of personal financial planning. The early years of this century, in particular, saw phenomenal growth in the property sector, not just in the amount of property investment activity, but also in the sheer numbers of people entering the property investment market. While the big flotations of the 1980s acted to spread investment in stocks and shares into all sectors of society, the early years of this century witnessed a similar spreading of property investment.

'Property investment' is a very wide term. At its simplest, buying your own home is usually most people's first property investment. Even this is not free from tax, as there will generally be Stamp Duty Land Tax (or its Scottish/Welsh equivalents) on the purchase and, of course, Council Tax to pay thereafter. Furthermore, any use of the property as anything other than your only or main private residence may have Income Tax and/or Capital Gains Tax consequences (all of which are covered in this guide).

Apart from buying their own home, many people go on to make further investments in property, such as:

- Developing or improving their home
- Buying a second home
- Buying business premises
- Investing in property as a long-term asset

We will look at all these types of investment, their tax consequences, and how to plan for them, in this guide.

But, while some property investments are held for other reasons, most properties apart from the investor's home (or homes) are rented out, with the investor thus becoming a landlord. And this, of course, is the main focus of this guide.

Some investors diversify beyond property letting, into other activities, such as renovation, conversion, and development. Others find different ways to invest in property, such as investing abroad, or clubbing together to invest through joint ventures, syndicates, or special purpose vehicles (SPVs). Beyond these, there also lie the fields of property trading and management.

All these different activities are subject to different tax regimes, and establishing the correct classification for each property investment can sometimes be difficult. One of my first tasks in this guide is therefore to help you understand how your property investments will be treated for tax purposes, and this is something we will consider in depth.

There are many reasons for becoming a property investor. Some fall into it by accident, finding themselves with a second property through marriage, inheritance, or other changes in personal circumstances. Others move into the property sector quite deliberately, seeing it as a safe haven providing long-term security and perhaps an income in retirement. Still others see the property market as a means to generate a second income during their working life.

Many landlords choose to enter the property business as a professional career. In fact, given the ever-increasing volume of rules and regulations the private rented sector has to contend with, a professional approach to property investment has become essential: whatever your reasons for entering the property market in the first place. This is no bad thing: a professional approach has always been desirable. Those who are prepared to devote substantial time and resources to their business are generally rewarded with better results, including those who plan their tax affairs carefully.

The last twenty years have seen enormous changes in the property market. The 2008/9 banking crisis and its aftermath challenged previously held views on the certainty of capital growth and the philosophy of 'you can't lose'. But, while the economic difficulties instigated by the crisis were disastrous for some, they created opportunities for others. The lower interest rates enjoyed by investors for many years afterwards brought healthy rental profits to many. Sadly, that 'golden age' has drawn to a close, as interest rates have risen again and, despite falling from their peak, seem likely to remain considerably higher than many investors had come to expect.

Each of us must form our own view of what the future is likely to hold. In the end, only time will tell but, whatever happens, periods of economic difficulty can be seen as part of an evolutionary process: the fittest property businesses weather the storm to survive as part of a stronger property sector.

Nonetheless, while the sector may grow stronger in the long term, there seems little doubt it will also be considerably leaner, with far fewer small or 'accidental' landlords than we have seen in the past. In fact, some fear the sector currently faces an extinction level event, meaning the degree to which it shrinks could be nothing less than catastrophic.

This is largely because economic uncertainty has, for many years, been compounded by a prolonged attack from Governments that appear hell-bent on the destruction of the private rented sector. In the last decade, we've seen the diabolical 'Section 24' restrictions on residential landlords' interest relief, the abolition of the furnished holiday letting regime, and outrageous hikes in Stamp Duty Land Tax and its devolved equivalents.

Worse still, the private rented sector in England is currently bracing itself for the impact of the Renters' Rights Act: with the main provisions coming into force from 1st May 2026.

And now, on top of all this, in the November 2025 Budget, we get the news that Income Tax rates on rental income will be increased from April 2027: no doubt, it will be the last straw for many landlords. Quite where the Government expects to house all the tenants losing their homes as a result of the prolonged attack on the private rented sector is a mystery to me!

But, while there is no doubt these are hard times for many in the private rented sector, demand for rental property continues to far outstrip supply. This trend will only increase, and accelerate, in the years ahead, as many landlords head for the exit. As a result, most commentators expect to see rents continuing to spiral upwards, meaning that, while these are hard times for some, they are lucrative times for others.

So, despite the difficulties it faces, I believe the private rented sector is here to stay. Naturally, it will have its ups and downs, as any business sector does; and it will need to grow stronger and leaner in the years ahead. But the idea of property investment as a career, or a pension plan, is now so well entrenched, it is impossible to imagine it ever disappearing.

Changes in both the economy and in tax legislation have always had a dramatic impact on the tax planning landscape, and will continue to do so. Tax and tax planning are a vital part of every business's strategy. Property businesses are no exception!

With the Government soon to be taking between 42% and 63% of many landlords' profits, PLUS what is effectively an additional penalty of between 20% and 41% on their mortgage interest; as well as 24% of their capital gains (a large proportion of which are usually down to inflation); and an extra 5% charge on their purchases; planning your tax affairs carefully is one of the best ways to ensure *your* property business is fit and lean enough to survive.

So, whatever your reasons for entering the property investment market, whatever type of property business you have, and whether you decide you've had enough, or want to enjoy your share of the opportunities that lie ahead, my aim in this guide is to give you a better understanding of how the UK tax system affects you, and show you how to minimise or eliminate your potential tax liabilities. In other words, as it says on the cover: How to Save Property Tax!

In the first two chapters, I will set the scene by looking at the different taxes you will meet as a property investor and how they apply to various types of property investments and property businesses.

Chapter 3 examines how annual income and profits from all types of property investments and businesses are dealt with under the UK tax system. In Chapter 4, I then focus on landlords, property letting businesses, and the taxation of rental and other income derived from property investment.

These chapters include a detailed examination of the deductions, reliefs, and allowances available to every type of property business.

In Chapter 5, we move onto Capital Gains Tax, and explore the rules, the tax rates, the reliefs and allowances available, and the reporting and payment obligations relating to this vitally important tax for all landlords, property investors, and second home owners.

Chapter 6 covers Stamp Duty Land Tax and its devolved equivalents in Scotland and Wales: information vital to anyone purchasing property anywhere in the UK. Chapter 7 then looks at VAT, critically important to anyone renting out commercial property, holiday accommodation, or providing significant additional services to tenants; as well as those carrying out renovations and conversions, and many others with property-based businesses. This chapter also covers other taxes that may affect property investors.

In Chapter 8, we look at the tax treatment of some other property-based businesses, each with their own quirks and nuances to be aware of.

Throughout the first eight chapters, there is an emphasis on simple, practical steps to minimise your tax burden, and to make meeting your tax obligations easier: so, there is plenty of helpful tax planning guidance to get your teeth into. However, in Chapter 9, we step it up a notch, by looking at some more specialised areas, and pulling everything together with more advanced tax planning strategies that could help reduce your tax burden even further.

Along the way, you'll find plenty of **'Tax Tips'** to help you minimise or delay your bills; **'Wealth Warnings'** to keep you away from treacherous pitfalls; and **'Practical Pointers'** to make your obligations as painless as possible.

I believe this guide is comprehensive enough to meet the needs of almost every individual property investor based in the UK and I hope, with its help, you will be able to enjoy a much larger proportion of the fruits of your endeavours.

Finally, I would like to thank you for buying this guide, and wish you every success with your property investments.

Scope of this Guide

This guide covers the current UK tax system applying to property, together with as much as we know, or can reasonably assume, about future tax changes. My aim is to help you deal with your current obligations; benefit as much as you can from the available deductions, reliefs, and allowances; and plan for the future. I will strive to cover as much as possible of the UK tax implications of investing in property personally, jointly with one or more other individuals, through a traditional partnership, a limited liability partnership, or via a trust.

The tax-planning strategies outlined in this guide represent a reasonably comprehensive catalogue of the main techniques available to individual property investors subject to UK property tax. Individuals with second homes, or who have had second homes in the past, will also benefit, as will those who wish to develop their home.

Although many of the principles applying to individuals apply equally to companies, or other corporate vehicles, investing in property, these entities are beyond the scope of this guide. The tax position of the owners of such entities is also beyond the scope of this guide. Detailed guidance on the UK taxation of property companies, and on the UK tax implications for individuals investing in property via a company, is contained in the Taxcafe guide *Using a Property Company to Save Tax.*

Apart from a brief summary, I will not be covering professional property developers, or property management businesses, in this guide. These are trading activities, subject to different tax regimes. Where carried out by an individual or a partnership, these activities are covered in the Taxcafe guide *Small Business Tax Saving Tactics*; for companies carrying out these activities, see either *Putting it Through the Company* or *Using a Property Company to Save Tax.*

I will, however, cover what one might call 'incidental' property development activities carried out by homeowners, landlords, and other property investors who are not professional property developers. I will also cover property trading.

While this guide primarily focuses on the forthcoming, 2026/27 tax year and the future, I will also cover the current, 2025/26 tax year, and will continue to include rules forming the basis for the preparation of tax returns for 2024/25. Rules applying in earlier years will only be included where they continue to be relevant. For more information on earlier years, see previous editions of this guide.

As far as tax *rates* are concerned, unless stated or implied to the contrary, the rates quoted throughout this guide are those applying for the tax year 2026/27: although I will, of course, also be covering the increase in Income Tax rates on property income from 2027/28 onwards.

This guide covers the four types of individual property investor who are subject to UK property tax:

(i) UK residents investing in UK property
(ii) UK residents investing in overseas property
(iii) UK residents investing in both UK and overseas property
(iv) Non-UK residents investing in UK property

For tax purposes, the UK does not include the Channel Islands or the Isle of Man, but comprises England, Scotland, Wales, and Northern Ireland.

The UK tax position for non-UK resident individuals investing in UK property is summarised in Section 2.10. Former non-UK residents, resident in the UK for no more than four UK tax years, are covered in Section 9.36.

Prior to 2025/26, those who were UK resident but non-UK domiciled were able to enjoy savings on income or gains derived from overseas property, but not remitted to the UK. Some potential savings may currently still be available under transitional rules. If you or your parents were born abroad, there is a strong possibility you may be non-UK domiciled. For more information on the concept of domicile, see the Taxcafe guide *How to Save Inheritance Tax*.

While the rest of this guide remains relevant to current or former non-UK resident, or non-UK domiciled, individuals, they may be able to employ more specialised tax-planning techniques not included in this guide. Unless stated to the contrary, it is assumed throughout this guide that individuals are UK resident and domiciled, and have been UK resident for more than four UK tax years.

Foreign tax implications are beyond the scope of this guide. Both UK residents investing in property overseas, and non-UK residents investing in UK property, may also face foreign tax on their property income and capital gains. Each country has its own tax system, and income or gains that are exempt in the UK may nevertheless still be liable to tax elsewhere. In some cases, citizens of another country who are resident in the UK for tax purposes may still have obligations and liabilities under their own country's tax system. The USA, for example, imposes this type of obligation on its expatriate citizens.

It is only when talking about taxpayers who are both UK residents and UK citizens, who are investing exclusively in UK property, and who are neither residents nor citizens of any other country, that we can be certain no other country has any right to tax income or gains.

Different Income Tax rates apply to Scottish taxpayers. We will look at these in Section 3.20. Throughout the rest of the guide, unless stated to the contrary, I will refer only to Income Tax rates applying to non-Scottish taxpayers. It is worth noting, however, it is only the tax *rates* that are different for Scottish taxpayers, and all other principles discussed throughout the guide remain equally applicable. At present, Welsh taxpayers pay the same overall rates of Income Tax as English or Northern Irish taxpayers, but these could change in the future.

To keep things simple, I will ignore student loan repayments (unless stated to the contrary). Although these are generally collected through the tax system, they are not, strictly speaking, a tax.

Property within designated Enterprise Zones, Freeports, or Investment Zones, may enjoy additional tax reliefs beyond the scope of this guide.

Elements of the Capital Gains Tax regime that are not relevant to property are ignored in this guide: these include investor's relief and tax on carried interest.

This guide incorporates all relevant Government proposals announced prior to the date of publication. Some proposals are not yet law and may undergo alteration before being formally enacted. It is also not unknown for Government proposals to be abandoned altogether (as we saw during Liz Truss's brief premiership in 2022).

This guide focusses purely on property taxation. Naturally, however, there are many legal issues surrounding property ownership, development, rental, change of use, sales, and other transactions involving property. The law governing property in Scotland, Wales, or Northern Ireland is also different to the law in England. As far as residential rental property in England is concerned, significant changes will arise when the provisions of the Renters' Rights Act come into force (mainly on 1st May 2026). While every effort has been made to ensure tax planning measures in this guide, or actions included within the examples, can be carried out in a manner compliant with all relevant legal requirements, such matters are beyond the scope of this guide. Dealing with tax is complicated enough!

Lastly, the reader must bear in mind the general nature of this guide. Individual circumstances vary and the tax implications of an individual's actions will vary with them.

For these reasons, it is always vital to get relevant local, professional advice regarding both tax and legal issues before undertaking any tax planning or other actions related to property. The author and Taxcafe UK Ltd cannot accept any responsibility for any loss that may arise as a consequence of any action taken, or any decision to refrain from action taken, as a result of reading this guide.

A Word about the Examples

This guide is illustrated throughout by many examples. Unless specifically stated to the contrary, it is assumed all persons are UK resident and domiciled for tax purposes, have been UK resident for at least four UK tax years, and are **not**:

i) Subject to the Child Benefit Charge (see Section 3.3)
ii) Subject to the Winter Fuel Charge (see Section 3.3)
iii) Claiming the marriage allowance (see Appendix A)
iv) Scottish taxpayers (see Section 3.20)
v) Using the cash basis of accounting (see further below)

In preparing the examples, I have assumed the UK tax regime will remain unchanged in the future, except to the extent of any formal Government announcements already made at the time of publication. Hence, unless stated to the contrary, the 2027/28 tax rates and allowances set out in Appendix A are used in respect of all years from 2027/28 onwards. However, if there is one thing I can predict with any certainty, it is the fact change *will* occur. The reader should bear this in mind when reviewing the results of examples in this guide.

All persons described in the examples are entirely fictional characters created specifically for the purposes of this guide. Any similarities to actual persons, living or dead, or to fictional characters created by any other author, are entirely coincidental.

For the sake of illustration, I have not checked whether dates in examples fall at the weekend or on a bank holiday. In reality, it will not be possible to enter into some transactions on a Saturday, Sunday, or bank holiday. Readers should take this into account when planning their affairs. Easter can be a particular problem, as it will often fall near 5th April!

On the subject of dates, it's worth noting that 2028 will be a leap year, making the 2027/28 tax year a 'leap tax year' of 366 days' duration. This will have a minor effect on a few calculations in the examples.

Accruals versus Cash

Historically, all accounts had to be prepared under the 'accruals basis' for UK tax purposes (this term is explained in Section 3.11). The position has changed in recent years, however, with the introduction of two alternative accounting methods using a 'cash basis': one for landlords (Section 4.22), and one for traders (see the Taxcafe guide *Small Business Tax Saving Tactics*). While we will examine the cash basis for landlords in detail, throughout the rest of this guide, it is assumed, unless stated to the contrary, that property investors continue to account for their income using traditional accruals basis accounting. My reasoning for this approach is explained in Section 3.11.

Abbreviations and Terminology

We don't like using jargon at Taxcafe: we want to keep our guides as simple as possible. However, to save some space, I have allowed myself a few abbreviations. I think they are fairly obvious and should not cause any confusion. Some, like UK or VAT, are in common usage. I will explain what the others mean the first time I use them, and they are set out again in Appendix C for ease of reference.

Large amounts of £1,000,000 or more are abbreviated by use of the letter 'm'. For example, £2,500,000 is written as '£2.5m'.

For the purposes of this guide, a 'spouse' includes a civil partner, but only includes spouses who are legally married (or legally registered civil partners). Similarly, a 'married couple' refers only to legally married couples or registered civil partners. Unmarried couples are subject to different rules for tax purposes.

While civil partners can, of course, also be business partners (as can any spouses), these are entirely different things.

Unless expressly stated to the contrary, all references to partnerships in this guide mean business partnerships and include limited liability partnerships (LLPs). Where it is necessary to distinguish LLPs from other business partnerships, the term 'traditional partnership' will be used to describe those other partnerships.

The term 'partner' may mean a business partner or an unmarried life partner, depending on the context. However, where there is any risk of confusion, I will use the more specific term 'business partner' to clarify the position. Whether this specific term is used or not, business partners include members of an LLP unless expressly stated to the contrary.

When I refer to a 'disposal' of property, this includes property sales. However, disposal is a broader term, as it also includes gifts or transfers to another individual, or to an entity such as a trust or company: which generally have the same tax consequences as a sale at market value (but see further in Section 5.7).

Any references to a furnished holiday let (FHL) in this guide, means a property that qualified under the special tax regime explained in Section 9.23. This is generally only relevant for tax years up to 2024/25.

For the avoidance of doubt: in this guide, the term 'business owner' includes landlords (but naturally includes other business owners too). References to 'trades' or 'trading businesses' include professions, such as doctors, lawyers, accountants, etc, but do not include landlords.

Chapter 1

What is Property Tax?

1.1 KNOWING YOUR ENEMY

You cannot begin to consider how to save property tax until you understand what property tax is. You must know your enemy in order to combat it effectively.

There is no single 'property tax' but rather a whole range of taxes that apply to property. There's no point saving one only to find yourself paying even more of another!

Horror stories of this nature happen all too frequently, such as the taxpayer who managed to avoid 1% Stamp Duty on part of his new house, only to find he was stuck with a 17.5% VAT bill instead. Worse still was the taxpayer who undertook some Inheritance Tax (IHT) planning on the advice of his lawyer only to find himself with a £20,000 Capital Gains Tax (CGT) bill, with no sale proceeds from which to pay it. If only they'd spoken to a *real* tax expert first!

In this introductory chapter we will therefore take a brief look at the taxes that affect the property investor and give some consideration to the relative importance of each. Later, when we begin to consider tax-planning strategies, it is vital to bear in mind it is the overall outcome that matters, not simply saving or deferring any single tax. In fact, I would go even further ...

> ***Bayley's Law***
> *The truly wise investor does not seek merely to minimise the amount of tax payable, but rather to maximise the amount of wealth remaining after all taxes have been accounted for.*

If this seems like no more than plain common sense to you, then all well and good. In practice, I am amazed how often people lose sight of this simple fact and, in trying to save tax at any price, actually end up making themselves worse off!

1.2 WHAT TAXES FACE A PROPERTY INVESTOR?

There seem to be an ever-growing number of UK taxes specific to property. Those that can (or will soon) apply to individuals include: Council Tax (residential property); Business Rates (commercial property); Stamp Duty Land Tax (SDLT) and its devolved equivalents (Section 1.4); the so-called 'Mansion Tax' (Section 7.7); and the proposed Visitor Levy (Section 7.6).

However, as much as these taxes can be a painful thorn in the side, they are rarely as important as some of the other taxes that apply. Property investment is exposed to a huge range of UK taxes. Tax is levied when property is purchased (SDLT), rented out (Income Tax), and sold (CGT); even when it is given away (CGT again).

Property investors have to pay tax when they buy goods or services (VAT), when they make their investments through a company (Corporation Tax), and even when they die (IHT).

Those who are classed as property traders pay Income Tax and National Insurance (NI) on profits from property sales. Investors carrying out property development activities may sometimes have to account for tax under the Construction Industry Scheme (CIS) when using sub-contractors for even the most routine building work.

Most property investors will be paying Insurance Premium Tax, and those who employ help will have PAYE and employer's NI to pay too. Many will pay Road Tax (Vehicle Excise Duty) and fuel duty as they travel on business. They may even be paying Air Passenger Duty if their business takes them far. Faced with this horrifying list, investors might be excused for turning to drink: only to find themselves paying yet more tax!

1.3 WHICH TAXES ARE MOST IMPORTANT?

For most individual property investors, two taxes comprise the majority of the tax burden they will face during their lifetime. These are Income Tax and CGT, and they are covered in detail in Chapters 3 to 5. The way these taxes apply to *your* property investments depends on what type of property investor you are.

For tax purposes, there are a number of different categories into which a property investment, or property business, might fall, and it is crucial to understand how your investments or business will be classified before you can plan your tax affairs. I will return to this question in Chapter 2.

For some classes of investor, NI will form what is effectively an additional layer of Income Tax, and we will examine this extra tax burden in Section 8.1. Other taxes that may also have a significant impact include VAT and the various forms of Stamp Duty. These are covered in Chapters 6 and 7.

For those investors using a company, Corporation Tax will become of equal, if not greater, importance to the two main taxes and IHT is likely to be a major concern for most property investors. These two important taxes are covered in the Taxcafe guides *Using a Property Company to Save Tax* and *How to Save Inheritance Tax*.

1.4 PROPERTY STAMP TAXES

There are different forms of Stamp Duty on purchases and transfers of UK property, depending on which nation the property is located in:

England:	Stamp Duty Land Tax
Scotland:	Land and Buildings Transaction Tax
Wales:	Land Transaction Tax
Northern Ireland:	Stamp Duty Land Tax

The rules are broadly similar and explained in Chapter 6. For the sake of simplicity, I will refer only to Stamp Duty Land Tax, or SDLT, throughout this guide, but readers should bear in mind different taxes apply in Scotland or Wales.

Chapter 2

What Kind of Property Investor Are You?

2.1 OVERVIEW

Before we begin to look in detail at how property investments are taxed in the UK, we should first pause to consider whether your activities amount to a business and, if so, what type of business it is. This is an essential step, as the tax treatment of property, or income derived from property, will vary according to the type of business or investment activities involved.

However, while it is an essential step, for most people the conclusion will be pretty clear and our pause will be a brief one.

One tax that always applies to any kind of property investment is IHT: and that's equally true whether I mention it or not. For UK property, the same can be said for SDLT (or its devolved equivalents).

Homeowners
If you buy a property purely for use as your own home, occupy it as your only or main private residence, and never use it for anything else, the only taxes you will generally need to be concerned with are SDLT (Chapter 6), Council Tax, and, ultimately, IHT.

This may change if you develop or improve the property, and we will look at this in Sections 9.14 to 9.16. For high value properties, worth over £2m, you will also be subject to the Mansion Tax (Section 7.7).

If you buy a second, or subsequent, home, you will be exposed to CGT. You may also be exposed to CGT if you use any of your home for other purposes, or if your home has extensive gardens or grounds. These issues are covered in Chapter 5.

Renting out your home will expose you to both Income Tax and CGT, although there are some important reliefs available in these circumstances, as we will see in Chapters 4 and 5.

Your Own Business Premises
Buying your own business premises as a sole trader does not make you a landlord. You will, however, be subject to SDLT (Chapter 6), Business Rates, CGT (Chapter 5), and, ultimately, IHT.

If you personally buy business premises for use by your own company, or a partnership in which you are a partner, you effectively become a landlord. Your position in these circumstances is covered in Section 9.25. Some additional points for partnerships are included in Section 9.33.

Landlords
If you buy properties purely for the purpose of renting them out, then lease them to tenants, and ultimately sell them, you are a landlord with a property investment business, and will be subject to Income Tax on your rental profits (Chapter 4) and CGT on your property sales (Chapter 5).

You will generally pay higher rates of SDLT (or its devolved equivalents) on residential property purchases (Chapter 6).

If you rent out commercial property, you will generally benefit by registering for and charging VAT (Chapter 7).

If you rent out residential property as furnished holiday accommodation, or other short lettings, you may be subject to the Visitor Levy (Section 7.6). You may also have to register for VAT. In some cases, you may benefit by registering for VAT voluntarily.

If you own high value residential property worth over £2m, you will be subject to the Mansion Tax (Section 7.7).

Developing, converting, or improving your rental properties may alter your position, and that is something we will be looking at over the rest of this chapter. However, it will never alter the Income Tax treatment of your rental income.

Property Investors with No Business
Property investment, in itself, is not always classed as a business. If you do not have a business, you cannot have a trade, and hence you cannot be classed as either a property trader or a property developer.

We will look at the factors that determine whether you have a business in Section 2.4. Not having a business does not usually mean your property investments are tax free, and will never change the way rental income is taxed, but it will alter how property disposals are taxed, as we will see in Section 2.6.

Property Traders
If you buy properties purely, or mainly, for the purpose of realising a profit on their sale, and you carry on this activity professionally, as a business (see Section 2.4), you are a property trader. This means the profits on your property sales will be subject to both Income Tax and NI, and not CGT. We will take a closer look at the tax treatment of property traders in Section 8.1. See also below regarding incidental rental income.

Property Developers
Buying properties with the sole or main intention of developing, converting, or renovating them, in order to make a profit on their sale, is property development.

If carried on as a business (see Section 2.4), this is a trading activity, subject to both Income Tax and NI. Even the most minor of conversion or renovation projects can lead to an investor being treated as a property developer if the property concerned was clearly acquired with the sole or main intention of realising a profit on its sale and the activity is carried on as a business.

The tax treatment of trading businesses is covered briefly in Section 8.1, but far more extensively in the Taxcafe guide *Small Business Tax Saving Tactics*. Beyond the brief summary in Section 8.1, professional property developers are not covered in this guide, but we will be looking at incidental development activities in both this chapter and Sections 9.14 to 9.16. See also below regarding incidental rental income.

Mixed Activities and Mixed or Unclear Intentions

So far in this section, we've covered all the main categories of property investor and summarised their tax treatment. Most people will fall into one of those categories, and their tax treatment will therefore be clear.

But, for some, the position will be less clear, and the way in which they are taxed will vary according to a number of factors that we will examine in this chapter.

None of this affects the tax on rental income, as this is always taxed in the same way, regardless of how casual, small, or incidental it may be. So, whether you're a full-time landlord with a large portfolio of rental properties, or a middle-aged couple renting out your home for a fortnight on Airbnb while you're away, the principles explained in Chapter 4 apply equally to your rental income (although the property income allowance covered in Section 4.17 may be enough to exempt your income in the latter case).

This fixed treatment for rental income also extends to the element of any lease premium classed as income in the hands of the lessor (Section 9.28).

It is the treatment of other sums derived from property that will vary according to whether you have a business and, if so, what type: principally, of course, the gain made on disposal of the property.

This issue can be hugely important. Let's say an individual who already has taxable income between £50,270 and £100,000, but no other capital gains in the same tax year, makes a £100,000 gain on disposal of a property in 2026/27. There are several possible outcomes:

i) If the property qualifies as their main residence throughout their ownership (see Chapter 5), there will be no tax to pay
ii) If the property is fully eligible for business asset disposal relief (Section 9.24), they will have CGT of £17,460 to pay
iii) If neither (i) nor (ii) apply, but their gain is not deemed to be trading income, they will have CGT of £23,280 to pay
iv) If their gain is classed as deemed trading income (see Section 2.5), they will have Income Tax of between £46,285 and £48,771 to pay
v) If their gain is classed as a trading profit, it will generally be subject to both Income Tax and NI, with a combined tax bill somewhere between £48,285 and £52,279.
vi) Other outcomes are possible where the gain is partly, but not wholly, eligible for private residence relief (Section 5.9) or business asset disposal relief.

With overall effective tax rates ranging from 0% to 52.3%, we can see that, whenever the position is not entirely clear-cut, it is vital to establish whether the investor has a business and, if so, what type. And that's what we're going to look at in Sections 2.3 to 2.8. But first, let's look at another important question.

2.2 DOES IT MATTER WHAT KIND OF PROPERTY YOU INVEST IN?

I can remember a time, not so long ago, when the answer to this question would have been, "No." But recent years have seen a growing trend for residential property to be treated less favourably (or should I say more harshly).

Residential property, naturally, means people's homes, and covers flats, houses, apartments, bungalows, cottages, etc. Also counted in this category are second homes and self-catering holiday accommodation.

Commercial, or non-residential, property covers a wide range of properties, including shops, offices, restaurants, pubs, doctors', dentists' and vets' surgeries, hotels, sports centres, warehouses, factories, workshops, garages, schools, hospitals, prisons... anything that isn't residential, basically.

It is important here to distinguish between owning commercial property and renting it out to other businesses: which is generally an investment activity; and actually occupying and using the commercial property yourself: which is generally a trade.

Example: *Basil owns a string of hotels that he does not run himself, but rents to a number of other businesses. Basil is therefore a landlord. He is taxed on his rental income as outlined in Chapter 4 (but is not subject to the restriction on interest relief in Section 4.7). Capital gains on a sale or transfer of his properties will be subject to CGT and will not be eligible for business asset disposal relief (Section 9.24), holdover relief (see Section 5.7), or rollover relief (Section 9.26).*

Sybil also owns a string of hotels, but she runs them herself (with the help of a few employees). She therefore has a hotel trade, which is taxed as outlined in Section 8.2.

Polly owns a string of hotels that she rents to her company, Manuel Ltd, which operates a hotel trade. Polly is also a landlord, but is taxed slightly differently to Basil. We will look at the position for people like Polly in Section 9.25.

Developing, or trading in, commercial property is also a trade (if carried on as a business: see Section 2.4), but a very different one to occupying and using that property in your own trade. Naturally, it follows the tax treatment of such trades is also different.

How Does This Affect What Type of Business You Have?

Assuming you are not actually occupying and operating a trade from your properties, the type of property in which you invest has no bearing on whether you have a business, or what type of business it is. The answers to these questions depend purely on the way you behave as an investor and not on the nature of the properties you own.

The guidelines set out in the remainder of this chapter therefore apply equally to both residential and commercial property investors, *except*, of course, to the extent we are considering issues related to residing in the property yourself: which can only apply to residential property. For this reason, it is more likely that investing in commercial property will amount to some sort of business, albeit the principles that determine what type of business remain unchanged.

Naturally, there are many other important differences between the tax treatment of residential property and commercial property and, indeed, in the tax treatment of different types of residential and commercial property. We will examine these differences as we progress through the following chapters. Note also it is quite possible to have both commercial and residential property within the same business.

2.3 PROPERTY BUSINESSES & TERMINOLOGY

So far, we have seen that a property investor may be:

i) Simply a homeowner with no business at all
ii) A pure investor who does not have a business
iii) A landlord with a property letting business
iv) A property developer
v) A property trader
vi) A sole trader investing in their own business premises
vii) A company owner who holds their company's business premises
viii) A business partner who holds the partnership's business premises

Regardless of what category you fall into, any rental income you receive becomes what is officially termed 'property income' and is taxed as set out in Chapter 4.

Landlords (category (iii)) are, of course, the main focus of this guide. They have what is officially termed a 'UK property business' or, in the case of overseas property, an 'overseas property business'. This type of business is also often called a 'property letting business' or a 'property investment business'. Whatever term is used, we are talking about landlords.

Confusingly, it is possible to have a property investment business, or to simply have property investments (category (ii)). Generally, it is letting out the property that turns it into a business, but we'll take a closer look at this distinction in Sections 2.4 and 2.6.

In addition to the categories listed above, there are many other property-based businesses that involve the provision of services far beyond what the normal property investor would provide. We will look at the tax treatment of these businesses in Chapter 8.

Is there any advantage in having a property investment business rather than a property development or property trading business?
Yes, there is often quite an advantage for an individual property investor (or partnership) in having a property investment business instead of one of the other types of business classified as trades for tax purposes.

The main reason for this is the fact property disposals are treated as capital gains, taxed under the CGT regime, and not income taxed under the Income Tax regime. This, in turn, enables the investor to benefit from CGT rates of just 24% at most, as well as providing the opportunity to utilise the many different CGT reliefs available (Chapter 5).

By contrast, the effective combined Income Tax and NI rates on trading profits range from 26% to 62% (even more in some cases), meaning we can sometimes see differences of 38% or more between the tax applying to a capital gain and the tax applying to a trading profit. The tax on a property disposal could be ***over twice as much*** for a property developer or property trader as for a landlord, second home owner, or other property investor.

However, it is always important to remember it is the way you carry on your business and handle your property investments that determines the tax treatment: it is not a matter of choice!

This makes it essential to take care that your business is classified correctly. With such a large differential applying to the tax at stake, you can be sure HMRC is going to be vigilant. In Section 2.8, we will return to this important issue and examine the borderline between investment and trading in greater detail.

Property Development, Renovations, Conversions, and Improvements
People who carry on these activities all the time, with a view to profiting from them are, of course, professional property developers with a trading business, and fall outside the scope of this guide (but can read the Taxcafe guide *Small Business Tax Saving Tactics* for a host of valuable tax planning tips).

What makes life complicated though, and what the next few sections are going to address, is where people whose main activities fall into another category, or who don't have a property business at all, carry out any property development, renovations, conversions, or improvements. This can have a number of possible outcomes, depending on the circumstances:

- The development activities are merely incidental to their main reason for holding the property. In this case, the expenditure becomes capital expenditure (see Sections 4.10 to 4.14, 4.23, and 5.7) and the property investor remains in whichever category (as above) they were in.
- They have become a property developer, and the profit from their development activities will be subject to Income Tax and NI (see Section 8.1).
- They have sought to profit from a development opportunity, but without becoming a professional property developer. In this case, the development profit will become deemed trading income subject to Income Tax, but not NI (see Section 2.5).

Uncertainty and Change
Another area of complication arises where an investor's intentions for a property are not clear, or change at some stage. We'll look at the implications of such uncertainty, or change, and how to protect yourself from additional tax costs in these cases below, and in Sections 2.7 and 2.8.

A Mixed Bag
The same individual may have property investments falling into two or more categories. Indeed, most landlords own their own home. Many may also invest in a development property, or buy a property to 'flip' (sell on at a profit), which could be classed as property trading (Section 8.1), or at least deemed trading income (Section 2.5).

In these cases, where the intentions for each property are clear from the outset, and never change, then each property falls into its own category and should be taxed accordingly.

Where the investor's intentions for a property are unclear, or change, however, then their overall pattern of behaviour for their property investments as a whole will be highly influential.

Example 1: *Fletcher purchases three properties off-plan, intending to hold them as long-term investments and rent them out. On completion of the properties, however, he sells one in order to provide funds for a new investment he wishes to make. Nevertheless, the other two properties are retained and rented out for a number of years.*

Although Fletcher sold one of the properties quickly, there was a good commercial reason for doing so. Hence, he may still be regarded as having a property investment business and the profit on his sale will be subject to CGT and not Income Tax or NI.

Example 2: *Godber purchases three old barns in September 2025 and converts them into residential property. The work is completed in August 2026 and he sells two of the former barns immediately.*

The third barn proves difficult to sell. In the meantime, in order to generate some income from the property, Godber lets it out as holiday accommodation. The property is never taken off the market and a buyer is found in January 2027, with completion taking place in March.

Although Godber let one of the properties out for a short period, his main business activity remained property development. His intention was clearly to develop the properties for sale at a profit. This was reinforced by the fact the property remained on the market throughout the rental period. Godber therefore has a property development business. The profits on all his property disposals will be taxed as trading income subject to both Income Tax and NI (Section 8.1), although his incidental rental income will be taxed as property income (Chapter 4).

This holistic approach is often favoured by the courts. Sometimes it can be beneficial (as it was for Fletcher), sometimes not (as for Godber). This means there can sometimes be a danger that any property development or property trading may effectively taint what would otherwise be a property investment business, with the result that HMRC might seek to deny you CGT treatment on *all* your property transactions. (Remember: the maximum CGT rate is 24%; a property trader or developer faces marginal tax rates of up to 62% or more on their profits.)

To avoid the danger of a property investment business being tainted by development or trading activities, it may make sense to take whatever steps you can to separate the businesses, such as:

- Drawing up separate accounts for the different businesses
- Using different bank accounts for the different businesses
- Using a different business name for the different activities
- Reporting the non-investment activities as a different business in your tax return
- Using a different legal ownership structure for the non-investment activities (e.g. put them in a company, or a partnership with your spouse, partner, or adult children)

On the other hand, such steps would have been a mistake for Fletcher in Example 1, as he benefited from the holistic, 'single business' approach. Nonetheless, a third example will perhaps demonstrate where this business separation could be beneficial.

Example 3: *Over the last few years, Heslop has purchased six properties. He has rented out two of them, but renovated or converted, and then subsequently sold, the other four: as was always his intention. Heslop therefore has both a property investment business and a property development trade.*

Heslop is now buying a seventh property. The new property is in need of extensive renovation, after which Heslop intends to rent it out. However, after completing the renovation work, Heslop gets an exceptionally good offer from a potential buyer and therefore decides to sell the property.

In principle, accepting an exceptional, or unexpected, offer should not alter the fact that an investor has acquired a property with the intention of holding it as a long-term investment that, ultimately, should be subject to CGT on its disposal. However, given the fact that Heslop already has a property development trade, there is a danger HMRC might seek to tax his gain on the sale of the seventh property as a development profit subject to Income Tax and NI. Hence, it is in these circumstances that separating out his businesses, as described above, could be beneficial.

Conversely, it is worth noting that combining a property investment business with a property development business may produce IHT savings: see the Taxcafe guide *How to Save Inheritance Tax* for more information.

Lastly, it's worth pointing out that a property developer or property trader who buys their own business premises retains CGT treatment on *that* property and may also be eligible to claim capital allowances on qualifying assets within it, or even on the property itself (Sections 4.10 to 4.14).

2.4 DO YOU EVEN HAVE A BUSINESS?

As stated in Section 2.1, rental income is always taxed in the same way, regardless of whether you have a business, or what type of business that might be. But the treatment of other sums derived from property, particularly property sale proceeds, depends on whether you have a business, and what type.

If there is a business, it may be a trade, and, as we have seen, this can make an enormous difference to your tax bill when you sell a property. But there cannot be a trade unless there is a business. There is an important distinction, therefore, between a professional property developer or property trader, and a casual investor. To be 'professional' in this context does not necessarily mean it must be a full-time activity, merely that it is more than casual.

To be a business, there needs to be some degree of serious intent involved. The investor must be undertaking the activity in a reasoned and methodical manner. In the context of a property business, the factors to consider in determining whether a business exists are whether the activity being undertaken is:

i) A serious undertaking earnestly pursued
ii) Actively pursued with reasonable or recognisable continuity
iii) Conducted in a regular manner on sound business principles

Where some or all of the tests are satisfied, the activity may constitute a business. However, as with many things in tax, it is the overall picture formed by looking at all the tests together, as well as the other facts of the case, that decides the position.

When it comes to property letting, the position is usually pretty straightforward. Buying property with the sole intention of renting it out will always represent a property investment business and the capital gain arising on the disposal of the property will be subject to CGT.

Other cases may be less clear, however, and we will look at some examples to further illustrate when a property business exists, and what the tax consequences are, in Section 2.6. First, however, we need to look at the issue of deemed trading.

2.5 DEEMED TRADING

One way or another, the profit or gain on disposal of a property is taxable. It may be subject to CGT, in which case the exemptions and reliefs covered in Chapter 5 will be available and sometimes the gain will be tax free. Alternatively, it may be subject to Income Tax, in which case there is likely to be a tax bill, unless the profit is covered by your personal allowance.

Usually, CGT treatment is best, as the maximum tax rate applying is just 24% (although there are exceptions, as we shall see later). However, this is not a matter of choice but depends on the circumstances.

In the absence of a business, the default position is that CGT will apply to the gain. However, the profit on disposal of UK property must be *treated* as trading income subject to Income Tax when the main purpose *or one of the main purposes* behind its acquisition is to realise a profit on disposal.

This broadens the scope of what might be considered *trading income*. It does not, however, alter the basic principles that determine when a trade exists (Section 2.4: remember, there cannot be a trade if there isn't a business). In other words, there is a middle ground where there is no actual trade, but where profits are simply *treated* as trading profits.

Fortunately, the simple *hope* of a long-term gain does not make this a main purpose behind the acquisition. In fact, HMRC guidance suggests very few disposals will be caught by the deemed trading legislation. They state this should not apply to *'transactions such as buying or repairing a property for the purpose of earning rental income or as an investment to generate rental income and enjoy capital appreciation,'* or *'straightforward long-term investment where the economic benefit arising to the owner is the result of market movement from holding that asset ...'*

The guidance also states long-term capital growth may be a reasonable expectation without it necessarily forming a main purpose of the acquisition.

The general thrust of the guidance seems to suggest it is only where a profit can already be anticipated due to the property's *current* value at the time of purchase, or where a profit is anticipated due to some action to be carried out by the owner (typically developing the property), that the deemed trading provisions can apply. Even then, the profit on disposal will generally need to be a main purpose behind the acquisition, development activity, or other actions carried out.

So, it is clear the mere hope or expectation of a long-term gain does not make this a main purpose behind the acquisition or other activity. There needs to be a more concrete strategy involving the realisation of a gain before this can be regarded as one of the main purposes behind the acquisition or other actions carried out. Nonetheless, it remains important for investors to be careful about documenting their intentions when acquiring property or carrying out development projects.

Applying the Rules in Practice

It is fair to say the deemed trading provisions cannot generally apply to landlords with a property investment business and nor can they generally apply to your own home (but we will revisit this in Sections 9.14 to 9.16).

However, I will sound two words of caution here. Firstly, the deemed trading provisions can apply where there is a significant change of intention relating to the property: we'll look at that in Section 2.7.

Secondly, while rental income will always be taxed as set out in Chapter 4, a small amount of rent received for a relatively short period will not necessarily create a property investment business. In such cases, it could still be that one of the main purposes behind the property's acquisition was to realise a profit on its disposal.

If the gain on a property disposal is deemed to be trading income, it will be subject to Income Tax instead of CGT. However, where no actual trade exists, it will not be subject to NI, or to the reporting requirements under Making Tax Digital (see Section 3.6).

In Section 2.6, we will see some examples of the type of investor who may be caught in this middle ground where they have no actual trade, but do have deemed trading income.

Another type of transaction that may be caught by the deemed trading provisions is so-called 'slice of the action' contracts. We'll look at these in Section 9.16. These contracts often apply to part of an individual's own home. We'll see more ways to benefit from the development potential of your home in Sections 9.14 and 9.15.

2.6 TAX TREATMENT OF PROPERTY DISPOSALS

So far, we have established that rental income is always taxed as set out in Chapter 4; the same applies to the income element of lease premiums (Section 9.28); but the tax treatment of property disposal proceeds and other property-based income depends on whether you have a property business and, if so, what type. In Section 2.5, we also saw gains on property disposals can be deemed to be trading income under certain circumstances.

In this section, I will further illustrate how these various rules apply to property disposals. When it comes to profits or gains on property disposals, we have to first consider whether there is a business (Section 2.4). Then, where there is no business, or the business is a property investment business, we must consider whether the deemed trading provisions apply (Section 2.5).

References in this section to 'the business tests' or to tests (i), (ii), and (iii), refer to the tests set out in Section 2.4.

Example 1: *Caroline bought a house in 2005 and used it as her main residence throughout her ownership. In 2012, she built an extension, which substantially increased the property's value. She continued to live in the house until eventually selling it in 2026.*

Caroline clearly does not have a business, as she simply bought a house to use as her own home. The fact she carried out some improvements (building the extension) does not alter this as she carried on using the house as her private residence for many years after. The gain on her property is subject to CGT, but will be exempt under private residence relief (Section 5.9).

Example 2: *Nicole buys a house with a buy-to-let mortgage, advertises it for rent on the open market and leases it to a family with whom she has no other connection.*

This is a straightforward property letting or property investment business and will be taxed as described in Chapter 4. Any gain on disposal of the property will be subject to CGT.

Where the property is held purely for rental purposes, this will always be the correct treatment. It does not matter that Nicole only has one rental property and it would not matter if she financed the purchase in a different way, bought the property from her savings, or acquired it through inheritance, divorce, or by way of a gift.

Example 3: *Debbie bought a house in 1998 and used it as her main residence for five years. In 2003, she moved into a new house and converted the first one into a number of flats. Following the conversion, she let the flats out until eventually selling the whole property in 2026.*

Debbie did not have a business until 2003, but from then onwards, she has a property letting business taxed as described in Chapter 4. Adopting a former home as a rental property turns it into a business asset.

Debbie's gain on the sale of the property will be subject to CGT as, although she carried out some conversion work, it was clearly intended as a long-term investment. She will have a partial exemption under private residence relief (see Sections 5.9 and 9.14).

Example 4: *Karen purchases a property and rents it to her elderly aunt for considerably less than market rent.*

This is not a business; it fails to meet test (iii) as it is not being conducted on sound business principles. However, Karen remains subject to Income Tax on any rental profit she makes (see Section 4.20). While there is no business, the property remains a long-term asset and any gain Karen makes on the disposal of the property will be subject to CGT. This is because her primary motive in acquiring the property was to provide a home for her aunt; any long-term gain is simply a hope rather than a main purpose behind the property's acquisition.

Example 5: *Helen inherits a run-down property from her mother. She carries out some repairs, redecorates the interior throughout, then sells the property, making a considerable gain compared with the probate value.*

This is not a business; it does not meet any of the business tests. Helen did not pursue the undertaking as she inherited the property; there was no continuity, as it was a one-off; and it was not conducted in a regular manner. There was no purpose to her acquisition as she did not purchase the property. Hence, the deemed trading provisions cannot apply and her gain is subject to CGT. She will be able to deduct the property's value at the date of her mother's death as her base cost (see Section 5.7).

Example 6: *Laura is a university lecturer. She purchases a run-down property considerably below market value. In her spare time, she carries out some repairs, redecorates the interior throughout, then sells the property, making a substantial gain. She reinvests the net sale proceeds in a new property, which she adopts as her main residence.*

Again, this is not a business. It meets test (i), the undertaking was earnestly pursued as Laura bought the property with the intention of doing it up. But it was a one-off, there is no recognisable continuity, and carrying out the work in her spare time is not conducting the activity on sound business principles, it is more like a hobby.

To some extent, Laura was speculating on the hope she might get a better price on the sale of the property. She did carry out some work, but it was only what any property owner might do to prepare a property for sale. On balance, while there is a degree of doubt, I would say the deemed trading provisions probably should not apply and Laura's gain should be subject to CGT.

Example 7: *Sandra is an office manager. She purchases a series of run-down properties considerably below market value. In each case, she repairs and redecorates the properties in her spare time then sells them at a profit and reinvests the proceeds in the next property.*

This meets both tests (i) and (ii), as Sandra is clearly undertaking these projects in a serious manner and there is a recognisable continuity to her activities. But she is still carrying out the work in her spare time and it is quite different to her main occupation. On balance, I would say she does not have a business.

However, the degree of repetition in her actions might indicate that one of the main purposes behind her acquisitions was to make a profit on the sale of the properties. Hence, while such things often end up at the whim of the courts, it is possible the deemed trading provisions could apply in this case and Sandra's gains may be subject to Income Tax (but not NI).

The position would be different if Sandra had other motives for her property acquisitions. If she had intended to rent the properties out, or to live in them, but ultimately decided to sell them instead, she may retain CGT treatment. In a case like this, there may even be the argument that she simply enjoys renovating properties and her main motive was one of personal satisfaction.

If Sandra actually did rent out the properties or live in them, this would strengthen her case further: although, if such periods of rental or occupation are only brief, this alone will not be conclusive.

Example 8: *Joanne is a chartered surveyor and a partner in a small construction firm. She regularly purchases run-down properties considerably below market value. In some cases, she will carry out some conversion or improvement work before she repairs and redecorates the properties. She sub-contracts some of the work but does most of the smaller jobs herself in her spare time. She sells the properties when the work is complete, reinvesting some of the profits, but keeping a portion to augment her partnership income.*

This is a business. It meets all of the business tests. The activity is earnestly pursued with recognisable continuity in a regular manner and appears to be conducted on sound business principles. This conclusion is reinforced by the fact the activity is closely aligned to Joanne's main occupation and she uses some of the profits to augment her income. Joanne will be taxed as a property developer, and the profits on her property disposals will be subject to both Income Tax and NI.

Example 9: *Sian, a wealthy woman with several other properties, bought a derelict barn in 2024. She developed it into a luxury home using the services of a building contractor. Immediately after the development work was complete, she put the property on the market and sold it in early 2027. She has never previously carried out any other building project and reinvests her sale proceeds on the stock market.*

This meets tests (i) and (iii): the activity was earnestly pursued and conducted on sound business principles. But it fails test (ii): it is a one-off, there is no recognisable continuity. Furthermore, Sian acts as an investor by contracting the work out rather than developing the property herself. Hence, Sian does not have a business.

However, unless Sian can demonstrate otherwise, it appears her main purpose in acquiring the property was to realise a profit on its disposal. Hence, the deemed trading provisions are likely to apply, meaning her profit will be subject to Income Tax (but not NI).

Nonetheless, it might be that Sian had intended to rent the property out or occupy it herself. If so, she might still successfully argue for CGT treatment. See Section 2.8 for guidance on helpful steps to take in these circumstances.

Example 10: *Clare is the managing director of an engineering company. She also regularly purchases derelict properties in her own name, and develops them into luxury homes using the services of a building contractor. The new homes are generally sold shortly after development work is complete although, if a buyer cannot be found reasonably quickly, Clare sometimes rents a property out as holiday accommodation for a short period.*

Clare has a business. She meets all the business tests: her property development activity is earnestly pursued with recognisable continuity and is conducted on sound business principles. She is a professional property developer and will be taxed as described in Section 8.1. Her profits on property disposals will therefore be subject to both Income Tax and NI, although NI will not apply to her rental income.

Example 11: *Susan bought an old farmhouse in 2026. She lived in the property for three months then moved out while substantial renovation work took place. After the work was completed, she let the property out as holiday accommodation but, three months later, she put it on the market and sold it with completion taking place the day her last tenants moved out.*

This would not appear to be a property development business: one cannot say the development activity was earnestly pursued in a regular manner, so it fails tests (i) and (iii). If it is a one-off project it will also fail test (ii). However, if Susan is like Clare (Example 10) and has several other development projects in hand, this property might be regarded as part of the same business, in which case Susan would be subject to both Income Tax and NI on her profit on disposal of the property.

Susan will be taxed on her rental income in the usual way, but it is far from clear whether she had a property investment business. Hence, in the absence of any other development projects, the tax position is going to hinge on Susan's motives.

This case warrants a much closer look at all the circumstances. The more Susan can do to demonstrate her intention had been to hold the property as a long-term investment, the better her chances of successfully arguing for CGT treatment. Her personal and financial circumstances could also be crucial. If she got married around the time of the sale, or got into unexpected financial difficulties that forced her to make the sale, she might successfully argue for CGT treatment.

Otherwise, it is possible (though far from certain) HMRC could argue one of Susan's main purposes in acquiring the property was to realise a profit on its disposal. Hence, the deemed trading provisions could apply, meaning her profit will be subject to Income Tax (but not NI in the absence of any other development projects).

2.7 CHANGES OF INTENTION

All or part of an existing property held as a long-term asset, whether for business or personal use, may become a trading asset where there is a change of intention. Where a property owner develops an existing investment property with a view to realising additional profit on its disposal, the profit arising after the change of intention will be a trading profit. Any increase in value prior to that point will remain a capital gain.

Example: *Louis bought a block of flats for £1m in 2019. He rented out the flats until 2026, by which time the property is worth £1.3m. He then redevelops the property into luxury apartments at a cost of £400,000. He sells all four apartments for a total of £2.4m.*

The costs used to calculate his development gain are the market value of the block before redevelopment (£1.3m) and conversion costs of £400,000, a total of £1.7m. This gives him a development gain of £700,000 (£2.4m – £1.7m).

The treatment of this development gain will depend on a number of factors: the most important being Louis' intentions at the time the redevelopment commenced. If it is clear the redevelopment was carried out with a main purpose of realising an additional profit on the disposal of the property then the development gain will be a trading profit subject to Income Tax.

However the development gain is treated, the gain of £300,000 arising prior to the start of development work will continue to be a capital gain subject to CGT.

In the case of a one-off development like this, it seems probable Louis does not have a property development trade. Hence, even where his development gain is a deemed trading profit subject to Income Tax, it should not be subject to NI.

However, if Louis already has an existing property development trade, any trading profit will be subject to both Income Tax and NI. This may also be the case where the development represents the first of a series of property developments, although the position here is less clear and will again depend on Louis' intentions at the commencement of the development work. It remains possible he intended this to be a one-off development and only later decided to start a full-on property development trade.

2.8 THE BOUNDARY BETWEEN INVESTMENT AND TRADING

The most important issue for property investors is whether your activities are treated as investments (including a property investment business), or trading (either a trading business or deemed trading). The major difference is in the treatment of profits arising on property disposals, but there are many other differences to be aware of, as we shall see as we progress through the guide.

By now, you've probably got a fair idea how you would *like* your property investments to be treated for tax purposes. However, as I have already pointed out, it is not a question of choice, but is determined by how you conduct your business, or handle your investments. Furthermore, not only is it a matter of how you actually behave, very often it will hinge on what your intentions were at the beginning of any particular project.

What Are Your Intentions?
In practice, a property investor's intentions may not always be clear. When I asked my clients to tell me their plans, I often heard answers like: *"I might sell it, or I might hang on to it for a while if I can't get a good price"; "We think we'll rent it out for a few years, but we might sell if we get a good offer"; or "We'll probably sell a few and rent the rest out."*

Naturally, any investor is going to do what produces the best result and, if an unexpected opportunity comes along, they would be foolish not to take it. For tax purposes though, we have to establish what the investor's main intentions were, at the outset, when the investment was made.

The trouble with intentions, of course, is they can be difficult to prove. Who but you can possibly know exactly what was in your mind when you purchased a property? Looking at it from HMRC's point of view, the only evidence they may have to go on is what actually transpired and this could be very different to what was intended.

> **Tax Tip**
> Document your intentions for your property business. This could take many forms. Some of the most popular are a business plan, a diary note, an email to your solicitor, or notes of a meeting with your accountant. Remember to date your documentary evidence.

Expect the Unexpected
A business plan that says, *'We will rent the properties out for five to ten years then sell them,'* may not ring true if you actually sell all the properties very quickly. In other words, merely having a business plan (or other documentation) that purports to

support your intention to hold properties as long-term investments may not be very persuasive if you actually start behaving blatantly like a property trader.

Example: *McLaren buys ten properties off-plan in April. He finances part of the purchase through a loan from a high street bank. To support his loan application, he draws up a business plan that states, 'I intend to hold properties in prime rental sites for a period of five to ten years.'*

Despite his business plan, McLaren sells all the properties in October; after having emigrated to Australia in August.

Any reasonably competent tax officer is going to question McLaren's motives and it is highly likely they would argue he was, in fact, a property trader, despite his business plan. But what if there is more to the story?

Example Part 2: *McLaren protests he had no intention of emigrating to Australia until the sudden, unexpected death of his great aunt Bunny in July. Bunny left McLaren a vast estate in Queensland and he had to move to Australia as quickly as possible to look after his inheritance. Running a UK property business now appeared impractical, so he sold his UK properties.*

Now we can see McLaren's behaviour was the result of an unexpected change in circumstances. His original business plan therefore regains more credence and might be sufficient to persuade HMRC he did indeed have a property investment business and not a property dealing trade.

An occurrence as dramatic as the one in the example probably speaks for itself, but more often it is some more subtle shift in circumstances that causes an investor to change their mind.

Documenting the reasons behind your change of plans is again the best way to proceed. A diary note to the effect of, *'Johnny got a place at Glasgow University instead, so we sold the flat in St Andrews and bought one there,'* for example, could save you thousands of pounds!

Acceptable reasons for changing your mind could include:

- An unexpected shortage of funds
- An unexpected and exceptionally good offer
- Relocation due to work, family, or other reasons
- Divorce or separation
- Bereavements and inheritance
- Health problems (yourself or a family member)
- Concerns over the property market in a particular location
- Funds are required for an investment opportunity elsewhere

Such changes leading to an early sale of a property do not mean you have changed your intentions, but rather you have simply responded to a change in circumstances. Accordingly, the early sale of the property does not alter the nature of your property investment and any profit arising on the disposal will generally continue to be subject to CGT, and not Income Tax.

Undertaking development work with a view to realising additional profit on a sale of all or part of your property is a different matter and does represent a change of intention. We saw the potential consequences of this in Section 2.7. Even participating in a development profit could lead to a change in tax treatment, as we will see in Section 9.16.

But Life Isn't Always That Simple

Many property investments quite clearly fall into one of the categories we have looked at in this chapter. But some can fall into the grey area where investment meets trading. It's not always so easy to be sure which side of the line you're on.

It is almost impossible to give a definitive answer to explain exactly when investment becomes trading. Here, however, are some useful guidelines:

Renovation and Conversion Work

Activity such as building, conversion, or renovation work may sometimes be indicative that there is a trading motive behind the purchase of land or property. However, the mere fact this work takes place does not in itself necessarily make it a trading activity. If you continue to hold the property for several years after completion of your building work, it is likely you still have an investment property.

On the other hand, if you sell the property immediately after completing the work, you may be regarded as a property developer *unless* your original intention had been to keep the property and rent it out, or adopt it as your own home (or business premises), but some change in circumstances led you to change your mind.

Frequency of Transactions

If you only sell a property once every few years, you are likely to be carrying on a property investment business. If you make several sales every year, representing a high proportion of your portfolio, you may be a property trader or developer.

Number of Transactions

As well as their frequency, the number of property transactions you have carried out can be a factor in deciding whether you are trading.

Many people like to buy a property, adopt it as their home while they 'do it up', then sell it and move on. If you do this once or twice, you're probably nothing other than a normal homeowner in the eyes of HMRC. If you do it every six months for ten years, I would suggest that somewhere along the way you may have become a property developer. (See Sections 2.6 and 9.14 for further guidance on the tax treatment of this type of activity.)

Finance Arrangements

Long-term finance arrangements, such as mortgages or longer-term personal loans are generally indicative of an investment activity. Financing your business through short-term arrangements, such as bank overdrafts will be more indicative of a development or dealing trade. Short-term finance tends to indicate short-term assets.

Length of Ownership
There is no definitive rule as to how long you must hold a property for it to be an investment rather than a trading asset. Like everything else, length of ownership is just one factor to consider. For example, many property developers hold land stocks for many years before commencing development (known as a 'land bank') but this does not alter the trading nature of their activities.

Where there is no obvious trading activity, I have heard it suggested an ownership period of three years or more is generally regarded as indicative of a property investment business: although there is no legal basis for this. This is not to say ownership for any lesser period cannot represent an investment where the facts of the case support it, and we have seen several examples of this already.

In practice, the longer you hold your properties, the more likely they are to be accepted as investments.

Renting the Properties Out
Renting properties out provides a good indication they are being held as investments, not trading assets. Like everything else on this list though, it may not be conclusive on its own (see Example 2 in Section 2.3).

Living in a Property
Living in the property is another way to evidence your intention to hold it as a long-term asset. Once again though, this may not be enough if the other facts of the case suggest otherwise. We will explore this area of planning in a great deal more detail later in the guide.

'Hands On' Involvement
Being actively involved in the renovation or development of a property makes you look like a property developer. Contracting all the work out looks more like property investment. But, like everything else, there are exceptions.

Property Management
In many cases, landlords have a minimal level of involvement in the day-to-day running of their business, and pay an agent to manage their property affairs. This is the model operated by many buy-to-let investors: who are thus generally regarded as having a property investment business.

But there are also many more 'hands on' property letting businesses, where the landlord is more involved in the management of the business on a day-to-day basis. For larger property letting businesses, the landlord's job even becomes a full-time one.

As long as properties continue to be held as long-term investments, the business generally remains a property investment business for tax purposes, regardless of the level of the landlord's involvement on a day-to-day basis. Managing your own properties does not, in itself, mean you have a property management business.

Where a landlord begins to provide services way beyond mere management, the business could eventually become a property-based trade of the type examined in Section 8.2. Generally, this requires some fairly extreme steps, but we will return to this issue and, in particular, some instances in which it may be beneficial, later in the guide.

That aside, we can generally regard property investment businesses and property letting businesses as one and the same for tax purposes. The only real difference lies in the level of administrative expenses that may justifiably be claimed, as we shall see in Chapter 4.

However, while managing your own properties does not mean you have a property management business, managing other, unconnected investors' properties would almost always be a trade (see Section 8.1).

Managing a mixture of your own and other people's properties might, in some circumstances, amount to a trade, and this can sometimes carry advantages. To be more certain of this treatment, the property management activities are usually better carried out through a separate entity, such as a company or partnership. See the Taxcafe guide *Using a Property Company to Save Tax* for further details.

In Summary

Each of the points examined above is just one factor in determining what kind of property business you have. Ultimately, it is the overall picture formed by your intentions, your behaviour, and your investment pattern that will eventually decide whether you have a property investment business; a property trade; no business at all, just investments (Section 2.4); or some mixture of these. In many cases, this overall picture will point to a fairly clear answer and the correct treatment of the business, or investments, will be obvious.

In some cases, the position may be more borderline and the correct treatment will not be clear. In these cases, it may be beneficial to adapt your behaviour a little, bearing the guidelines above in mind, in order to produce a clearer picture of the nature of your business and secure a more beneficial treatment for tax purposes.

2.9 JOINT OWNERSHIP & PROPERTY PARTNERSHIPS

Before we move on to the detailed tax treatment of property businesses, it is worth pausing to think about the impact of joint ownership. The first point to note is joint ownership, in itself, does not alter the nature of your property business.

In England and Wales, joint ownership comes in two varieties: joint tenancy, and tenancy in common. Don't be confused by the word 'tenancy' here, this is terminology only and doesn't affect the fact you jointly own the freehold, leasehold, etc.

Joint Tenancy

Under a joint tenancy, ownership of each person's share passes automatically on death to the other joint tenant. This is known as survivorship. Furthermore, neither joint owner is normally able to sell their share of the property without the consent of the other.

Each joint owner is treated as having an equal share in the property. In effect, joint tenants are regarded as joint owners of the whole property.

Tenancy in Common

Under a tenancy in common, the joint owners are each free to do as they wish with their share of the property and there is no right of survivorship. The joint owners' shares in the property do not have to be equal. In effect, tenants in common each own a separate share in the property.

A tenancy in common generally provides more scope for tax planning than a joint tenancy. We will see more on the potential benefits of tenancies in common in the following chapters.

Scotland

In Scotland, joint ownership of property comes predominantly in one major form called 'pro indivisio'. As far as the tax position is concerned, this is more or less the same as a tenancy in common.

Property Investment & Joint Ownership

When it comes to a property investment business, all joint ownership usually means is that each individual has their own property investment business, and is taxed on their share of rental profits and capital gains accordingly. The joint ownership does not affect the nature of the underlying business.

Joint owners carrying on a property investment business will not generally constitute a business partnership unless they formally create one.

There are opportunities for joint owners to split the income from their property in a beneficial manner. The position differs depending on whether the joint owners are a married couple or any other combination of two or more individuals (see Sections 9.6 and 9.9).

Property Development or Property Trading

Joint owners engaged in property development, property trading, or any other property-based trade will generally form a business partnership under basic legal principles. This is because two or more individuals engaged in the mutual pursuit of commercial trading profits are, in law, generally deemed to constitute a partnership.

Example: *Ingrid and Lenny buy an old barn and some disused farm land as tenants in common. They convert the barn into a pair of semi-detached dwellings and build two new houses on the disused land. They then sell all the newly developed properties and share the profit equally. This is one of a series of construction projects the pair have carried out together, so it represents a business (Section 2.4). Ingrid and Lenny are therefore in a trading partnership.*

It nevertheless remains possible for joint owners of a property used in a property development to be engaged in a joint venture, rather than a business partnership, if the terms of the arrangements between the parties do not amount to the mutual pursuit of profit.

Example: *Luke owns an old farm. At the edge of the farm is a small field Luke is no longer able to farm profitably. Ives comes to Luke with a proposition, "If you sell me a half interest in your field for its current agricultural value, I'll get planning permission to build some houses and then, after I've built and sold them, I'll pay you the residential use value for your remaining half interest."*

While this proposition does involve joint ownership of development land, it does not amount to a trading partnership, as Luke is not participating in Ives' development profit.

A property trading partnership may also exist without joint ownership.

Example: *Norman holds a piece of land on which he has planning permission to build ten houses. Unfortunately, he does not have the funds or expertise to carry out the development. Norman approaches Stanley, a wealthy property developer and suggests they carry out the development jointly and share the profit equally. While Norman is the sole owner of the land, his arrangement with Stanley may constitute a trading partnership.*

A partnership usually exists where both parties share, whether equally or not, in the same risks and rewards. There must also be a business (Section 2.4).

Where one party's income is fixed, or determined without reference to the other party's overall profit, this is more akin to a joint venture. Where a joint venture exists, each party has their own business and it is even possible for one of them to have a property investment business while the other has a property development business. In fact, as we will see in Section 9.16, it is also possible for one of them to have no business at all.

Where a trading partnership is formed under general legal principles, this will be a traditional partnership. To form an LLP, it is necessary to go through a formal registration procedure with Companies House, similar to forming a company.

Property Partnerships
Unlike an LLP or a company, traditional partnerships in England and Wales are not recognised as separate persons with their own legal status. Hence, traditional partnerships in England and Wales cannot own property in their own name. This is reflected in the fact it is not the partnership that has any capital gain on the sale of a property, but the individual partners.

The problem of legal ownership is generally circumvented through the use of nominees. Between two and four partners will usually own the partnership's property as nominees. For legal reasons, it is wise to ensure there are at least two nominee interests, as a single nominee could claim to own the property outright!

LLPs have their own legal status, as do Scottish partnerships, and these entities can own property in their own name. The tax position remains the same, however, with the partners themselves being taxed on any capital gains made by the partnership.

The nature of the business carried on by a property partnership is determined under exactly the same criteria as we have examined earlier in this chapter.

For tax purposes, the partnership income is allocated to the individual partners in whatever shares have been established between them and continues to be treated as property income or trading income, as appropriate. Hence, a partner may be in receipt of partnership trading income subject to both Income Tax and NI or partnership property rental income subject to Income Tax only. Or both!

The calculation of the tax due on each partner's share of the partnership income is exactly the same as if they had received an equal amount of the same type of income directly from their own individual business. The way in which the income must be reported does, however, get a little more complicated and we will return to this in the next chapter.

2.10 NON-RESIDENTS

The taxation of non-UK residents is subject to the terms of any double taxation agreement between the UK and their country of residence, although most agreements allow the UK to tax non-UK residents on income, profits, or gains derived from UK property. Non-UK residents investing in UK property are therefore generally subject to the same UK taxes as UK residents, including:

Income Tax: UK Income Tax is payable on rental profits derived from UK property by non-UK resident individuals. UK Income Tax is also payable by non-UK resident individuals developing, or trading in, UK property (non-UK residents are not subject to NI, however). The deemed trading rules covered in Section 2.5 apply equally to non-UK residents.

Where non-UK residents are subject to UK Income Tax, they pay at the main UK rates (Scottish rates cannot apply). However, only certain classes of non-UK residents are entitled to a personal allowance. These include British Nationals resident abroad, nationals of states within the EEA (see Section 3.5), Crown servants, residents of the Isle of Man or Channel Islands, and residents of other countries with a suitable double taxation agreement with the UK.

Stamp Duty Land Tax (and its equivalents per Section 1.4): An additional SDLT surcharge (currently at 2%) applies to purchases of residential property in England or Northern Ireland by non-UK residents (see Section 6.4 for details). Subject to this, these taxes apply in the usual way for non-UK resident purchasers acquiring UK property.

Inheritance Tax: Non-UK resident individuals generally remain subject to UK IHT on UK property. Some non-UK residents who have only recently left the UK may be subject to UK IHT on all property worldwide. See the Taxcafe guide *How to Save Inheritance Tax* for details.

VAT: Non-UK residents making taxable supplies in the UK are generally subject to UK VAT in the same way as UK residents (see Chapter 7).

Capital Gains Tax: Non-UK resident individuals are subject to UK CGT on disposals of UK property. For residential property, the element of the gain arising after 5th April 2015 is taxable. For non-residential property, it is generally only the element of the gain arising after 5th April 2019: however, where the owner has used the property in a trade carried on in the UK through a branch, agency or other permanent establishment, the full gain arising will be chargeable.

Non-UK residents are subject to the report and pay regime, and attendant 60-day deadline, on *all* disposals of UK land or property (see Sections 5.20 and 5.21).

Other Taxes: Both the Mansion Tax and the Visitor Levy are expected to apply to non-UK residents in the same way as UK residents (see Sections 7.7 and 7.6).

Non-Residents and Overseas Property

Overseas property held by non-UK residents should generally be outside the scope of UK taxation: with the exception of IHT on property held by certain non-UK resident individuals; and CGT on property disposals made during a period of temporary non-residence (generally less than five years).

Indirect Ownership

Individuals owning UK property indirectly, via an overseas company, partnership, trust, or other entity, must register as the ultimate beneficial owner on the Register of Overseas Entities held at Companies House. Further details of the UK tax consequences of such indirect ownership are included in the Taxcafe guides *Using a Property Company to Save Tax* and *How to Save Inheritance Tax*.

Chapter 3

How to Save Income Tax

3.1 INTRODUCTION TO INCOME TAX

Income Tax was introduced by William Pitt (the Younger) in 1799 as a temporary measure to fight the Napoleonic Wars. Bonaparte may have met his Waterloo in 1815, but it seems the British taxpayer is still paying for it! The tax was initially charged at a rate of just two shillings in the pound (10%), but the top rate rose to a (previous) all-time high of 95% under Harold Wilson's Labour Government in the 1960s.

Rates remained fairly high (with a top rate of 60%) until Nigel Lawson's tax-cutting Budget of 1987 established 40% as the top rate. This remained the top rate until Alistair Darling introduced the additional rate (currently 45%) in 2010. At the same time, the withdrawal of personal allowances for those with income over £100,000 created an effective rate of 60% (currently on income between £100,000 and £125,140). In 2013, George Osborne went further, with additional tax charges that created even higher effective rates for many parents (currently those with income between £60,000 and £80,000), conceivably ***over 100%***, although this is now extremely rare.

Sadly, given all the doom-saying we've had from new Labour Chancellor, Rachel Reeves, the era of high Income Tax rates looks set to remain with us for the foreseeable future. Furthermore, in the November 2025 Budget, she reneged on her promise to end the current freeze in Income Tax thresholds in 2028 (as predicted by yours truly), and extended it to at least 2031. Worse still, she announced increases to the Income Tax rates on property income from 2027/28 onwards (we'll get to that later).

The long history of Income Tax may go some way towards explaining some of its quirks. Badly needed modernisation is often slow in coming. It was only in 1998 that the expense of keeping a horse for the purposes of travel to the taxpayer's place of work ceased to be allowable.

The roots of how Income Tax affects property investors lie in the schedular system introduced in the 19th Century. The schedules were abolished in 2005, but their legacy is still with us in the way each type of income is classified and taxed separately. Under the Income Tax (Trading and Other Income) Act 2005, rental income and certain other property-based income is referred to as 'property income'. The act's rather lengthy name is often shortened to 'ITTOIA', which, as a fan of Ms Wilcox, I refer to as 'I Toyah': sounds like an early 1980s album doesn't it?

Until 1995, the rules governing tax on rental income were somewhat archaic. The system then underwent an overhaul, which resulted in more sensible rules that applied for over twenty years and, quite rightly, treated property letting as a business. Property letting is still treated more or less as a business, but the sensible era came to an end in 2017, when outrageous restrictions on relief for interest costs came into force.

We will examine the current tax regime for property income in Chapter 4: including the dreadful restrictions on interest relief, and the proposed increase in tax rates from 2027/28 onwards. Where the taxpayer is deemed to be trading, or to have deemed trading income, the income falls under a different set of rules, which we will look at in Chapter 8.

Despite the many changes we have seen, Income Tax has reached the grand old age of 227 with some of its greatest peculiarities still intact. Indeed, in recent years, our Governments have seemed determined to add to them. Perhaps the greatest oddity of all, the UK's peculiar tax year, has surprised many of us by surviving well into the 21st Century!

3.2 INCOME TAX PRINCIPLES

The UK tax year runs from 6th April each year to the following 5th April. The year ending 5th April 2027 is referred to as '2026/27' and the tax return for this year is known as the '2027 Return'.

From 2026/27 onwards, some individuals will be required to comply with a new system, called Making Tax Digital (MTD), while others will continue to be subject to the old self-assessment system. Partnerships and trusts will also remain under the self-assessment system for the foreseeable future.

MTD does not affect how much tax is due or when it is payable: it only alters an individual's record-keeping and reporting obligations. We'll look at the timetable for the introduction of MTD, who will be required to comply, and the requirements they will need to meet, in Section 3.6.

Individuals, partnerships, and trusts subject to the self-assessment system must complete and submit a tax return each year. The return is normally due by 31st January following the end of the tax year (31st October for paper returns). We will look at the self-assessment tax return in Section 3.5. In addition to submitting a return, the taxpayer must calculate the amount of tax due, although most tax return software will do this for you. For the minority who still submit a paper return, HMRC will do the calculation if the return reaches them by the due date.

Most landlords and other property business owners remain in the self-assessment system for 2025/26, although a small number of individual landlords and sole traders have voluntarily moved to MTD early (no-one is *required* to comply with MTD before 2026/27).

Whether you are subject to MTD or self-assessment, the Income Tax system is also used to collect NI on self-employed or partnership trading income (Section 8.1), some CGT, and certain student loan repayments ('student persecution payments' as my children call them). However, only Income Tax and Class 4 NI are subject to the six-monthly payments on account system described below.

The tax due is the taxpayer's total liability for the year, less any amounts deducted at source (e.g. under PAYE). Regardless of whether the taxpayer is subject to MTD or the old system, we call this the self-assessment liability, and it is normally payable as follows:

- A first instalment or 'payment on account' on 31st January during the tax year
- A second payment on account on 31st July following the tax year
- A balancing payment (where appropriate) on 31st January following the tax year

Additional CGT payments on account need to be made in respect of disposals of UK residential property (or *any* UK property in the case of non-UK residents). See Section 5.20 for further details.

Where the payments on account exceed the final liability for the year, no balancing payment will be due and the taxpayer will receive a repayment of the excess (or may set it against the first payment on account due for the next year).

Each of the six-monthly payments on account is usually equal to half the previous tax year's self-assessment liability for Income Tax and Class 4 NI. However, payments on account need not be made when the previous year's self-assessment liability for Income Tax and Class 4 NI was either no more than £1,000, or less than 20% of the individual's *total* liability for the year (including tax deducted at source).

Applications to reduce payments on account may be made when there are reasonable grounds to believe the following year's self-assessment liability for Income Tax and Class 4 NI will be lower.

Individuals in employment, or in receipt of a private pension, may apply to have self-assessment liabilities of up to £3,000 collected through their PAYE codes for the following tax year. This produces a considerable cashflow advantage.

A *disadvantage*, however, arises where HMRC attempt to collect some of an individual's self-assessment liability for the current year through PAYE. At present, taxpayers have the right to appeal against such adjustments to their PAYE codes which, at best, accelerate tax payments considerably, and, at worst, may lead to overpayments. While such overpayments should eventually be repaid, there will seldom be any compensatory interest payments.

Sadly, the Government is now looking at changing the rules so that, in future, HMRC will be able to *force* taxpayers with employment or private pension income to pay some of their self-assessment liability in advance through PAYE. Our ever-greedier Government is also considering enforcing 'timelier' (i.e. earlier) tax payments for everyone subject to self-assessment: we, at Taxcafe, have a nasty feeling this may be tied in with the introduction of MTD (Section 3.6).

3.3 INCOME TAX RATES

The UK Income Tax rates and allowances for 2025/26, 2026/27, and 2027/28 are set out in Appendix A. Property income is currently taxed at the same rates as most other income: 20%, 40%, and 45%.

From 2027/28 onwards, however, property income will be subject to increased rates: 22%, 42%, and 47%. In effect, a 2% increase 'across the board'. These new rates will be known, respectively, as the 'property basic rate', 'property higher rate', and 'property additional rate'.

Individuals with total taxable income in excess of £100,000 lose £1 of their personal allowance for every £2 by which their income exceeds this threshold. This currently creates an effective Income Tax rate of 60% on taxable income falling into the band between £100,000 and £125,140. From 2027/28 onwards, the effective Income Tax rate on taxable property income falling into this band will be either 62% or 63% (see Section 3.10).

The Child Benefit Charge (CBC)
An additional Income Tax charge is levied on the highest earner in a household where any household member has taxable income in excess of £60,000, and Child Benefit is being claimed.

The additional charge is equivalent to 1% of the Child Benefit claimed in the same tax year for every £200 by which the highest earner's taxable income exceeds £60,000. Once the highest earner's taxable income reaches £80,000, the whole of the Child Benefit will effectively have been withdrawn and the charge will have reached its maximum.

Those affected by the charge in 2025/26 or 2026/27 will have overall effective Income Tax rates on taxable income between £60,000 and £80,000 as follows:

No. of Qualifying	Effective Tax Rates	
Children	**2025/26**	**2026/27**
1 Child	46.8%	47.0%
2 Children	51.3%	51.7%
3 Children	55.7%	56.3%
4 Children	60.2%	61.0%
Each additional child	+4.5%	+4.65%

These rates can all be expected to rise by at least 2% from 2027/28 where taxable property income falls into the £60,000 to £80,000 bracket (except the addition for each additional child).

As an alternative to the Income Tax charge, the claimant can apply to stop their child benefit payments instead. This is clearly only worth doing where it is certain the highest earner's taxable income for the year will exceed £80,000. Furthermore, it is sensible to claim child benefit, even if you apply to stop the payments, as the claimant gets a credit for state pension entitlement purposes (where at least one child is under 12) and the payments stopped can still be claimed any time within two years of the end of the relevant tax year if your circumstances should change such that you are, in fact, entitled to some or all of the payments after all. If no claim were made, it would only be possible to backdate a future claim by a maximum of three months.

The highest earner's total annual income for the purpose of the charge is their 'adjusted net income'. This means taxable income less grossed up personal pension contributions and gift aid payments, making these reliefs extremely valuable to individuals subject to the CBC.

We will look at other ways of avoiding, or at least mitigating, the CBC in Section 9.31. In all other sections of this guide, unless expressly stated to the contrary, it is assumed the CBC does not apply.

The Winter Fuel Charge
From 2025/26 onwards, winter fuel payments (or their devolved equivalents in Scotland and Northern Ireland) will be clawed back through the tax system for eligible individuals (broadly those over state pension age) with income over £35,000. This will effectively add an additional tax charge of between £100 and £305 for affected individuals, *including* residential landlords over state pension age whose income is deemed to be more than £35,000 because of the outrageous restrictions on interest relief (Section 4.7).

While I will ignore this additional tax charge for the rest of this guide, it is worth noting the £35,000 threshold operates as a 'cliff edge': taxable income of £35,000, you keep all your winter fuel payment; taxable income of £35,001, you lose the lot!

Future Income Tax Rates
As previously stated, the Income Tax rates on property income will be increased from 2027/28. Increases to Income Tax rates on dividend income from 2026/27, and on savings income (interest, etc) from 2027/28, were also announced in the November 2025 Budget.

At the same time, Chancellor Rachel Reeves announced that both the personal allowance and the higher rate tax threshold will remain frozen at their current levels (£12,570 and £50,270 respectively) until at least 2030/31, breaking her previous promise to increase them after 2027/28.

For the sake of illustration, in the rest of this guide, I will assume there will be no other changes to Income Tax rates, thresholds, etc, in the foreseeable future. This is not a prediction, merely a simplification. In reality, we may see more changes.

3.4 CALCULATING THE INCOME TAX DUE

Another change coming into force from 2027/28 onwards is that the personal allowance, basic rate band, and other relevant Income Tax bands must be allocated in a strict order, as follows:

i) Employment income, self-employment income, and pension income
ii) Property income
iii) Savings income
iv) Dividends

At present, property income is simply bundled in with any income under (i), as this doesn't make any difference, and an individual can allocate their personal allowance in whichever way produces the lowest overall tax bill (this also seldom makes any difference, but can occasionally produce a small saving where the individual has savings or dividend income).

Since, for earlier tax years, the current rules will produce exactly the same result as the rules applying from 2027/28 in the vast majority of cases, I will apply the new rules now.

The best way to explain how an individual's self-assessment liability for Income Tax is calculated is by way of an example. To keep things simple for the time being, I will assume the restriction on relief for interest and finance costs, covered in Section 4.7, does not apply in this case.

The example will also demonstrate the impact that beginning to receive untaxed income, such as rental or trading profits, may have on the timing of an individual's tax liabilities.

Example: *In the tax year 2026/27, Meera receives a gross salary of £45,000. She suffers Income Tax deductions totalling £6,486 under PAYE. If Meera had no other income during 2026/27, she would have no self-assessment liability: the tax deductions made at source would cover all her Income Tax for the year. Many people are in this situation before commencing a property business.*

However, for the first time in 2026/27, in addition to her salary, Meera also has profits of £15,000 from a property business. Her Income Tax calculation is therefore as follows:

Employment income	
£12,570 @ 0% (personal allowance)	*£0*
£32,430 @ 20%	*£6,486*
Property income	
£5,270 @ 20% (remaining basic rate band)	*£1,054*
£9,730 @ 40%	*£3,892*
Total tax for the year:	*£11,432*
Less: Tax paid under PAYE	*£6,486*
Tax Due under Self-Assessment	***£4,946***

Not only does Meera have a considerable amount of tax to pay for 2026/27, her liability is too great to pay through her PAYE coding and she must make payments on account in respect of 2027/28. Hence, unless Meera has reasonable grounds for claiming her 2027/28 self-assessment tax liability will be less than for 2026/27, she will have to make payments as follows:

By 31st January 2028:

Tax due for 2026/27:	*£4,946*
First instalment for 2027/28:	*£2,473*
Total payment due:	*£7,419*

By 31st July 2028:

Second instalment for 2027/28:	*£2,473*

By 31st January 2029:

Balancing payment (or repayment) for 2027/28
First instalment for 2028/29

And so on, every six months thereafter for as long as her self-assessment liability exceeds £1,000 per year (or until the Government changes the rules: see Section 3.2).

Readers may wonder why I bothered to include Meera's employment income in the calculation and didn't simply calculate the tax on her property income (since the tax suffered under PAYE is simply deducted again). However, the tax paid under PAYE isn't always correct (in fact, in my experience, it seldom is unless you have very simple tax affairs).

As the example demonstrates, when you begin to receive income that is not taxed at source, such as property rental income, or trading profits, the tax liabilities arising in the first year can be horrendous. You will need to find the tax on two years' worth of profits within the space of six months: most of it on a single day. This is what I call the 'double whammy' effect of self-assessment!

Of course, once you're in the system and things settle down, you should be paying broadly similar levels of tax every six months. Nevertheless, every time your taxable rental or trading income increases significantly, you will be hit by this double whammy effect again. Furthermore, as we are talking about *taxable* income here, and not actual, real income, many landlords suffer this effect even when their income is static, or falling: due to the impact of the interest relief restrictions discussed in Section 4.7.

A mini double whammy also awaits many landlords as a result of the increase in Income Tax rates on property income in 2027/28. Let's say, for instance, that Meera from our example has the same income in 2027/28 as in 2026/27. This means her annual self-assessment liability will increase by £300, from £4,946 to £5,246.

But she won't just pay £300 extra on 31st January 2029, she'll have to pay ***£450 extra***, plus another £150 of extra tax on 31st July 2029, and every six months thereafter, as long as the current system lasts.

3.5 TAX RETURNS UNDER SELF-ASSESSMENT

Nowadays, most people submit their tax returns online and many use specialised software for the purpose, so you may be less aware of which boxes or pages your entries will actually appear in on the final return. However, the way in which property businesses should be reported on the self-assessment return (or returns) is summarised below.

I will include trading profits here, in order to cater for property traders and other property-based trades (see Chapter 8). I will also cover deemed trading income (Section 2.5) and casual income, which must be reported differently.

Unless expressly stated to the contrary, references to boxes or pages on the tax return throughout this edition of the guide are to the full 2025 UK Self-Assessment Tax Return for individuals (form SA100 and its supplementary pages): the latest version available at the time of writing.

Although some minor variations in box or page numbers occur from time to time, they can generally be expected to remain much the same for the foreseeable future. One key exception is that the separate boxes relating to furnished holiday lets (FHLs) will be removed from 2025/26 onwards, due to the regime's abolition. We'll discuss the current position for FHLs in more detail in Section 9.23. For the rest of this section, we will cover the position for tax returns for previous tax years, up to 2024/25.

UK Rental Income
Rental income from UK land and property should be detailed on Pages UKP 1 and UKP 2 of the tax return (the UK property supplement: SA105).

Page UKP 1 begins with a few general questions including the number of rental properties you had during the relevant tax year (Box 1). This may seem like a pretty trivial question, but it is important to get it right as HMRC will compare this figure with the details of the properties you hold at the land registry. Hence, when completing Box 1, remember to include:

i) UK properties only (see below for furnished holiday lets in the EEA)
ii) Rental properties you hold jointly with another person
iii) UK properties let as furnished holiday lets
iv) Properties not let on arm's length commercial terms (Section 4.20)
v) Property on which rent-a-room relief is claimed (Section 4.16)
vi) All your UK rental properties (Section 4.3), including any from which you actually received no rental income during the year

If you hold any of these properties jointly with another person you should put an 'X' in Box 3. (We will look at joint lettings and their potential benefits in Section 9.2.) We will deal with the significance of Boxes 2 and 4 in Chapter 4. For tax returns for years up to 2024/25, the rest of Page UKP 1 deals with income from FHLs (Section 9.23).

Details of other UK property lettings should be entered on Page UKP 2: total gross rents and other income received (see Section 4.21) in Box 20; the element of any lease premium subject to Income Tax (see Section 9.28) in Box 22; reverse premiums and other inducements in Box 23; and expenses categorised as explained in Section 4.2.

Furnished Holiday Lets in the European Economic Area (EEA)
Although it may seem rather odd, the UK property supplement should also be used to report income from FHLs in the EEA (in tax years up to 2024/25). The EEA

comprises the 27 member states of the European Union, plus Iceland, Liechtenstein, and Norway.

Where you also have a UK property rental business, you will need to complete two UK property supplements: one for your UK property business and one for FHLs in the EEA. When completing a UK property supplement in respect of an FHL business in the EEA, Boxes 1 to 4 should be completed in respect of that business only, with an 'X' placed in Box 18 on Page UKP 1.

Any foreign tax suffered on income from FHLs in the EEA should be detailed on Page F 6 of the foreign supplement (see further below), with a suitable explanation in Box 19 on Page TR 7 of the main tax return form (SA100). Remember to include the relevant amount in the sum entered in Box 2 on Page F 1 of the foreign supplement.

Other Overseas Rental Income

Income from land and property overseas is treated as a different source of income. With the exception of income from qualifying FHLs in the EEA, this income should be detailed on Pages F 4 and F 5 of the foreign supplement (SA106). Any foreign tax on this income should be detailed on Pages F 4 and F 5.

To claim relief for foreign tax suffered on all your overseas property income (including FHLs in the EEA), you should include the total eligible amount in the sum entered at Box 2 on Page F 1.

Property Trades

Where your property business is deemed to be a trade for tax purposes, you will need to complete the self-employment supplement. A short, two-page version (SA103S) can be completed in some cases where your tax affairs are relatively simple and your total gross business income for the year is less than the VAT registration threshold (currently £90,000). Gross business income for this purpose means total sales before deducting expenses. Those able to complete an SA103S may report total allowable expenses as a single figure in Box 20 if they wish, without the need to break it down into categories.

In other cases, you will need to complete the full six-page version of the supplement (SA103F), categorising business expenditure as appropriate.

Multiple Sources

If you have both investment and trading activities then you will need to complete both the UK property supplement (and/or the foreign supplement, as appropriate) and the self-employment supplement.

Deemed Trading Income and Casual Income

Deemed trading income that does not arise from an actual property trade (Section 2.5) and casual income of the kind described in Section 8.4, should be entered in Boxes 17 to 19 on Page TR 3 of the main tax return form (SA100), with a suitable description in Box 21.

Joint Owners
Where property is held jointly, but not as a partnership, each joint owner must include their own share of property income and expenses on their tax return each year, as appropriate.

Partnership Income
Where a property business is operated by a partnership (see Section 2.9), the partners must each report their share of partnership income on the partnership supplement. The full version (SA104F) will be required where there is partnership rental income, or deemed trading income, but the short version (SA104S) can be used where there is only partnership trading income (from an actual trade).

A separate partnership tax return (form SA800 plus appropriate supplements) must be completed on behalf of the partnership, in addition to the partners' individual tax returns.

Short Returns
HMRC issues short returns (SA200) to selected taxpayers. These are only four pages long, compared with the usual full tax return of eight pages plus supplements. Some property investors whose tax affairs are simple may receive a short return.

Note, however, that it remains your legal obligation to ensure all your income and gains are reported. In some cases, despite being issued with a short return, you will still need to complete the normal full return, and it is your responsibility to ascertain whether this is the case. HMRC's guidance note SA211 sets out the conditions you must meet to use the short return.

Additional Information (White Space)
On the main tax return (form SA100) and some of the supplementary pages, you will find additional information boxes, sometimes known as the 'white space'. In cases where there is no prescribed form, election, or signed declaration required, this is the best place to advise HMRC of anything you think they ought to know, such as why your repairs expenditure is so high this year. Using the white space like this is often beneficial and could save you from the stress of a tax enquiry.

3.6 MAKING TAX DIGITAL

After years of delay and confusion, we finally have a detailed timetable for the introduction of MTD for Income Tax: for individuals at least!

Individual landlords (including joint owners) and sole traders will be required to comply with MTD from the following dates, based on their total gross income (see further below):

Income over £50,000: April 2026
Income over £30,000 but not over £50,000: April 2027
Income over £20,000 but not over £30,000: April 2028

HMRC also intends to introduce MTD for partnerships at some stage, but there is no date proposed at present: it seems unlikely to be before 2028 at the earliest. Trusts are currently outside the scope of MTD.

There are exemptions for those who are 'digitally excluded', but these will rarely apply in practice. Those who do not have a NI number are also exempt. Non-UK resident landlords will be exempt for 2026/27, but may be brought into MTD later if they have a NI number and sufficient gross qualifying income from UK properties.

Gross Qualifying Income

Individual landlords and sole traders will be required to comply with MTD if their total gross annual income from all qualifying sources exceeds the thresholds set out above. Gross income for this purpose is before deducting any expenses.

Your gross income for 2024/25, will be used to test whether you exceed the £50,000 threshold requiring you to comply with MTD for 2026/27. Your gross income for 2025/26, will be used to test whether you exceed the £30,000 threshold requiring you to comply with MTD for 2027/28. Thereafter, your gross income for each subsequent tax year (from 2026/27 onwards) will determine whether you have to comply with MTD for the tax year falling two years later, based on a threshold of just £20,000.

For example, a landlord with annual gross rental income of £35,000 will be required to comply with MTD from April 2027; a landlord with annual gross rental income of £25,000 will be required to comply from April 2028; a landlord with annual gross rental income of £15,000 will *not* be required to comply with MTD. (These examples assume a steady level of income each year and no other qualifying income from another source.)

A landlord with gross rental income over £50,000 in 2024/25 will be required to comply with MTD from April 2026.

The sources you must include for this purpose are all forms of rental income (including the income element of any lease premiums received: Section 9.28) and any self-employed trading income as a sole trader. You do not need to include any partnership income, or income that is wholly covered by rent-a-room relief, the property income allowance, or the trading income allowance. Income from real estate investment trusts and open-ended investment companies is also excluded.

Landlords with jointly owned property should include their own individual share of the gross rental income received. As explained in Section 2.9, joint ownership is different to having a partnership.

This means many joint owners with total gross rental income of up to £40,000 between them (and no other qualifying income sources) will not be forced to comply with MTD in the foreseeable future.

Note that, where a source of income included on an individual's tax return is for a period of less than twelve months, it must be adjusted pro-rata to determine whether the above thresholds have been exceeded.

For example, if a landlord started letting out their first rental property on 6th October 2024, and received gross rental income of £26,000 between then and 5th April 2025 (a period of six months), this has to be adjusted to £52,000 (£26,000 x 12/6) for the purpose of the qualifying thresholds, meaning they will be forced to comply with MTD from 2026/27.

Preparing for MTD

If, and when, you are subject to MTD, the first thing you will need to do is get some 'functional compatible software'. This is software that incorporates an 'application programming interface', or 'API' that enables two-way communication with HMRC's systems. In practice, there are three ways of doing this:

a) Use MTD-compatible accounting software to maintain your business records and submit the required returns to HMRC,
b) Use an API-enabled spreadsheet with an inbuilt function allowing it to submit the required MTD returns, or
c) Keep your business records on a normal spreadsheet (e.g. Excel) and use MTD-compatible bridging software to submit the required returns

My preference is option (c), but it's really a question of personal choice (and I have been using spreadsheets for over forty years). If you do go for this option, the link between your spreadsheet and the bridging software must also be digital (i.e. it must not involve any retyping of figures).

Having sorted out your software, you will need to register for MTD: HMRC will not do this for you (even though they will have all the necessary information to know you need to register).

> **Wealth Warning**
>
> Mandatory MTD is going to arrive as a very unwelcome shock for many landlords and sole traders on 6th April 2026. There will be a huge number of people trying to obtain the right software, and get registered for MTD, before this deadline. If your gross property income, plus any gross trading income you had, was over £50,000 in 2024/25, you will be caught in the MTD net, so you need to act as soon as possible to beat the rush and be ready in time!
>
> A similar rush will happen again leading up to 6th April 2027, when the second batch of landlords and sole traders will be caught by MTD. Be ready for that rush if your gross property income, plus any gross trading income you have, is over £30,000 in 2025/26 (but not over £50,000 in 2024/25).

MTD Requirements

Once you are subject to MTD, you will be required to maintain digital records: essentially, this means keeping your business records (details of income and expenses) on a computer or other electronic device, using your functional compatible software.

Digital records must include, for each transaction, the amount, date, and category. The categories to be used for this purpose in a property letting business are:

Income:

- Rental income
- Other income from property (see Section 4.21)
- Lease premiums (element subject to Income Tax: see Section 9.28)
- Reverse premiums and other inducements

Expenses:

- Rent, rates, insurance, and ground rents
- Property repairs and maintenance
- Non-residential property finance costs
- Residential property finance costs
- Legal, management, and other professional fees
- Cost of services provided, including wages
- Travel expenses
- Other allowable property expenses

Finance costs include interest. For further details of the meaning of these categories, see Section 4.2. Different categories apply to trading businesses.

Quarterly Updates

Those caught in the MTD net will be required to submit quarterly updates to HMRC using the same software, summarising your results for the relevant period.

Landlords or sole traders with total gross income not exceeding the VAT registration threshold (currently £90,000) will only need to report total income and total expenses for the relevant period. Those with a higher level of income will need to report totals for each category of income and expenses, as detailed above, as well as (for landlords) unused residential property finance costs brought forward (see Section 4.7).

The quarters for MTD operate on a cumulative basis to 5th July, 5th October, 5th January, and 5th April in each tax year: unless you elect to use calendar quarters ending on 30th June, 30th September, 31st December, and 31st March instead. (Naturally, you start again from scratch in the next tax year: the cumulative approach is only within each tax year, not permanent.)

The deadline for submitting each quarterly update is the 7th of the month, one month after the end of the quarter (the same as the VAT return deadline, for those familiar with this). There will be no penalties for 2026/27 but, from 2027/28 onwards, there will be penalties for late submission (although not for errors: at least, not to begin with).

Hence, for example, a landlord subject to MTD in 2026/27 is required to submit a quarterly update with details of their income and expenditure for the period from 6th April to 5th July 2026 by 7th August 2026; their next quarterly update will cover the period from 6th April to 5th October 2026, and will be due by 7th November 2026, and so on...

Alternatively, if the landlord has elected to use calendar quarters, their first two quarterly updates would cover the period from 1st April to 30th June 2026 (due by 7th August 2026), then the period from 1st April to 30th September 2026 (due by 7th November 2026). And so on...

If you have more than one business (e.g. a sole trade and a property letting business), the MTD requirements will apply separately to each business. Whichever accounting basis you use (accruals or cash), the same basis applies for the purpose of all MTD requirements, thresholds, etc.

The quarterly updates do not need to include accounting adjustments (where the accruals basis is being used), capital allowances, other allowances, or tax relief claims: these will be dealt with through your digital tax return.

Landlords can choose to exclude expenses (but not income) relating to jointly owned property from their quarterly updates and will be able to keep less detailed records relating to these properties. They will still need to report all the relevant income and expenditure on their digital tax return, however.

The Digital Tax Return

For those forced into (or volunteering for) MTD, a new, digital tax return is to replace the old self-assessment tax return (Section 3.5), with the same deadline for submission (31st January following the tax year).

The digital tax return will include all the individual's sources of income, as well as any relevant accounting adjustments, capital allowances, other allowances, or tax relief claims. As with the old self-assessment tax return, there will be penalties for *both* late submission and any negligent, careless, or deliberate errors or omissions.

All four quarterly updates for the relevant tax year must be submitted before you can submit your digital tax return.

3.7 AMENDING PRIOR YEARS' TAX RETURNS

After reading one of our Taxcafe guides, many readers realise they have missed out on legitimate claims they could have made in previous years. However, it is often still possible to make claims in respect of earlier years following one of the procedures detailed below.

The Previous Year

Tax returns may be amended any time up to twelve months after the normal online filing deadline. For example, you may submit an amended tax return for 2024/25 any time up until 31st January 2027. (It is for this reason I generally continue to cover the tax rules for 2024/25 throughout this edition.)

Amending the previous year's tax return is a relatively straightforward matter and may be used to make a number of claims, elections, etc, which might not initially have seemed desirable, or which might simply have been missed, such as:

i) Claims to set off trading losses against other income
ii) Claims to set the capital allowances element of a rental loss off against other income (Section 4.18)
iii) Disclaimers of capital allowances (Section 4.13)
iv) Rent-a-room relief claims (Section 4.16)

The previous year's tax return may also be amended to implement claims for business expenditure that has previously been missed, such as:

v) Use of home (Section 3.14)
vi) Business mileage (Section 3.15)
vii) Repairs expenditure initially thought not allowable (Section 4.8)

Amendments to the previous year's return under this simple procedure are quite common and a normal part of the self-assessment regime.

Wealth Warning
Amending an earlier year's return means it is open for enquiry once again (for a period of twelve months) and HMRC may investigate any aspect of the return. While this should not prevent legitimate claims being made, it is something to bear in mind.

Earlier Years
Earlier years can only be amended by making a formal tax repayment claim. This facility is only open where errors or mistakes have arisen. Claims must be based on the general understanding of the law at the time the return was originally submitted. HMRC will, of course, interpret this as meaning *their* understanding of the law!

The facility cannot be used to make claims based on a change in the general understanding of the law and is only available for a period of four years following the end of the relevant tax year. For example, a tax repayment claim for 2021/22 must be made by 5th April 2026.

Amending earlier years' returns under the tax repayment claim facility is a more formal procedure and can only be used if there are errors in the original return. Generally, it cannot be used to make a claim that has simply been missed, such as those detailed at (i) to (iv) above.

It could be used to claim expenditure that has been omitted, such as items (v) to (vii) above. However, tax repayment claims under this facility are a more exceptional occurrence and should not be undertaken lightly as they are, in effect, a clear admission that you got it wrong. The Wealth Warning above therefore becomes even more important. Hence, while this is a useful facility that I have used several times to obtain tax repayments for new clients, it should generally only be used where there are significant amounts at stake and you are absolutely certain of the grounds for your claim. If in doubt, take professional advice.

Note that the items listed at (i) to (vii) above are by no means an exhaustive list and I have encountered many other examples of items that might warrant an amendment to the previous year's tax return, or a more formal tax repayment claim. The key is to be sure your claim is worthwhile, bearing in mind the points made above.

3.8 CLAIMS AND ELECTIONS DEADLINES

The deadline for making most claims and elections for Income Tax purposes is generally twelve months after 31st January following the end of the tax year. Hence, for example, the deadline for claims and elections in respect of 2026/27 will generally be 31st January 2029.

Different deadlines apply to joint elections required for capital allowances purposes (Section 4.10). Subject to this, the usual deadline described above is the deadline for making any other Income Tax claims or elections covered in this guide, unless specifically stated to the contrary.

3.9 REGISTERING A NEW PROPERTY BUSINESS

Landlords starting a new property letting business should notify HMRC by registering for self-assessment. As a landlord, you are not classed as self-employed (this only relates to trading businesses) and should use the 'For another reason' route when following the registration process at: www.gov.uk/register-for-self-assessment.

The law requires you to register by 5th October following the tax year in which your letting business is deemed to commence (see Section 4.3). It is probably better to get it done sooner rather than later: however, some taxpayers registering a new business with HMRC within the same tax year as they commenced their business have been issued a notice to deliver a tax return for the previous year. Once a notice has been issued, there is an obligation to complete a tax return, and hence unnecessary extra work has been created. HMRC can withdraw a notice to deliver a tax return where it has been issued unnecessarily, but requesting this will also require unnecessary extra work, so it is still best avoided in the first place!

My recommendation for new landlords is therefore to register for self-assessment shortly after the end of the tax year in which your business is deemed to commence. If you are already registered for self-assessment due to another (current) source of income, there is no need to register again, but you will need to ensure your tax return includes details of your property income and is submitted on time.

You do, however, need to register again if your previous registration has lapsed (i.e. you were not required to submit a tax return last year).

When completing form SA1, in response to the question 'Why do you need to complete a tax return?' you should tick the box 'I'm getting income from land and property in the UK': unless your rental income comes from an overseas property, in which case tick the box 'I'm getting taxable foreign income of £300 or more'. In either case, enter the date your property letting business is deemed to commence (see Section 4.3).

Strictly speaking, a taxpayer is required to notify HMRC of any new source of income by 5th October following the tax year. A new source for this purpose means the commencement of a property business, rather than a new property within an existing business. It is not necessary to advise HMRC every time you rent out a new property!

However, as explained in Section 4.3, when someone with a UK property business rents out their first overseas property, this does amount to a new source. The same is true for anyone renting out their first UK property, including non-UK residents.

In practice, there are not usually any penalties for a delay in reporting a new property investment business, as long as you are registered for self-assessment, your tax return includes the new source of income, and the return is completed and submitted on time.

However, for anyone not already within the self-assessment system, it is essential to report the new source of income by the 5th October deadline, so that a Unique Taxpayer Reference (UTR) number can be issued in time to complete and file a tax return by the due date. It is almost impossible to file a tax return without a UTR and there is a considerable delay in issuing new numbers. If you have not reported your new source of income by 5th October, you will have no legitimate excuse for filing your return late just because you did not receive your UTR in time.

Property Trades

When you commence a new property trade, you will generally need to register with HMRC as a self-employed trader within three months from the end of the calendar month in which you commence your trade. Failure to register within three months of commencement is subject to a penalty of £100.

In the case of a partnership or joint owners, each individual must register. If an individual is already registered due to some other existing source of self-employment trading income, there is no need to register again.

3.10 MARGINAL TAX RATES EXPLAINED

A great deal of tax planning revolves around marginal tax rates and this is a phrase you will see me use a few times in this guide. An individual's marginal tax rate is the effective rate of tax they pay on each additional £1 of income. Or, to put it another way, it is the amount of tax they can save on every £1 by which they are able to reduce their taxable income. So, it's an important concept.

Your marginal tax rate is mostly a product of your total taxable income for the year. It also depends on the type of income involved, and can be further affected by the amount and type of other taxable income you receive in the same tax year. Subject to this, the position for property income falling into the relevant tax brackets is generally as set out below.

Marginal Tax Rates on Property Income

Taxable Income	Current	Future
Up to £12,570	0%	0%
£12,570 to £50,270	20%	22%
£50,270 to £100,000	40%	42%
£100,000 to £125,140	60%	62% or 63%
Over £125,140	45%	47%

The current rates have applied each year since 2023/24 and continue to apply up to 2026/27. The future rates are expected to apply each tax year from 2027/28 until at least 2030/31.

The marginal tax rate on property income falling into the £100,000 to £125,140 bracket from 2027/28 onwards is 62% if you also have at least £12,570 of income from other sources (excluding interest and dividends), but is generally 63% otherwise.

As illustrated by the example in Section 3.4, income from other sources (excluding interest and dividends) will generally push property income into a higher tax bracket.

Savings or dividend income will not affect the marginal tax rate on your property income, but may affect your *overall* marginal tax rate. This does not affect most people, however, as there is no effect if dividend income does not exceed £500 and total income, excluding dividends and interest, is at least £17,570. The main people who are affected are small company owners: see the Taxcafe guide *Salary versus Dividends* for further information.

The principles (and figures) behind the marginal tax rates set out above are explained in Section 3.3 and Appendix A. For the purposes of these rates, property income derived from residential lettings must be calculated before deducting interest and finance costs (see Section 4.7). In other words, for residential landlords, their taxable property income is their rental profit before interest.

See Section 8.1 for the marginal tax rates on trading profits and deemed trading income.

Marginal tax rates on taxable income between £60,000 and £80,000 will be increased where the CBC applies. The Winter Fuel Charge does not affect marginal tax rates, as this dreadful attack on the elderly operates on a 'cliff edge' basis: nonetheless, it is worth bearing in mind. See Section 3.3 for further details on both these additional charges.

The marginal tax rates applying to Scottish taxpayers are different (mostly higher). See Section 3.20 for details. Welsh taxpayers may also have different Income Tax rates in future (no changes are proposed at present).

3.11 ACCOUNTING METHODS: ACCRUALS VERSUS CASH

Most landlords have a choice between accounting for their property income under the traditional 'accruals basis', or under the 'cash basis'. The Government are very keen to encourage as many people as possible to use the cash basis. Personally, for reasons I will explain later, I am generally rather more cautious about the cash basis, although there are cases when it can be highly beneficial.

The basic idea behind the cash basis is simple enough: income is taxable when it is received; expenses are deductible when they are paid (provided they qualify in the first place). In fact, those unfamiliar with accounting principles probably assume this is how things work anyway: and yes, under the cash basis, you'd be right.

Historically, however, all businesses, including landlords, were required to prepare accounts under the accruals basis for tax purposes. Under the accruals basis, income is taxable when it is *due*; expenses are deductible when they are *incurred* (again, provided they qualify in the first place).

Let's look at a basic example to illustrate the difference between the two methods.

Example: *Meghan is a higher rate taxpayer renting out residential property, and prepares accounts to 5th April each year. In March 2027, she has some roof repairs carried out at a cost of £5,000, although the builder does not invoice her until May and she does not pay until July. On 1st April 2027, she receives £1,200 rent in respect of the month of April.*

Under the ***cash basis****, the full £1,200 of rent due for April 2027 is taxable in 2026/27, but Meghan cannot claim the cost of her roof repairs until 2027/28.*

Under the ***accruals basis****, only £200 (£1,200 x 5/30) of the rent due for April 2027 is taxable in 2026/27 (the proportion relating to the five days falling into 2026/27), the remaining £1,000 will fall into 2027/28. Furthermore, Meghan can claim the cost of her roof repairs in 2026/27, as she had already incurred this expenditure by her accounting date.*

In this example, if we assume there are no other differences between the two methods, Meghan will have an additional £6,000 of taxable profit in 2026/27 under the cash basis (compared with the accruals basis), thus increasing her Income Tax bill for the year by £2,400 (at 40%).

Accelerating £6,000 of her taxable profit into 2026/27 may, of course save Meghan £2,520 in 2027/28 (at 42%) if she is a higher rate taxpayer again, giving her an overall net saving of £120. However, it is questionable whether it is worth joining the cash basis for such a small saving, especially as it carries a significant cashflow disadvantage.

The cash basis is now the default basis of accounting for most landlords, and applies automatically if you qualify, unless you opt out. We will take a closer look at the cash basis for landlords, including the qualifying conditions, and how to opt out if you don't want to use it, in Section 4.22.

We will also look at the process of joining or leaving the cash basis: which, to say the least, can be rather complex (though sometimes beneficial).

A separate cash basis is available to sole traders and partnerships with trading businesses: see the Taxcafe guide *Small Business Tax Saving Tactics* for details.

While using one of the cash bases largely only alters the timing of taxable profits, there are some crucial restrictions on deductible expenditure, particularly capital expenditure, and we will look at this in Section 4.23.

Approach Taken in this Guide

Since most landlords now have the choice between using the accruals basis or the cash basis, I will be covering both in this guide.

However, while the cash basis has its advantages (and I will examine these in detail) *my* default basis (as opposed to HMRC's) is to assume accounts are being prepared, and hence taxable profits calculated, using traditional accruals basis accounting.

Hence, unless stated to the contrary, throughout this guide, it is assumed the individual, partnership, trust, or other business entity concerned is using the accruals basis. My reasons for taking this approach are as follows:

- For landlords, the cash basis will generally lead to an acceleration of taxable profits (as we saw in Meghan's case in the example above).
- Some landlords remain ineligible for the cash basis.
- A significant amount of capital expenditure that is deductible under the accruals basis cannot be deducted under the cash basis.
- Those who have operated the accruals basis up to now face complex transitional rules if they wish to move to the cash basis. While I will guide you through those transitional rules in Section 4.22, and they can provide some excellent tax planning opportunities, the complexity they create inevitably represents another barrier to entry for the cash basis.

I must stress, these are only the reasons why I am adopting the approach of using the accruals basis as *my* default basis in this guide. They do not mean the cash basis is never suitable for landlords or other property business owners. Indeed, the cash basis may be advantageous to specific individuals or partnerships and/or may also provide significant tax planning opportunities.

We'll look at all this later in the guide but, for now, just remember, my basic assumption, unless stated to the contrary, is that you are using the accruals basis.

Irrelevant Sections?

If you are using the cash basis there are, inevitably, some sections in this guide that are not directly relevant to you. I'll point these out when we get to them.

While not directly relevant, however, these sections will remain important as they will show you what the alternative treatment would be and hence the consequences of leaving the cash basis, whether compulsorily or voluntarily.

Taxes Affected
The choice between the accruals basis and the cash basis will affect your Income Tax position, as well as Class 4 NI if you are operating a trading business. It has no effect on other taxes.

3.12 CLAIMING TAX DEDUCTIONS

Whatever kind of business you have, there will usually be expenses that can be claimed as a deduction from your profits. Some deductions are very much dependent on the type of business, and we will therefore examine some of the specific categories of deductible expenditure most relevant to landlords in Chapter 4. Firstly, however, it is worth dealing with some of the basic principles applying to deductions claimed in any kind of business.

Wholly and Exclusively
All expenses must be incurred wholly and exclusively for the purposes of the business and, naturally, must actually be borne by the taxpayer. The term 'wholly and exclusively' is enshrined in tax law, but is not always interpreted quite as literally as you might think.

Example: *Saleema pays £50 per week for gardening services. This covers the upkeep of her own garden and that of the house next door, which she also owns and rents out. This is what we call 'mixed use'. The gardening costs are partly private expenditure and partly incurred for Saleema's property business. This does not mean all the gardening expenditure falls foul of the wholly and exclusively rule. The correct interpretation is to say part of the gardening expenses are incurred wholly and exclusively for business purposes and thus claim an appropriate proportion.*

Expenditure has mixed use where it serves more than one purpose, but in a way that can be separated or sub-divided. Where it is possible to separate out the business element of the expenditure, this can be claimed for Income Tax purposes. This is why landlords and other business owners are able to claim business mileage in respect of business use of their car (see Section 3.15).

Conversely, where expenditure serves more than one purpose at the same time in a way that cannot be separated or sub-divided, we call this dual-purpose expenditure and, where one of those purposes is to provide a benefit for the taxpayer or their family, none of that expenditure can be claimed as a deduction for tax purposes. One of the best examples of this is normal office clothing, where the business purpose of looking smart and professional cannot be separated from the personal functions of providing warmth and decency, which are provided simultaneously by the same clothing.

In summary, where it is possible to make a reasonable apportionment between the business and private elements of the expenditure, the business element may be claimed. But, where the business and private elements take place simultaneously, the expenditure generally cannot be claimed at all.

Revenue versus Capital

In the tax world, all business expenditure is either revenue or capital. The term 'revenue expenditure' refers to expenditure incurred on an ongoing basis in order to earn revenue (i.e. income) in the business. Expenditure on the acquisition or enhancement of a long-term asset of the business will generally be capital expenditure.

Under traditional accruals basis accounting, expenditure must generally be revenue expenditure in order to be claimed for Income Tax purposes. No direct Income Tax deduction is allowed for capital expenditure under the accruals basis.

Some capital expenditure is, however, eligible for a form of tax relief known as capital allowances, and we will explore these in detail in Sections 4.10 to 4.14. Residential landlords may also claim replacement of domestic items relief, which we will look at in Section 4.9. These reliefs do not apply where the cash basis is being used (except for expenditure on cars). We will look at relief for capital expenditure under the cash basis in Section 4.23.

Whether expenditure is capital or revenue depends not only on the nature of the expenditure, but also on the type of business you have. Capital expenditure is a particularly significant issue for landlords, as a great many of your expenses will be deemed capital for tax purposes. We will cover some more specific examples relevant to landlords in the next chapter. Before that, however, let's look at a simple example to illustrate the difference between capital and revenue expenditure.

Example: *Willie runs a chain of sweet shops. As part of his expansion programme, he opens two new shops, one in Midchester and one in Normingham. He buys the freehold of the Midchester shop, but rents the premises in Normingham. The Midchester shop is a long-term capital asset of Willie's business. The cost of buying the freehold is therefore a capital expense, deductible only for CGT purposes if and when Willie decides to sell the property. This treatment also extends to costs incurred in the purchase, such as legal fees and SDLT, (but see Sections 4.5 and 4.6 for the treatment of interest and finance costs).*

The Normingham shop, however, is only rented and Willie does not own any long-term asset. The rent paid is a direct cost of making sales of sweets in Normingham and thus represents a revenue cost Willie may deduct against his profits for Income Tax purposes.

Interest and finance costs generally remain a revenue cost, even though these are often incurred in order to acquire a long-term asset (particularly a property). The definition of finance costs goes a lot further than you may think, as we will see in Section 4.6.

Capital expenditure on property, property improvements, fixtures, and fittings will often (though not always) be deductible for CGT purposes on the sale of the underlying property. That sale may take place many years from now. It is important, therefore, to keep receipts and other documentary evidence of this expenditure in a safe place: as it may save you a significant amount of CGT one day!

Assets Bought on Hire Purchase, Etc.
Hire purchase and similar types of contract represent a blend of both capital and revenue expenditure. The cost of the asset itself is generally capital expenditure, but the interest and finance charges arising under the contract are revenue costs. In most cases, the two elements must be dealt with separately, including:

- All cars purchased under hire purchase, etc.
- Anyone using traditional accruals basis accounting
- Anyone claiming fixed rate mileage allowances (see Section 3.15)
- Residential landlords

It is only in the case of a property business owner with no residential lettings, using the cash basis, purchasing an asset other than a car, and not claiming fixed rate mileage allowances (if it is a van or motor cycle), that hire purchase payments can effectively be regarded as a single business expense that doesn't need to be separated into the two elements.

Grants & Insurance Claims
Grants or insurance claims should generally be deducted from the underlying expense (whether that expense is revenue or capital). Some grants may, instead, form additional taxable income.

If you incur deductible expenditure that is also the subject of an insurance claim, you may claim the expenditure as and when it is incurred and need only credit the insurance claim (as a negative expense) back into your accounts when it's received. This could be in a later tax year, giving you a tax cashflow advantage to partly compensate for the cashflow disadvantage you suffer while waiting for your claim to be sorted out.

Where a property is destroyed, or damaged so badly it cannot be used again, the relevant insurance claim may sometimes represent disposal proceeds for CGT purposes rather than a negative expense.

VAT on Expenses
If you are unable to recover the VAT on an expense then, as long as the underlying expense itself is deductible, you may also include your irrecoverable VAT in the deduction claimed. This is a simple reflection of the fact that, in such cases, the business expense incurred is the VAT-inclusive cost. (Most residential landlords cannot recover VAT, but we will return to the question of when VAT may be recoverable in Chapter 7.)

Commencement & Pre-Trading Expenditure
You may incur some expenses for the purposes of your property business before it even starts. Such expenses incurred within seven years before the commencement of your business will usually still be allowable if they would otherwise qualify under normal principles. The expenses may be claimed as if they were incurred on the first day of the business. The expenses do, however, need to relate to the same business as the one you eventually start. In the case of a property letting business, it is important to remember that UK properties and overseas properties must be treated as different businesses (where letting commenced before 6th April 2025, FHLs in the UK or EEA were also classed as different businesses: see Section 9.23).

Discounts, Reductions, Rent Holidays, Etc.
Any discounts, reductions, etc, agreed with customers or tenants simply reduce your taxable income. Such reductions do not represent a bad debt expense (Section 4.15). However, a waiver of a debt already due should usually be dealt with as a bad debt.

Fines and Penalties
As a basic principle, no deduction can be claimed for any fine or penalty imposed by the authorities. This generally includes parking fines but, for a more detailed discussion of this issue, see the Taxcafe guide *Small Business Tax Saving Tactics.*

A commercial penalty imposed under contract, or otherwise charged by a private organisation, is a different matter, and this cost may be claimed when incurred in the course of the business. This includes parking penalty charges imposed by a commercial organisation.

In accounting terms, rent repaid under a rent repayment order represents negative income. I would expect to see this treatment replicated for tax purposes: i.e. a rental loss would be created, to be dealt with as explained in Section 4.18. However, I have yet to see a test case on the subject.

3.13 ADMINISTRATIVE EXPENSES

One category of expenses common to any type of business is administrative expenses, or business overheads. This heading is very broad and can extend, among other things, to the cost of running an office, motor and travel costs, and support staff's wages.

In Sections 3.13 to 3.18, we will look at the most common types of administrative expenditure in a property business. While the amounts involved may not always be significant, it is well worth claiming the deductions you are rightfully entitled to. Many property business owners overlook some of these expenses and pay more tax as a result but, with a little extra effort, claiming these items can help reduce your tax bill.

The items covered in Sections 3.14 to 3.18 are not meant to be an exhaustive list. Almost anything that meets the wholly and exclusively rule, and which qualifies as revenue expenditure (see Section 3.12), may be claimed for Income Tax purposes; although, sadly, most entertaining expenditure is specifically excluded.

3.14 USE OF HOME & OTHER PREMISES COSTS

Many people run their property business from home. In these cases, the business owner may claim an appropriate proportion of their household bills as a business expense.

Generally, the proportion to be used is based on the number of rooms in the property, excluding bathrooms, toilets, kitchens, landings, and hallways.

The claim should be further restricted where there is also some private use of the part of the property used in the business.

Example: *Shakira spends about 30 hours per week running her property business from a small room in her house. The house also contains a living room, a kitchen, a bathroom, and two bedrooms. Shakira's house therefore has four rooms that count for the purposes of our calculation. The room Shakira uses for business also has some private use, which she estimates amounts to around 10% of the room's total use. Shakira may therefore claim 90% of one quarter, or 22.5%, of her household bills as a business expense.*

In practice, where the private use of the part of the house used in the business is negligible, HMRC has not usually sought a further reduction in the *proportion* of household expenses claimed.

> **Wealth Warning**
> Exclusive business use of part of your home can have a detrimental effect on your CGT position, as we shall see in Chapter 5.

Household expenses to be included in the office cost calculation generally comprise:

- Heating and lighting (electricity, gas, oil, coal, etc.)
- Cleaning (cleaners' wages and/or cleaning materials)
- Council Tax
- Water rates or metered water supplies
- General repairs to the fabric of the building
- Insurance
- Mortgage interest or rent

If part of the taxpayer's mortgage interest on their home is already being claimed on the basis it has been used to fund business expenditure (e.g. the deposit on a rental property), that part must be excluded from the household expenses used to calculate the claim for business use of the home (i.e. it cannot be counted twice!)

Sections BIM 47800 to 47825 of HMRC's Business Income Manual provide instructions to tax officers telling them to accept reasonable claims for an appropriate proportion of the above costs. (It may be useful to refer them to these sections if you encounter any resistance to a claim.)

HMRC's instructions acknowledge there are a variety of acceptable methods for apportioning household expenses where there is business use of the home and no method is mandatory.

The instructions do, however, draw a distinction between running costs (heating, lighting, cleaning, and metered water) and fixed costs (all other items listed above). They then go on to suggest running costs should be apportioned according to actual use, whereas fixed costs should be apportioned according to the room's availability: although their own examples do interpret this in different ways.

In practice, the key point is to be reasonable. Where the business use is quite extensive (say 20 hours or more per week) it will generally be reasonable to claim the same proportion of all household costs (as in Shakira's case above).

Where there is only moderate business use, however, (say less than 20 hours per week) it will usually be reasonable to restrict the claim for fixed costs to a lower proportion. One potential method for doing this is illustrated in the example below.

Example: *Rhodri has five rooms in his house excluding the kitchen, bathrooms and hallway. One of these is his study, which he uses for business nine hours per week. The study is also used privately for an average of one hour per week. Rhodri's household costs for the year comprise fixed costs of £12,000 and running costs of £5,000.*

Rhodri uses his study for business purposes nine hours per week out of total actual usage of ten hours per week on average. He therefore claims the following proportion of his running costs: £5,000 x 1/5 x 9/10 = £900.

Rhodri also considers that his study is available for use 16 hours per day (it has no bed, so cannot be used at night). This equates to 112 hours per week. He therefore claims the following proportion of his fixed costs: £12,000 x 1/5 x 9/112 = £193. His total claim in respect of household expenses is thus £1,093 (£900 + £193).

The number of rooms method is not compulsory and any other method that produces a reasonable result may be applied instead. Some consistency in the method used would generally be expected, however.

Any mortgage interest element within a residential landlord's claim for use of home needs to be separated out and treated in accordance with the regime described in Section 4.7. For example, if £10,000 out of the £12,000 of fixed costs incurred by Rhodri represents mortgage interest, and he is a residential landlord, then £161 (£10,000 x 1/5 x 9/112) of his use of home claim will need to be separated out and dealt with as an interest cost subject to restricted relief, as shown in Section 4.7.

Minimal Use

HMRC's instructions also suggest small claims not exceeding £2 per week, or £104 per year, will be acceptable for even the most minimal business use. This simple claim is available to all property businesses as an alternative to the more complex calculations considered above. For those with minimal business use of their home, it will make sense to simply claim this small deduction.

The claim should be restricted, as appropriate, where the business has not been running for a full year. Some actual business use of the home is required, even if only minimal.

Some people have interpreted the £6 per week (£312 per year) allowed where an employer reimburses an employee required to work from home as also applying to property business owners. This approach is seldom challenged, although it is not strictly correct.

Flat Rate Deductions

A system of flat rate deductions for business use of the taxpayer's home is available for *trading businesses*. Strictly speaking, this system is not available to landlords with property letting businesses.

However, HMRC's manuals tell their inspectors where 'there is only minor business use of the home, you may accept a reasonable estimate.' It is hard to see what grounds they could have for not accepting the use of the same flat rate deductions that are available to other businesses as a reasonable estimate.

Having said that, the flat rate deductions are not exactly generous, so I find it difficult to believe many landlords working from home at least 25 hours a month (the minimum requirement) will want to use them. Anyone who feels it is not worth performing complex calculations to arrive at a suitable proportion of household expenses can still claim the simple deduction of £2 per week described above in any case (and this is available even if you only work from home one minute a month).

The flat rate deductions are an alternative method available *instead* of the proportionate calculation discussed above. The amount of the deduction is calculated on a monthly basis, according to the number of hours spent wholly and exclusively working on business matters at the home during the month. The rates applying are:

25 to 50 hours	£10 per month
51 to 100 hours	£18 per month
101 hours or more	£26 per month

Business Premises

If your property business grows to the point where you need to rent premises from which to run it, the rent, business rates, and other running costs you incur will generally be an allowable expense.

Expenditure on purchasing or improving your own business premises will always be treated as capital in nature, whatever type of business you have.

If you buy a property to run your business from, you will be able to claim any interest and finance costs incurred. The principles outlined in Section 4.5 (for rental property purchases) will apply to determine which interest and finance costs qualify for relief. For residential landlords, the restrictions in Section 4.7 will also apply to interest and finance costs on funds used to buy your own business premises.

The running costs, including business rates, of a property you purchase for use as your business premises may be claimed as business overheads.

Having business premises does not prevent you from also making a use of home claim if you continue (as most business owners do) to carry out some work at home. The principles outlined above remain the same, although, of course, the amount of hours you spend working at home is likely to be reduced.

3.15 MOTOR EXPENSES

The cost of running vehicles used in your business may be claimed as a business expense. Generally, the vehicle will also have some private use, so an appropriate proportion is claimed. (Or a proportion is disallowed, depending how you look at it and how you draw up your accounts.)

The appropriate proportion to claim will vary from one taxpayer to the next. If you were to buy a vehicle purely for use in your business, a 100% claim might be justified. Typically, however, for landlords with property letting businesses, the business use of a vehicle will tend to be fairly low, perhaps 15% to 30%; but this is only a rough guide, and the appropriate claim may be considerably higher or lower in some cases.

You will need to work out the appropriate proportion to apply in your own case based on the specific facts supporting your claim. Keeping a mileage log to record your business journeys is the best way to do this and is highly recommended (although not everyone does this). For guidance on what can be regarded as a business journey, see Section 3.16.

The exact percentage of business use will vary from one year to the next, but a reasonable average rate is usually acceptable unless there is a significant change in your overall pattern of behaviour.

Mileage Rates
Alternatively, you may claim fixed mileage rates instead of the appropriate proportion of actual running costs. For cars and vans, the rate is 45p per mile for the first 10,000 business miles travelled in each tax year, and 25p per mile thereafter. For motorcycles, a single flat rate of 24p per business mile may be claimed. If claiming fixed mileage rate deductions, it is essential to keep a mileage log (a mileage log is advisable in any case).

This method has the advantage of simplicity, but does have some drawbacks. If claiming business mileage rates, you cannot also claim any running costs for the vehicle, and nor can you claim any of the purchase cost, neither under the capital allowances regime (Section 4.12), nor as a direct deduction under the cash basis (Section 4.23). You can, however, still claim a suitable proportion of any finance costs, where relevant (subject to the restrictions discussed in Section 4.7 in the case of residential landlords).

Once you have chosen a method (either fixed mileage rates, or a proportion of actual costs), you must normally stick to that method throughout your ownership of the vehicle. You are, however, free to choose again in respect of any new vehicle you acquire: in other words, the choice is made on a vehicle-by-vehicle basis.

Leased Vehicles
Similar principles apply where a vehicle is held under a lease. The business owner has the choice of claiming an appropriate proportion of lease payments plus other running costs, or claiming the fixed rate mileage allowances described above.

Under traditional accruals basis accounting, lease payments for a car with more than 50g/km of CO_2 emissions are subject to a statutory 15% disallowance, in addition to the appropriate adjustment for private use.

Hence, for example, if a landlord is making monthly lease payments of £1,000 for a car with 40% business use, they can only claim £340 per month (£1,000 – 15% = £850 x 40%). This additional 15% disallowance does not apply under the cash basis.

Double Cab Pick-Ups
Double cab pick-ups purchased or leased under an agreement entered into before 6th April 2025 will generally be treated as vans for all tax purposes, except that the 15% statutory disallowance for lease payments discussed above will apply to payments after 30th September 2025 where the accruals basis is being used.

Purchases or leases under later agreements will generally be treated as cars (though not usually for VAT purposes). See the Taxcafe guide *Small Business Tax Saving Tactics* for further details.

3.16 TRAVEL AND SUBSISTENCE

Travel costs incurred for business purposes should generally be allowable. This might include the cost of:

- Visiting existing rental properties
- Scouting for potential new properties
- Visiting your bank, mortgage broker, solicitor, or accountant
- Visiting hardware stores to purchase goods for your business
- Visiting property shows, exhibitions, courses, etc.

Where your trip necessitates an overnight stay, you will additionally be able to claim accommodation costs and subsistence (meals, etc.). Care needs to be taken, however, in the case of any travel with a dual purpose. Travel, subsistence and accommodation costs will only be allowable if your trip was purely for business purposes, or if any other purpose was merely incidental.

If you travel to Brighton for a day to view some properties, for example, the fact you spent a spare hour at lunchtime sunbathing on the beach will not alter the fact this was a business trip. If, on the other hand, you take your whole family to Brighton for a week and spend just one afternoon viewing a few properties, then the whole trip will be private and not allowable for tax purposes (except for any additional costs incurred specifically in order to carry out the viewings).

Historically, HMRC has taken the view that subsistence costs may only be claimed where connected with an overnight stay while travelling on business. However, current generally accepted practice is that reasonable expenditure incurred while some distance away from your home and business base may usually be claimed.

For more information on what constitutes business travel, and what kind of subsistence claims are reasonable, and when, see the Taxcafe guide *Small Business Tax Saving Tactics.*

3.17 TRAINING AND RESEARCH

Many property investors spend a good deal of money on training and research. The first thing to note is the fact this expenditure is often incurred before the business starts is not, in itself, a barrier to claiming it as a business expense. (Unless it was incurred more than seven years before the business started!)

Any costs incurred in researching potential purchases, looking at available mortgage deals, attending property shows, and anything else to help you set up, or expand, your business should generally be allowable.

The cost of books, magazines, and other information purchased for business purposes is usually allowable. This covers not only industry-specific publications, like trade magazines, but also books and other publications you buy to help you meet your legal and taxation obligations. Books like this one, and many of Taxcafe's other guides, which keep you updated with developments in the field of property taxation, are therefore generally tax deductible.

The expenditure must be relevant to your business. If you are planning to invest in Spanish property, then the cost of an English-Spanish dictionary might be allowable. A self-help book on diet and yoga, however, would be pushing it too far, even if it does somehow make you a better landlord.

Training Costs, Seminars, Courses, Etc.

If you have employees, staff training costs will generally be allowable. For the business owner themselves, the position is, unfortunately, a little more nuanced, and can sometimes be a bit of a grey area.

When an individual business owner undertakes training aimed at updating or expanding their knowledge or expertise in their existing area of business, the cost will generally be allowable.

HMRC also accept training in ancillary skills that help the owner to run their business more efficiently, such as bookkeeping or computer skills, is usually an allowable cost.

However, HMRC takes the view that training which is unrelated to the business owner's *existing* area of business is something they call a 'personal capital expense', and cannot be claimed. Personally, I find this a preposterous concept, but I'm afraid that doesn't help, as HMRC's view is generally accepted and, while it depends on the facts of each case, can be expected to be held up in court.

All this leaves a number of questions: What is the owner's existing area of business? How far does this extend? And what is an ancillary skill?

HMRC have recently updated their guidance in this area and this can be found in their manuals at BIM 35660. For once, the updated guidance is fairly helpful, especially as it includes a number of examples that are particularly focussed on what they accept to be within the scope of the owner's existing business, and what they would regard as ancillary skills.

However, HMRC's guidance does not cover property businesses (plumbers are as close as they get). So where does all this leave landlords?

As far as property seminars and courses are concerned, the question of whether you are updating or expanding knowledge in an existing area of business can sometimes be a difficult distinction to draw.

Certainly, for an existing landlord, the cost of attending courses run by organisations such as the National Residential Landlords Association or the Scottish Association of Landlords should generally be allowable.

And, we can also safely include basic training in ancillary skills such as bookkeeping, property tax, computer skills, and your legal obligations: training on the Renters' Rights Act provisions is a prime example at the moment.

Basic training in things like plumbing, or how to do your own PAT testing, should also be allowable, provided you only intend to use these skills within your existing property business.

For the more expensive, 'boot camp' type courses some people attend, the position may be less clear. Arguably, if you already know how to do something (e.g. how to buy property) and the course is only intended to help you do it better, it must surely amount to the allowable cost of simply updating or expanding an existing area of knowledge.

But prospective landlords attending these types of courses before commencing their property business may find some resistance to claims for these costs, especially as they can run into many thousands of pounds.

In the end, the decision over expense claims of this nature will inevitably require you to use your own judgement, based on the exact circumstances of the case and the principles outlined above.

3.18 OTHER ALLOWABLE COSTS

Some other items of administrative expenditure worth considering are discussed below. However, as explained in Section 3.13, this is not an exhaustive list.

Telephone and Broadband
The cost of business calls and other business use of telephone lines, broadband, etc, may be claimed. Strictly, a detailed analysis of business and private use should be carried out but, in practice, a reasonable estimated allocation will usually be acceptable. A suitable proportion of line rental and other service charges can also be claimed.

Staff Entertaining
Most entertaining expenditure is not allowable for Income Tax purposes. The only exception, for a business large enough to have employees, is staff entertaining.

Please don't take this as carte blanche to have continual parties and meals out on the business, as this represents a benefit in kind on which the employees will have to pay Income Tax, and you will have to pay 15% in employer's NI.

There is, however, an exemption for one or more annual staff parties or similar functions costing no more than £150 per head in total. For most businesses, this is sufficient to ensure no-one gets taxed on the annual Christmas party. Naturally, before you can make use of this exemption, you need to have some employees!

And Don't Forget...
Other items worth mentioning include: postage and stationery; professional subscriptions (where relevant to your business); computer and IT costs (where these are capital in nature, they can be claimed for capital allowances purposes: see Sections 4.10 to 4.13, or as a direct cost where the cash basis is being used).

Just remember, if it's revenue expenditure, and it meets the wholly and exclusively rule (Section 3.12), it's probably allowable: unless it's business entertaining!

3.19 THE TAX RELIEF CAP

There is an annual limit, or cap, on a number of Income Tax reliefs. The total amount an individual may claim in any tax year, under all the affected reliefs taken together, is limited to the greater of £50,000, or 25% of their adjusted total income. Broadly speaking, adjusted total income means total taxable income for the year in which relief is being claimed: after deducting gross pension contributions (including tax relief at source); but before other reliefs. For individual property investors, the most important reliefs affected by the cap are:

Property loss relief: The ability to set capital allowances within property rental losses against other income for the same tax year or the next (see Sections 4.18 and 4.19).
Trading loss relief: Individuals with trading losses can set them off against their other income in the same tax year or the previous one. Additional relief applies in the early years of a trade.
Qualifying loan interest: Relief for interest on personal borrowings used to invest in a qualifying company or partnership (see Sections 9.33 and 9.34).

3.20 SCOTTISH INCOME TAX RATES

The Scottish Parliament has control over Scottish Income Tax rates and thresholds. It may not, however, alter:

- The personal allowance
- The Child Benefit Charge (Section 3.3)
- The Winter Fuel Charge (Section 3.3)
- The withdrawal of personal allowances on income over £100,000
- Tax rates on dividends, interest, and other savings income (Scottish taxpayers pay Income Tax at normal UK rates on this income)
- Capital allowances

It also has no power over other taxes, such as NI, VAT, CGT, and IHT. Scottish taxpayers pay these taxes at the same rates as other UK residents.

The amount of income on which a Scottish taxpayer is liable for tax is computed in exactly the same way as other UK resident taxpayers: only the rates of tax differ. Hence, the vast majority of this guide remains equally valid for Scottish taxpayers: it is only the amount of tax that can be saved (or may be suffered) that will vary.

Scottish Income Tax rates apply to a Scottish taxpayer's property income, regardless of where their properties are located. In other words, a Scottish landlord pays Scottish Income Tax rates on income derived from property both within and outwith Scotland. Other taxpayers pay Income Tax at normal UK rates on all their income, even if it is derived from property in Scotland.

The Scottish Parliament has set six different Income Tax rates. Combining these with the relevant parts of the UK tax regime means Scottish taxpayers will pay Income Tax at the following rates in 2026/27:

Up to £12,570	0%	Personal allowance
£12,570 to £16,537	19%	Starter rate
£16,537 to £29,526	20%	Basic rate
£29,526 to £43,662	21%	Intermediate rate
£43,662 to £75,000	42%	Higher rate
£75,000 to £100,000	45%	Advanced rate
£100,000 to £125,140	67.5%	Personal allowance withdrawal
Over £125,140	48%	Top rate

The rates for 2025/26 are broadly the same, except for the following differences:

£12,570 to £15,397	19%	Starter rate
£15,397 to £27,491	20%	Basic rate
£27,491 to £43,662	21%	Intermediate rate

Comparing the Scottish rates with the main UK rates in Section 3.3 and Appendix A, we can see Scottish taxpayers will suffer higher rates of Income Tax on all income over £29,526 in 2026/27, or £27,491 in 2025/26 (except dividends, interest, etc, as explained above).

Worst of all, while taxpayers in the rest of the UK are now enjoying a higher rate threshold of £50,270, Scottish taxpayers are stuck with a threshold of just £43,662. That's ***still less than the higher rate threshold*** of £43,875 all ***UK taxpayers had 17 years ago*** in 2009/10!

Most importantly, the lower threshold for Scottish taxpayers means up to £6,608 extra taxable income is exposed to higher rate tax. Not only does this lead to tax increases for those with genuine income in excess of the Scottish higher rate threshold, it also significantly increases the burden for Scottish landlords whose taxable income is pushed over this level by the restrictions on interest relief examined in Section 4.7.

Practical Impacts

Every Scottish taxpayer has two different sets of tax bands: Scottish bands that apply to employment, self-employment, rental and pension income; and UK bands applying to dividends, interest and savings income and for CGT purposes.

Example: *In 2026/27, Wallace has total gross rental income of £51,000 from residential property, allowable interest costs of £8,000, and other qualifying expenses of £3,500. This gives him a taxable rental 'profit' of £47,500. As he is a Scottish taxpayer, he will pay Income Tax on this sum as follows:*

£12,570 @ 0%	*£0*
£3,967 @ 19%	*£754*
£12,989 @ 20%	*£2,598*
£14,136 @ 21%	*£2,968*
£3,838 @ 42%	*£1,612*
Less: £8,000 @ 20%	*(£1,600) basic rate relief on allowable interest*
Net total due	*£6,332*

Wallace also has a taxable capital gain of £20,000 on a residential property sale (after deducting his annual exemption). His final CGT bill will be:

£2,770 @ 18%	*£499*
£17,230 @ 24%	*£4,135*
Total	*£4,634*

*£2,770 of his **UK** basic rate band is available for CGT purposes (Section 5.2).*

If Wallace had been living in a different part of the UK, he would have remained a basic rate taxpayer and his Income Tax bill would have been £946 less. However, his CGT bill would still have been the same.

Practical Pointer

Scottish taxpayers have the same tax bands for CGT purposes as other UK taxpayers. The CGT planning techniques explored in this guide will produce the same savings for Scottish taxpayers.

The interest relief restrictions detailed in Section 4.7 cost Scottish taxpayers more than other taxpayers for a number of reasons:

i) They have a lower higher rate tax threshold (this alone cost Wallace an extra £768; the cost for other Scottish taxpayers can be as much as £1,322)
ii) The higher rate is 2% more (this cost Wallace a further £77; the cost for other Scottish taxpayers can be as much as £627)
iii) Interest relief at the basic rate of 20% does not cover the cost of profits before interest being taxed at the intermediate rate of 21% (Wallace had £4,162 of interest relieved at basic rate where the corresponding profit before interest was being taxed at the intermediate rate: this cost him a further £42; the cost for some Scottish taxpayers can be as much as £141 in 2026/27)
iv) The advanced rate of 45% applies to taxable income over £75,000 (this could cost some Scottish taxpayers up to £2,507 in extra tax)

v) The Scottish top rate on taxable income over £125,140 is 3% more than the UK additional rate

The interest relief restrictions imposed by the UK Government cost Wallace an extra £887 because he is a Scottish taxpayer. Without the interest relief restrictions, his Income Tax bill would only be £60 more than a non-Scottish taxpayer.

Scottish landlords are suffering the worst of both worlds. The higher tax rates and lower higher rate threshold applying to Scottish taxpayers mean they are seeing even greater increases in their tax bills as a result of the UK Government's interest relief restrictions. In 2026/27, Scottish landlords with rental profits before interest of £50,270 or more will pay at least £1,555 more tax than their counterparts elsewhere in the UK.

Generally speaking, therefore, the Income Tax planning techniques explored throughout this guide will produce even greater savings for Scottish taxpayers.

Trading Profits

The upper earnings limit for NI purposes (see Section 8.1) remains at the UK level for Scottish taxpayers. At 2026/27 rates, this gives Scottish taxpayers below state pension age an overall marginal tax rate of 48% on trading profits falling into the gap between the Scottish higher rate threshold of £43,662 and the UK higher rate threshold of £50,270.

Future Scottish Income Tax Rates

The Scottish Government has announced an intention to maintain the freeze in the higher, advanced, and top rate tax thresholds until at least 2028/29. However, with elections to the Scottish Parliament coming in May 2026, it remains to be seen whether this current Government will still be around until then!

The Scottish Budget for 2026/27, published on 13th January 2026, notes that the Scottish Parliament expects to have the power to set separate Income Tax rates on property income received by Scottish taxpayers from 2027/28 onwards. There are no proposals at present but my crystal ball tells me a 2% 'across the board' increase is highly probable. Nonetheless, we will have to wait and see what happens.

Who Is a Scottish Taxpayer?

You are classed as a Scottish taxpayer if you are UK resident and your main place of residence in the UK is in Scotland. Your main place of residence must be determined as a question of fact, and it is important to remember, for ***this*** purpose:

- It is not possible to elect which property is treated as your main place of residence
- Only property in the UK is counted
- It is not necessary to have any legal or equitable interest in the property: any type of abode may be counted, including hotel rooms, and berths on ships and oil rigs
- Each person must be considered individually (married couples are not treated as a single unit)

Hence, while your main place of residence for this purpose will often be the same as your main residence for CGT purposes (see Chapter 5), the rules are slightly different and may sometimes lead to a different result.

See Section 5.15 for guidance on the factors to be considered in determining a main place of residence. Issues such as where your spouse lives, or whether you have any legal title in the property, are not critical for the purpose of determining if you are a Scottish taxpayer, but continue to be among those factors.

If you move to or from Scotland during the tax year, you will be classified according to where your main place of residence in the UK is for the majority of the year.

If it is not clear whether your main place of residence is in Scotland for any given tax year, the question of whether you are a Scottish taxpayer that year is based on where you have spent the most days. You become a Scottish taxpayer if you are present in Scotland at midnight on at least as many days as you are present in any of England, Wales, or Northern Ireland (taking each country separately).

Non-UK residents cannot be Scottish taxpayers.

Chapter 4

Saving Income Tax on a Property Business

4.1 THE TAXATION OF RENTAL INCOME

As we saw in Chapter 3, Income Tax rates on property income will be increased by 2% 'across the board' from 2027/28 onwards.

In other respects, property letting is generally treated much like any other business for Income Tax purposes, but it also has many quirks that set it apart. In essence, it is treated as a business, but not as a trade, and this leads to some fundamental differences in tax treatment, as we shall see to both our frustration and our delight (but mainly frustration, I'm afraid).

From 2025/26 onwards, property letting needs to be divided into two categories for tax purposes: UK property letting and overseas property letting. Each category is effectively treated as a separate business. Most of the rules we will examine in this chapter apply equally to each category, but there are a few variations applying to overseas property.

Each category needs to be accounted for and reported on your tax return separately. Hence, you will need to draw up accounts for each category to detail all your income and expenses. Quarterly updates for each category will also be required where you are subject to MTD (Section 3.6) and have both UK and overseas properties.

All properties within each category are effectively treated as a single business: referred to as either a 'UK property business' or an 'overseas property business', as the case may be. Hence, for example, if you are letting a number of UK properties on a commercial basis, this will be treated as a single UK property business and one set of accounts will usually suffice (although many landlords prefer to have a separate set of accounts for each property).

Separate accounts will, however, be required for any non-commercial lettings (Section 4.20) within either category.

All rental income must be included within the appropriate category, no matter how modest, unless it is fully covered by rent-a-room relief (Section 4.16) or the property income allowance (Section 4.17).

Technically, landlords may draw up accounts for any period. However, landlords must generally be taxed on the rental profits arising for the tax year ending on 5th April. Hence, while landlords could draw up accounts for a different period and then time-apportion the results to produce appropriate figures for the tax year, this would seldom produce any significant advantage, and it is far simpler to just produce accounts for the year ending 5th April.

One alternative that is accepted is to draw up accounts for the year ending 31st March. This has long been accepted as a sufficiently good enough approximation to the tax year: an approach that has now been given statutory backing by legislation.

For the rest of this chapter, unless stated to the contrary, I will assume landlords are drawing up accounts for the year ending 5th April each year. (But see Section 4.13 for some issues to be aware of it you are using a different accounting date.)

Many landlords have the option to choose whether to use traditional accruals basis accounting, or adopt the cash basis. Indeed, for those who qualify, the cash basis is the default option and those who wish to use the accruals basis need to opt out.

In Section 4.22 we will look at the cash basis for landlords, who qualifies, and some of its advantages and disadvantages. On balance, my view is that, under normal circumstances, the cash basis will generally be disadvantageous for landlords and, for this reason, unless stated to the contrary, it is assumed throughout this guide that landlords prepare accounts using traditional accruals basis accounting.

Nonetheless, for those who qualify, the cash basis is worth considering, as it will be advantageous in some cases. In particular, where a landlord's taxable income is likely to increase in a future tax year, pushing them into a higher tax bracket with a higher marginal tax rate, there may be opportunities to turn the cash basis to advantage and use it as a means to accelerate income into an earlier tax year when the landlord has a lower marginal tax rate: thus producing an overall saving.

Furthermore, as a result of the current cost of living crisis, it is likely the cash basis will be advantageous to more landlords at present, so we will take a closer look at the further potential benefits in Section 9.32. For an explanation of how both the cash basis and the accruals basis work, see Section 3.11.

Earlier Years

For tax years up to 2024/25, there were four categories of property business for tax purposes, as qualifying FHLs within the UK or the EEA were treated as separate businesses. We will look at both the tax regime for FHLs that applied up to 2024/25, and the transitional rules applying when the regime was abolished on 6th April 2025, in Section 9.23.

4.2 TAX DEDUCTIONS

The rules on what types of expenditure may be claimed as deductions in a property letting business are generally similar to those for other types of business, although there are some important differences. Some of the main deductions are listed below, collected under the somewhat arbitrary (and sometimes counter-intuitive) categories used on the tax return. Please note, this is not meant to be a comprehensive list, more like highlights, and I have not repeated anything I feel is self-explanatory.

The box numbers quoted here are from Page UKP 2 of the tax return, as it applies to UK property letting, although most of the deductions listed may also be claimed in an overseas property letting businesses.

Rent, Rates, Insurance, and Ground Rents (Box 24)
Includes service charges, etc. Costs such as Council Tax incurred by landlords during void periods can also be included.

Property Repairs and Maintenance (Box 25)
Includes both repairs to the property itself and repairs to furniture and equipment supplied with a property. See Section 4.8 for details of what may be claimed as a repair.

Non-Residential Property Finance Costs (Box 26)
Interest and finance costs related to non-residential property (see Sections 4.5 and 4.6). You should also include any finance costs not related to borrowings (e.g. bank charges on a current account in credit), even if related to a residential property letting business.

Legal, Management, and Other Professional Fees (Box 27)
Includes:

- Letting agent's fees
- Advertising for tenants
- Accountancy fees
- Legal and professional fees (see Section 4.4)

Costs of Services Provided, Including Wages (Box 28)
Includes:

- Heating, lighting, and other utilities, if borne by the landlord. Again, costs incurred during void periods can be included.
- The cost of cleaners, gardeners, etc, where relevant

Other Allowable Property Expenses (Box 29)
Includes:

- Bad debts (Section 4.15)
- Licence fees (e.g. for an HMO licence or selective licensing scheme)
- Professional subscriptions (e.g. membership of the National Residential Landlords Association or the Scottish Association of Landlords)
- Training and research (Section 3.17)
- Landlord's administrative expenditure (Sections 3.13 to 3.18)

Costs of Replacing Domestic Items (Box 36)
This covers replacement of moveable items within a residential letting. See Section 4.9 for further details.

Residential Property Finance Costs (Box 44)
Interest and finance costs related to residential property letting (see Sections 4.5 and 4.6). As explained in Section 4.7, these are not allowed as a proper deduction anymore and only provide basic rate relief: hence why they have to go in a different box on the tax return. This did not apply to FHLs up to 2024/25: the relevant costs went in Box 7 on Page UKP 1 instead.

If your total gross income from all property letting is less than the VAT registration threshold (currently £90,000), you can, if you wish, put the total of all items falling into Boxes 24 to 29 relating to your UK property letting into Box 29.

If your tenant contributes part of an otherwise allowable expense, you may claim only the net amount you actually bear yourself.

As explained in Section 3.12, expenses incurred before you begin your letting business may usually be included as pre-trading expenditure.

In the next few sections, we will take a closer look at some of the more common areas of expenditure typically encountered in property letting businesses and examine what determines whether these expenses may be deducted for Income Tax purposes. This is not an exhaustive list, however, and other expenditure that meets the general principles outlined in Section 3.12 will often be allowable. In particular, the administrative expenses described in Sections 3.13 to 3.18 should not be forgotten (in my experience, they often are!)

4.3 WHEN IS A PROPERTY A RENTAL PROPERTY?

You will frequently see me refer to 'rental property'. Whether a property is a rental property at any given time is often crucial in determining whether (or how much of) an item of expenditure is allowable.

Quite obviously, a property is a rental property while it is rented out. For most tax purposes, a property is usually also a rental property when it is:

- Available for letting but currently vacant
- Being prepared for letting
- Being renovated between lettings, with the intention of letting it out again thereafter

In each case, the property's rental property status would be lost if it was actually used for something else (e.g. a family holiday for the owner's spouse and children). Nevertheless, merely sleeping there overnight, while preparing the property for subsequent rental, should not usually harm the property's status.

Strictly speaking, a vacant property ceases to be a rental property once a decision is taken to sell it. In practice, however, this rule will not usually be applied where the period between the decision and the sale is relatively brief and there is no other use in the interim.

HMRC generally regards the day on which your first UK rental property is let out for the first time as the first day of your UK property business. Similarly, the day on which your first overseas property is let out for the first time is the first day of your overseas property business.

However, any eligible expenditure incurred within the seven-year period before your first property in ether category is first let should remain claimable as pre-trading expenditure (see Section 3.12). This sometimes means the expenditure must be claimed in a later tax year.

Eligible expenses relating to your second, and subsequent, rental properties within each category may generally be claimed as incurred, even if the relevant property is not let by the end of that tax year.

Remember, however, you have to treat UK property lettings and overseas property lettings as separate businesses. Hence, a first overseas rental gets treated as a first property even if you already have a portfolio of UK properties. The same goes for your first UK rental when you have a portfolio of overseas properties (or, up to 2024/25, your first FHL, etc).

4.4 LEGAL AND PROFESSIONAL FEES

Legal fees and other professional costs incurred for the purposes of a property business may fall into one of four categories for tax purposes:

i) Revenue expenditure
ii) Capital expenditure
iii) Costs of obtaining loan finance
iv) Abortive capital expenditure

See Section 3.12 for an explanation of the difference between revenue expenditure and capital expenditure.

Revenue Expenditure
Revenue expenditure may be claimed as a deduction against rental income. These are the costs incurred year in, year out, in earning rental profits. They will include items such as debt collection expenses, agent's fees, and accountancy fees for:

- Submitting your quarterly updates under MTD (where required, and where done by your accountant on your behalf)
- Preparation of your annual accounts
- Preparing the business element of your tax return

> **Tax Tip**
> If your property business is the only reason you are required to submit a tax return, then it will be reasonable to claim a deduction for all the fees incurred for preparing and submitting the return rather than merely the business element.

Legal and professional costs relating to a tenant's lease are generally allowable (e.g. legal fees for preparing the lease). Costs incurred in amending leases to be compliant with the Renters' Rights Act will also be allowable.

HMRC regards any expenses connected with the first letting of a property for a fixed term of more than one year as a capital expense that cannot be claimed. Costs relating to subsequent leases will generally be allowable provided the new lease is on broadly similar terms, for a period of less than 50 years, and the property has not been used for another purpose in the interim. These issues are generally only relevant to non-residential property.

Capital Expenses
Legal fees and professional costs incurred for the purchase or sale of properties cannot be claimed for Income Tax purposes in a property letting business. If the

purchase or sale goes through, they may be claimed for CGT purposes when the property is disposed of (Chapter 5).

This category would include:

- Legal fees
- Estate agent's fees
- SDLT
- Survey fees (but see below if carried out for a lender)
- Valuation fees (but see below if carried out for a lender)
- Professional costs incurred on a successful planning application

Costs of Obtaining Loan Finance

It is only the costs of actually purchasing a property itself that must be regarded as capital expenditure and cannot be claimed for Income Tax purposes. Any costs relating to obtaining finance (typically a mortgage) may be claimed as a finance cost. As we will see in Section 4.6, this extends much further than many property investors realise.

Sadly, when these costs relate to residential property, they are subject to the wretched 'Section 24' restrictions described in Section 4.7. But even basic rate Income Tax relief will often be preferable to a CGT deduction at some uncertain time in the future. Furthermore, since HMRC has been known to deny CGT relief for costs that could have been claimed for Income Tax purposes, it will generally be sensible to claim Income Tax relief when you can.

Costs such as survey or valuation fees incurred when re-mortgaging a property for business purposes may also be claimed as finance costs. This includes cases where the new borrowings qualify under the capital introduced principle (see Section 4.5).

Abortive Capital Expenditure

As we all know, sometimes a purchase or sale will not go through. In these cases, the investor will often incur costs such as survey or legal fees. Unfortunately, HMRC takes the view that costs related to purchases or sales which do not proceed are not generally allowable for Income Tax and neither will they be allowable for CGT purposes. These are what we sometimes call 'tax nothings'.

There is, however, a strong argument that any costs incurred before making a final decision whether to purchase or sell a property are part of the regular overhead costs of the property business and are therefore properly claimable as revenue expenditure.

Example: *Noah is considering buying an investment property in the Newcastle area. He spots a potential purchase in Gosforth and has a survey done on the property. However, he is unhappy with the result and decides not to pursue this purchase. Noah may claim the cost of the survey as an allowable business expense.*

Noah moves his attention to Durham and finds another potential investment property. He has a survey carried out and, happy with the results, this time he decides to proceed with the purchase.

Things go well until the owner of the Durham property is made redundant and is forced to take it back off the market. By this time, Noah has incurred substantial legal fees.

Noah's legal fees were incurred after he decided to purchase the Durham property. These fees are therefore abortive capital expenditure that Noah is unable to claim. Noah will, however, still be able to claim the cost of the survey fees for the Durham property as, once again, these were incurred before he made a decision to purchase the property.

To assist claims for 'pre-decision' expenditure of this nature, it is useful to retain documentary evidence showing the final decision to purchase or sell had not yet been taken.

In other cases, the claim for pre-decision abortive expenditure might reasonably extend further, perhaps to include a proportion of the legal fees. I have even heard the argument that a final decision cannot have been made until contracts are exchanged (or missives completed in Scotland). In practice, it all depends on the facts of the case.

While I believe claims for pre-decision abortive expenditure incurred for the purposes of a property business are perfectly valid, this is a view HMRC may not necessarily share. Some dispute over claims of this nature may therefore arise. However, I can say that, in over thirty years as a tax adviser, I never had such a claim overturned.

Professional costs incurred on an unsuccessful application for planning permission are also regarded as 'tax nothings', and generally cannot be claimed for either Income Tax or CGT purposes. However, if you can show the same costs led to a later, successful, application, they may still be regarded as part of the capital cost of the project for CGT purposes.

Abortive capital expenditure is not allowable when the landlord is using the cash basis. See Section 4.23 for further details.

4.5 INTEREST RELIEF: WHAT IS ALLOWABLE?

As most property investors know, there are restrictions on the ***rate*** of tax relief available to residential landlords for interest and finance costs. I will look at those restrictions, often known as the wretched 'Section 24', in Section 4.7. Firstly, however, I am going to look at ***which*** interest and finance costs are eligible to be claimed in the first place.

When Can Interest be Claimed?

Interest is allowable and may be claimed against rental income if it is incurred for the purposes of the property business. There are two ways this can occur:

i) The interest arises on funds that have been utilised in the business, **or**
ii) The interest arises on capital introduced into the business

The Capital Introduced Principle

The second heading above provides enormous scope for property investors to claim interest relief for Income Tax purposes.

When a property is rented out for the first time, the value of the property at that date represents capital introduced into the business. Any other capital expenditure incurred on a rental property also represents capital introduced into the business, including SDLT and legal fees paid on the purchase and the cost of furnishing the property, where relevant. The fact that a deduction cannot generally be claimed for these expenses does not prevent them from being capital introduced into the business.

Hence, subject to 'the catch' explained below, interest relief will generally be available on any borrowings against a rental property up to its original value when first rented out PLUS all the other capital expenditure incurred in purchasing it and preparing it for letting. ***It does not matter what the borrowed funds are used for!***

Later, additional, capital expenditure on a rental property, such as capital improvements, counts as further capital introduced (see Section 4.8 regarding the difference between repairs and capital improvements). You cannot double-count the same expenditure, however. For example, if you build an extension on a property before letting it out, its value when first rented out will be increased by this expenditure, so you cannot add it on again as further capital introduced.

For borrowings in excess of the capital introduced in respect of a property, we must rely on the first heading above. In other words, interest relief will only be available on these additional borrowings if the borrowed funds are used for business purposes. (Some interest arising under the first heading alone may not be allowable if the landlord is using the cash basis: see Section 4.22 for details.)

Example 1: *Matthew buys an investment property for £125,000 and immediately begins to rent it out. He finances his purchase with a buy-to-let mortgage of £90,000 and pays the remainder in cash. He also pays SDLT of £6,250 and legal fees of £1,500, of which £1,100 represents a capital cost (see Section 4.4). Naturally, he is able to claim relief for the interest on his buy-to-let mortgage against his rental income from the property.*

A few years later, Matthew re-mortgages the property and borrows an additional £50,000 to bring his total borrowings up to £140,000. He spends the new funds on personal items unrelated to his property business. Despite this, Matthew remains entitled to interest relief against his rental income for the first £132,350 of his borrowings: i.e. an amount equal to the property's value when first rented out plus the SDLT and capital element of the legal fees paid on the purchase. The last £7,650 of his borrowings are not eligible for relief, however, as these are in excess of the capital introduced into the business and have not been used for other business purposes either.

After a few more years, Matthew borrows a further £25,000 against the property. This time, he spends £15,000 taking his partner on a luxury cruise but uses £10,000 to improve another rental property. He cannot claim any interest relief on the £15,000 used personally as this does not represent capital introduced into the business. He can claim interest relief on the £10,000 used to improve another rental property as this has been used for business purposes.

Matthew therefore now has a total of £142,350 of eligible borrowings for interest relief purposes out of his overall total of £165,000. (We will look at how investors should calculate their interest relief in this situation later.)

Another way to look at the position for interest relief is:

i) Borrowings against a rental property up to a sum equal to the original value of that property when first rented out PLUS any other capital expenditure relating to that property are generally allowable (subject to avoiding any double-counting and 'the catch' described below)
ii) Other borrowings are allowable when the funds are used for business purposes

Interest will therefore always be allowable if it arises on funds used to purchase or improve rental properties or otherwise expended for the purposes of the property business (subject to the points in Section 4.22 where landlords are using the cash basis).

Example 2: *Mark takes out a personal loan and spends the funds on improvements to a flat that he subsequently lets out. The interest on his loan is allowable because it has been incurred for the purpose of his property business.*

Example 3: *Luke has a large property rental business and employs several staff. While the business is generally buoyant, Luke runs into cashflow difficulties in December 2026 and has to borrow an extra £10,000 to pay his staff's wages. Luke's borrowings were used for business purposes and hence the interest he incurs will be allowable for tax purposes.*

Example 4: *John borrows an extra £60,000 by re-mortgaging his home. He uses these funds for the deposits on two new rental properties. He may claim the interest on the £60,000 of new borrowing as it is used for business purposes.*

In a case like John's in our last example, there will usually be the practical difficulty of establishing just how much interest should be claimed. John will already have an outstanding balance on his mortgage, so it would not be right for him to claim all his interest. In practice, we must do an apportionment.

Example 4 Resumed: *Prior to re-mortgaging, John had a balance of £125,000 on the mortgage on his home. The extra £60,000 took that balance up to £185,000. John should therefore claim 60/185ths of his mortgage interest for tax purposes.*

Repayment Mortgages

Interest calculations are fairly straightforward in the case of an interest-only mortgage but what about repayment mortgages? The first and most important point to note is you can only claim relief for the interest element of your loan or mortgage payments. The capital repayment element may not be claimed. Your mortgage provider will usually send you an annual statement detailing the interest charged.

Where you have a repayment mortgage that is only partly allowable for business purposes, an apportionment must be made, as outlined above. However, as you repay capital, the total outstanding balance on the account will reduce, so how do you do your apportionment then?

The usual approach is to stick with the apportionment ratio you derived when you first did the re-mortgaging (e.g. 60/185ths in John's case).

Some, more aggressive, accountants might suggest all repayments should be treated as repaying the original non-business element of the loan. This approach may, however, be subject to challenge by HMRC.

> **Tax Tip**
> To maximise the business element within your interest payments, arrange for the new funds obtained on re-mortgaging to be allocated to a separate mortgage loan account with the bank. Make the new account interest-only, while leaving the original mortgage account as a repayment account. In this way, you can put beyond doubt the fact that the capital repayment element belongs exclusively to the non-business part of your mortgage.

'The Catch': What Counts as Capital Introduced?

Our last example raises another important point. John was able to claim interest relief for part of the mortgage on his home because he spent the funds for business purposes: as deposits on rental properties.

Those deposits, however, also count as part of the capital introduced into the business. In other words, this restricts the investor's ability to obtain further relief for additional borrowings against the rental property.

Let's say John used £30,000 from the mortgage on his home as a deposit on a buy-to-let property purchased for £117,500 and the other £87,500 was made up of £7,500 in cash and £80,000 from a buy-to-let mortgage. Let's also assume he paid a further £7,250 in purchase costs (SDLT, legal fees, etc).

Hence, at this stage, as far as this property is concerned, John has introduced capital of £124,750 into his property business (the value of the rental property plus his purchase costs), but is already claiming interest relief on borrowings of £110,000: a buy-to-let mortgage of £80,000 and £30,000 of the additional mortgage on his home.

John can therefore only *automatically* claim interest relief on further borrowings against the rental property of just £14,750: the same amount he originally funded in cash (£7,500 + £7,250). Any further borrowings will only be eligible for interest relief if the funds are used for business purposes.

What John can do, however, is borrow further funds against his rental properties to repay some or all of the additional £60,000 mortgage on his home. This would mean he was replacing one qualifying loan with another, so he would continue to obtain interest relief on the new borrowings.

HMRC's View on the Capital Introduced Principle

HMRC generally accepts the principles outlined above, although some resistance does arise from time to time. If any problems do arise over this issue, refer HMRC to Example 2 in BIM 45700 in their own manuals.

What Happens When Properties Are Sold or Cease to Be Used in The Business?
Interest on borrowings used to finance the purchase or improvement of a property will generally cease to be allowable if that property ceases to be used in the rental business (e.g. if it is subsequently adopted as the owner's residence). However, in other cases, the eligibility of interest for tax relief will follow the use of the underlying funds.

Example 5: *In 2026, Abel borrows £180,000 secured on his home, Eden Cottage, and uses the money to buy a rental property, Babel Heights. At this stage, the interest on his £180,000 loan is clearly allowable.*

In 2029, Abel sells Babel Heights and uses the sale proceeds to buy a new rental property, Ark Villa. Abel's interest payments on the £180,000 loan continue to be allowable as the underlying funds have been reinvested in the business.

In 2031, Abel sells Eden Cottage and moves into a new house in Gomorrah. Abel's mortgage on the Gomorrah property exceeds the balance on his Eden Cottage mortgage. The new mortgage therefore includes the original £180,000 borrowing used to acquire a business property and hence the appropriate proportion of Abel's interest payments should still be allowable.

In 2032, Abel sells Ark Villa in order to finance the costs of an extension he is building on his Gomorrah home. At this point, the interest on his £180,000 borrowings ceases to be allowable for Income Tax purposes.

As well as tracking the underlying funds, there is also the possibility that interest relief may continue to be available under the capital introduced principle (i.e. our second heading at the start of this section).

Example 6: *Naamah owns a rental property in Canaan Street that she bought for £150,000 some years ago and which has no mortgage against it. In 2026, she takes out a mortgage of £125,000 on the property and uses this money to buy a second rental property in Judea Gardens. Clearly, at this stage, her mortgage interest is allowable against her rental income.*

A few years later, she sells the property in Judea Gardens but the mortgage on her Canaan Street property remains outstanding.

She has sold the property that was purchased with the borrowed funds, but the interest on her Canaan Street mortgage remains allowable because it is also a rental property and the mortgage is less than its value when first rented out.

Existing Property Introduced into the Business
The interest on a mortgage over a property that is newly introduced into the rental business becomes allowable from that point onwards. Hence, the interest on a mortgage on your former home may be claimed from the date on which you make it available for letting.

Furthermore, as the entire value of the property at that date represents capital introduced into your business, you could also re-mortgage the property and all the interest payable on loans secured on the property, up to its value on the first day you rent it out, will be allowable for tax purposes.

Example 5 Revisited: *By 2034, Abel's Gomorrah property is worth £750,000 and his outstanding mortgage is £325,000. Abel re-mortgages the Gomorrah property, realising an additional £250,000, which he uses to buy a new home in neighbouring Sodom.*

Abel now starts to rent out his Gomorrah property. The entire interest payable on Abel's £575,000 mortgage will now be allowable against his rental income.

Where an existing property, such as a former home, is introduced into the rental business, the capital introduced will be its value when first rented out. Previous capital expenditure on the property, such as legal fees paid on the purchase, cannot also be counted in this case. The current value of any contents rented out with the property (furniture, etc) can, however, be included.

Loans in Joint Names, etc

Strictly, for interest to be claimed as an allowable cost, it must be a liability of the owner of the business. This generally means the underlying loan must be in the name of the property investor themselves.

By concession, however, HMRC will allow qualifying interest paid by a property investor to be claimed when the underlying loan is in joint names with their spouse, or even in the sole name of their spouse. Where the loan is in the spouse's sole name, it is vital the interest is actually ***paid*** by the property investor themselves, even though it is their spouse's liability.

Naturally, the interest is still only allowable if incurred for the purposes of the business, as detailed above.

4.6 FINANCE COSTS

The Government often talks about 'finance costs' and you will have seen me refer to 'interest and finance costs'. To be technically correct, finance costs *include* interest (which is usually the biggest element), but they also include other costs, such as loan arrangement fees. Furthermore, as we saw in Section 4.4, finance costs include professional fees incurred in obtaining loan finance, typically a mortgage.

The good news about finance costs is that, provided they are incurred for the purposes of your property business, they are allowable for Income Tax purposes.

The question of whether finance costs are incurred for the purposes of your property business follows the same principles as for interest (Section 4.5). In other words, these costs will generally be allowable where the borrowed funds either represent capital introduced into the business, or are otherwise used for business purposes. In some cases, the costs may need to be apportioned where they are only partly allowable: again, this will follow the principles we looked at in Section 4.5.

The bad news, sadly, is that, like interest, finance costs are subject to the wretched 'Section 24' restrictions (Section 4.7) when they relate to residential rental property. Nonetheless, finance costs are a much-overlooked source of tax relief, so it's well worth us taking a closer look at them.

Aside from interest, finance costs may include:

- Loan arrangement fees
- Mortgage broker's fees
- Lender's survey or valuation fees
- Land registry fees for registering a charge over a property
- A portion of the legal fees for a purchase partly funded by way of mortgage
- Early redemption fees (aka early repayment penalties)
- Facility arrangement fees
- Guarantee fees

A purchaser's own survey fees remain a capital expense (see Section 4.4). It is only additional lender's survey or valuation fees that can be claimed as a finance cost.

Land registry fees are typically paid by the purchaser's lawyer then passed on to the purchaser through the final settlement: so watch out for these in the settlement statement.

While it is perfectly reasonable to claim a portion of the legal fees related to dealing with a lender, registering the security, etc, not everyone does this as it is not always apparent what a suitable proportion might be.

> **Tax Tip**
> Part of the legal fees arising on the purchase of a property will often relate to the raising of finance: i.e. the mortgage. It may therefore be worth arranging to have this element of the fees invoiced separately, so they can be claimed for Income Tax purposes as a finance cost. Alternatively, a reasonable estimate of the appropriate proportion may be used instead. This will typically be in the region of a quarter to a third, although it varies from case to case.

Lender's survey or valuation fees are allowable both when purchasing a property for rental, or when re-mortgaging a property for business purposes: including cases where the new borrowings qualify under the capital introduced principle (see Section 4.5).

Claiming Relief for Finance Costs

Under the accruals basis, general accounting principles usually dictate that finance costs should be spread over the life of the relevant loan. Where this applies, the tax treatment will follow the same principles.

Example: *In June 2026, Eve purchases a property partly funded with a buy-to-let mortgage. The bank charges her a loan arrangement fee of £2,500. She also pays a mortgage broker's fee of £700, pays £400 for a lender's survey, and pays legal fees of £2,400. Her lawyer says around a third of the legal fees relate to dealing with the lender and registering the security. Eve funded the deposit for the rental property by re-mortgaging her home, for which she paid an additional fee of £600. She is able to claim the following finance costs:*

Loan arrangement fee	*£2,500*
Broker's fee	*£700*
Lender's survey	*£400*
Legal fees (£2,400 x 1/3)	*£800*
Re-mortgaging fee	*£600*
Total	*£5,000*

The buy-to-let mortgage has a twenty-year term, so Eve can claim these costs at £250 per year for twenty years (for the sake of illustration, we'll assume the same term applies to the re-mortgaging of her home).

Under the accruals basis, the timing of relief for loan arrangement fees, etc, is unaffected by whether the investor pays them at the outset or adds them to the value of their loan. We will look at the position under the cash basis in Section 4.22.

Where fees incurred for business purposes are added to the value of a loan, the subsequent interest charges on this additional balance are allowable in the same way as interest on the main loan balance.

Accelerating Relief

Spreading relief for finance costs over the life of the loan is based on generally accepted accounting principles. However, it is important to understand those principles only require the costs to be spread over the useful life of the loan and not necessarily its full legal life.

Hence, if you take out a twenty-year loan, but fully expect to refinance your property again after five years, then it would be quite reasonable to claim your finance costs over five years rather than twenty.

Where you decide to claim relief over a shorter period than the legal term of your loan, it is important to retain evidence of your rationale for doing so, such as a business plan that includes your financing policy.

Re-Financing: A Claims Bonanza!

When I was in practice, I always enjoyed it when one of my landlord clients refinanced one of their rental properties. There are three elements to the potential 'claims bonanza' that may be available on such an occasion:

i) The remaining finance costs relating to the old loan that have not yet been claimed
ii) Any early redemption fee relating to the old loan
iii) The finance costs relating to the new loan

Example Revisited: *Eve claimed £250 of her finance costs each tax year from 2026/27 to 2030/31 (five years). In June 2031, however, she refinances the property with a different bank. The new mortgage is again for a twenty-year term but, this time, Eve knows she will probably refinance again after five years. Her old bank charges her an early redemption fee of £1,750; the loan arrangement fee and other finance costs relating to the new loan total £3,500. This is what Eve can claim in 2031/32:*

Remaining balance of finance costs re old loan	
£5,000 x 15/20 =	*£3,750*
Early redemption fee	*£1,750*
Finance costs re new loan (year one of five)	
£3,500 x 1/5	*£700*
Total claim	*£6,200*

These costs will only produce relief at the property basic rate (which will be 22% at this time), but that's still a saving of £1,364.

To keep things simple, I have assumed the new loan paid off both the old buy-to-let mortgage and the additional amount Eve borrowed by re-mortgaging her home, but the new loan balance does not exceed the purchase price of the rental property.

If Eve had not paid off the additional amount she borrowed by re-mortgaging her home, some of the remaining balance of her old finance costs should arguably not be claimed in 2031/32. As the amount concerned is small, however, there is unlikely to be any challenge on this point.

If the new loan balance exceeded the purchase price of the property, Eve would have to restrict the third part of her claim unless she has used the excess for business purposes.

In the past, HMRC tended to regard early redemption fees as a personal cost rather than a business cost and did not generally consider them allowable for Income Tax purposes. However, it is now generally accepted that refinancing is a normal, commercial, part of a property business, and early redemption fees will generally be accepted as an allowable cost for Income Tax purposes, provided there is a good business reason for the early redemption (like paying less mortgage interest, for example).

4.7 INTEREST RELIEF RESTRICTIONS (SECTION 24)

In utter defiance of one of the most fundamental principles under which businesses are taxed in the UK, the Government has imposed restrictions on tax relief for interest and finance costs paid by residential landlords. Before we look at these dreadful restrictions, often known as Section 24, it is worth pointing out they do **not** affect landlords renting out non-residential property, or investors renting out property via a company (see the Taxcafe guide *Using a Property Company to Save Tax* for more information).

Interest and finance costs relating to qualifying FHLs were also exempt from the Section 24 restrictions up to 2024/25.

Nonetheless, the restrictions do now apply to *all* individuals renting out residential property (in the UK or overseas), including those operating as an individual in their own name, as joint owners, through a partnership, or through a trust.

The Restrictions

Tax relief for interest and finance costs relating to residential property lettings is restricted to basic rate only, currently 20%. From 2027/28 onwards, relief will be given at the property basic rate of 22%.

Example 1: *Adam is a higher rate taxpayer with a salary of £60,000. He also receives annual rental profits of £40,000 from a residential property portfolio: before deduction of interest and finance costs amounting to £30,000. The true profit from Adam's rental business is therefore just £10,000, but his tax liability on this income for 2026/27 is as follows:*

Profit before interest: £40,000 x 40% =	*£16,000*
Less: interest relief: £30,000 x 20% =	*(£6,000)*
Income Tax due:	*£10,000*

As a result of these terrible restrictions, Adam is suffering an effective tax rate of 100%!

Things are likely to get even worse for Adam in future, as any increase in his taxable income will mean he starts to lose his personal allowance. We'll look at the effect of this in more detail later.

Even if his income remains at the same level, Adam will suffer more tax in 2027/28 as follows:

Profit before interest: £40,000 x 42% =	*£16,800*
Less: interest relief: £30,000 x 22% =	*(£6,600)*
Income Tax due:	*£10,200*

It's worth pointing out that, because the rate of tax relief for residential finance costs is increasing by 2% at the same time that the Income Tax charges on taxable rental profits (before deducting interest) are also increasing by 2%, landlords will only suffer a tax increase on their true profits after interest. The rate of tax effectively suffered on their interest costs will generally remain the same.

Hence, in this example, Adam suffered a £200 tax increase, equating to 2% of his true rental profit of £10,000. But, it's still pretty bad: his effective tax rate has risen to 102%!

The agony of Section 24 is not confined only to genuine higher rate taxpayers like Adam. The impact of these outrageous restrictions extends to many landlords who would otherwise be basic rate taxpayers; even to some who are making rental losses.

Example 2: *Delilah has a salary of £30,000. She also has a portfolio of residential rental properties yielding annual profits (before interest and finance costs) of £33,000. She pays interest of £35,000 each year. Overall, she is making a loss of £2,000. However, Delilah's self-assessment tax liability on her rental income for 2026/27 is calculated as follows:*

Salary	*£30,000*
Rental profits before interest	*£33,000*
Total taxable income	*£63,000*
Less: Personal allowance	*(£12,570)*
	£50,430
Income Tax at 20% on basic rate band of £37,700:	*£7,540*
Income Tax at 40% on remaining £12,730:	*£5,092*
Less: Tax deducted under PAYE (basic rate tax on salary less personal allowance)	*(£3,486)*
Interest relief against property income £33,000 x 20% (see below)	*(£6,600)*
Income Tax due	*£2,546*

Thanks to the Government's vicious attack on landlords, Delilah has a tax liability of £2,546 despite making a loss of £2,000. This now gives her an overall after-tax loss of £4,546, which is more than she can possibly bear. How anyone can call such an outcome 'fair' defies belief: but the architect of this disaster has long since disappeared to his cushy job at the Evening Standard.

As we can see from the example, interest costs in excess of the individual's rental profit before interest do not attract relief. Before the Section 24 restrictions were introduced, Delilah's loss of £2,000 would have been carried forward in the form of a rental loss, deductible against any future rental profits from the same business. Now her loss is termed 'unused residential property finance costs' and can only be carried forward for relief at basic rate against future profits from residential lettings within the same business (i.e. either UK property or overseas property, as applicable).

I will refer to a loss of this nature as 'unrelieved interest', which is a bit easier on the eye (and brain) than HMRC's official term.

How Much Interest Attracts Basic Rate Tax Relief?

The amount of interest and finance costs on residential property that attracts basic rate tax relief is the lowest of three amounts:

i) The total qualifying interest and finance costs on residential property for the year (as established under the principles set out in Sections 4.5 and 4.6), plus any unrelieved interest brought forward
ii) The taxable residential rental profits for the year (before interest and finance costs)
iii) The landlord's total taxable income for the year, excluding dividends, interest, and savings income; and after deducting their personal allowance

Unrelieved interest brought forward means interest that can only be relieved at basic rate; it does not include interest that is fully deductible and is included within some older rental losses brought forward.

As an example, let's look at these three amounts for Delilah in 2026/27:

Her total qualifying finance costs for the year are £35,000. To this we add any unrelieved interest brought forward. Let's say this totals £10,000 for the sake of illustration, giving us £45,000 for amount (i).

Amount (ii), Delilah's taxable residential rental profits for the year, is £33,000.

Delilah's total taxable income for the year is £63,000. Deducting her personal allowance of £12,570 gives us £50,430 for amount (iii).

The lowest of the three amounts is amount (ii), £33,000, and this is the amount on which Delilah can claim basic rate tax relief.

If we go back to the earlier example of Adam, we see amount (i) (his total qualifying interest and finance costs) was the lowest amount and was thus the amount on which he claimed basic rate tax relief. This will generally be the case for most profitable rental businesses, but exceptions may arise for landlords with little or no other taxable income.

Example 3: *In 2026/27, Sheba has residential rental profits of £30,000 before deduction of interest and finance costs. She has no other income. She has £20,000 of allowable interest and finance costs. However, the amount eligible for relief is restricted to £17,430: the amount by which her taxable income of £30,000 exceeds her personal allowance of £12,570.*

Sheba therefore has no tax to pay and unrelieved interest and finance costs of £2,570 to carry forward. These carried forward costs could save her some tax in a later year when her rental profits are higher.

This example illustrates the only bit of good news about the interest relief restrictions: landlords like Sheba, whose overall income is quite low, are able to carry forward some of their interest and finance costs rather than set them against income covered by their personal allowance.

In other words, such landlords will get effective tax relief for their interest and finance costs (albeit in the future and restricted to basic rate) rather than wasting them as a deduction against income that would not have been taxed anyway.

Further Implications

Changing interest and finance costs from a deduction to a relief (at basic rate) means the landlord's total taxable income increases. We have already seen how this impacts on the use of the personal allowance and basic rate band, but the increase in total taxable income also affects:

- The Child Benefit Charge (see Section 3.3)
- The Winter Fuel Charge (see Section 3.3)
- Withdrawal of personal allowances if taxable income is over £100,000
- The additional rate tax threshold (see Appendix A)
- The savings rate band and personal savings allowance (see Appendix A)
- Scottish tax thresholds (Section 3.20)
- CGT rates (see Section 5.2)

Example 4: *Job has residential rental profits of £200,000 before deduction of interest costs totalling £150,000. He has no other income. He and his wife have three small children, so his wife claims child benefit of £3,268 (in 2026/27).*

If landlords were still subject to a reasonably sensible tax system (by which I mean if the Section 24 restrictions did not apply), Job would have taxable income of £50,000, meaning he remained a basic rate taxpayer and was not subject to the CBC. His Income Tax bill would amount to just £7,486, leaving him with after tax income of £42,514.

Instead, Job is treated as having taxable income of £200,000 and his Income Tax calculation for 2026/27 is as follows:

Income Tax at 20% on £37,700	*£7,540*
Income Tax at 40% on £87,440	*£34,976*
Income Tax at 45% on £74,860	*£33,687*
Child Benefit Charge	*£3,268*
Less: Basic rate relief on interest: £150,000 @ 20%	*(£30,000)*
Total tax due	*£49,471*

Unlike Adam (our first example in this section), Job has (just about) enough profit to cover his tax bill. Nonetheless, his effective tax rate for 2026/27 is still a whopping 98.9%!

And it will be worse for Job next year (2027/28). Even assuming no increase in the CBC (there probably will be in reality), his tax bill will increase by a further £1,000 (£50,000 x 2%), to £50,471: an effective tax rate of almost 101%!

Job works hard running his property portfolio, providing homes to tenants that need them. Yet the Government sees fit to take all but a mere £529 of his income from him. And, even that won't be enough for them next year, when they'll demand ***all*** his income, plus a bit more on top!

An arms manufacturer making weapons that kill would get full interest relief, but those who provide something incredibly valuable (a home) are being persecuted.

The Cost of Section 24

Section 24 means many residential landlords are taxed on hypothetical profits they are not actually making: i.e. their interest costs. In effect, the landlord pays tax at the normal marginal rates we saw in Section 3.10 on their genuine profits and then further tax on their interest and finance costs.

The effective rates of additional tax on interest and finance costs in tax years up to and including 2026/27 are as follows:

Effective Tax Rates on Interest and Finance Costs to 2026/27

'Income' Bracket	
Up to £50,270	0%
£50,270 to £100,000	20%
£100,000 to £125,140	40%
Over £125,140	25%

Landlords subject to the CBC (see Section 3.3) suffer further additional tax on interest and finance costs falling into the £60,000 to £80,000 'income' bracket. Older landlords may suffer the Winter Fuel Charge on their interest and finance costs (see Section 3.3).

The 'income' bracket the interest and finance costs fall into is generally the top part of the landlord's taxable income (with the exception of those with dividend income, as this is always the top part). Of course, we all know it is not really income, but that, in effect, is how it is treated under the lunacy of Section 24.

If we go back to Adam in Example 1, he had a salary of £60,000, genuine rental profits of £10,000, and interest costs of £30,000. Hence, his interest costs made up his taxable income from £70,000 to £100,000 and thus suffered an effective tax rate of 20%. That gave rise to a tax cost of £6,000 (£30,000 x 20%). Adding this to the tax on his genuine profits (£10,000 x 40% = £4,000) produced his tax bill of £10,000 for 2026/27.

While this is a good way of analysing the cost of Section 24, it does not mean, as some people fear, that an increase in interest costs will lead to an increase in your tax bill. For example, if Adam's interest costs increased by £1,000, his genuine profit would reduce to £9,000 and the tax on it would then be £3,600 (£9,000 x 40%) in 2026/27. Meanwhile, his interest costs of £31,000 would give rise to a tax cost of £6,200 (£31,000 x 20%). His total tax bill for 2026/27 would thus reduce by £200 to £9,800, reflecting the basic rate tax relief on his additional interest cost.

In other words, in most cases, the marginal tax rate applying to any increase, or reduction in residential landlords' interest costs is 20%.

For example, paying £5,000 more interest will generally mean paying £1,000 less tax. This, of course, is different to the marginal tax rates, and thus the rate of tax relief, for other expenses paid by landlords, as discussed in Section 3.10.

So, when it comes to interest and finance costs for residential landlords, the marginal rate of tax relief provided by those costs (generally 20%) is quite distinct from the effective cost of Section 24.

Example 4 Revisited: *In 2026/27, Job has genuine rental profits of £50,000 and interest costs of £150,000. He is subject to the CBC as his wife is claiming child benefit for their three small children. The extra tax arising on his interest costs under Section 24 can be calculated as follows:*

First £270 @ 0%	*£0*
Next £49,730 @ 20%	*£9,946*
Next £25,140 @ 40%	*£10,056*
Next £74,860 @ 25%	*£18,715*
Child Benefit Charge	*£3,268*
Total	*£41,985*

Adding this to the £7,486 Job is paying on his genuine profits gives us the total tax bill of £49,471 we saw before.

At Least It Won't Get Much Worse

As explained previously, while the Income Tax rates on genuine rental profits are increasing by 2% in 2027/28, the effective rates of additional tax on interest and finance costs will not generally increase and will largely remain as set out in the table above.

The one exception is for landlords with interest and finance costs falling into the 'income' bracket from £100,000 to £125,140, where the effective marginal rate on this hypothetical income will increase to 41% in some cases. However, this only applies if the landlord does not have income from other sources (excluding dividends and interest) of at least £12,570.

In Adam's case (Example 1), there was no increase in his Section 24 tax cost and the only increase he suffers for 2027/28 is an extra 2% tax on his genuine profits of £10,000.

The position for Job (Example 4) is different. Although the net result is that his tax bill for 2027/28 increases by £1,000, or 2% of his genuine profit of £50,000, this is not how it looks in terms of marginal tax rates.

Without Section 24, Job's tax bill for 2027/28 would be £8,235. His genuine profit of £50,000 less his personal allowance, £12,570, leaves £37,430, which is taxed at the new property basic rate of 22%. The extra tax arising for Job in 2027/28 because of Section 24 can then be calculated as follows:

First £270 @ 0%	£0
Next £49,730 @ 20%	£9,946
Next £25,140 @ 41%	£10,307
Next £74,860 @ 25%	£18,715
Child Benefit Charge	£3,268
Total	£42,236

Adding this to the £8,235 Job is paying on his genuine profits gives us his total tax bill for 2027/28 of £50,471 (see above).

Hence, in Job's case, the £1,000 tax increase he suffers in 2027/28 is made up of an extra £749 (£8,235 – £7,486) on his genuine profit and a £251 (£42,236 – £41,985) increase in the additional tax he suffers because of Section 24.

That same £251 increase in the cost of Section 24 will apply to any landlord with rental profits before interest of at least £125,140, genuine rental profits of no more than £100,000, and no other sources of income (apart from interest and dividends).

Further Hidden Costs of Section 24

There are other hidden costs of Section 24 that can affect residential landlords with dividend, interest, or savings income.

Example 5: *Joseph has a portfolio of rental properties that produce a profit of £40,000 before deducting his interest costs of £25,000. He also has interest income of £3,500 and receives dividends of £31,770 from his own company.*

If Joseph's rental properties are commercial properties, he will be able to deduct his interest costs in full, giving him taxable property income of just £15,000. The first £2,570 of his interest income will then fall into the starting rate band and the remainder will be covered by his personal savings allowance, leaving him with no tax to pay on this income. As a basic rate taxpayer, he will pay Income Tax at just 10.75% on £31,270 of his dividend income in 2026/27 (after deducting his £500 dividend allowance).

But, if Joseph's property income comes from residential lettings, Section 24 will mean his taxable property income is £40,000. He will still obtain basic rate tax relief for his interest costs, meaning the property income itself does not suffer any additional tax.

However, Section 24 will still give rise to significant additional tax costs for Joseph. His total taxable income will now be £75,270 (£40,000 + £3,500 + £31,770), making him a higher rate taxpayer. None of his interest income will fall into the starting rate band and his personal savings allowance is reduced to just £500. Hence, he will suffer Income Tax of £600 (£3,000 x 20%) on his interest income in 2026/27.

Far worse, £25,000 of Joseph's dividend income for 2026/27 will now be subject to Income Tax at 35.75% instead of 10.75%, increasing his tax bill by a further £6,250.

Hence, in this example, while the diabolical Section 24 has not led to any direct increase in the tax on Joseph's property income, it has still cost him an extra £6,850 (£6,250 + £600) in tax on his other income.

See Appendix A for the 2026/27 tax bands, rates, and allowances used in this example. The rates applying to dividend income are lower in 2025/26, but the impact of Section 24 in Joseph's case is the same. The rates applying to interest income are increasing in 2027/28, and this will increase the tax Joseph will have to pay on his interest income to £660 (£3,000 x 22%), meaning Section 24 will then be costing him an extra £6,910 in total (£6,250 + £660).

As we can see from the example, where Section 24 increases a landlord's taxable income so that more dividend income is pushed into the higher rate tax bracket, the effective tax cost is 25%. Further, additional costs can also arise where the landlord has interest and savings income.

And we mustn't forget that a number of tax charges are based on the landlord's *total* taxable income, including interest and finance costs on their residential lettings, meaning that Section 24 can also lead to further indirect tax costs, including the CBC, the Winter Fuel Charge, and the withdrawal of the landlord's personal allowance where total taxable income exceeds £100,000.

If, for example, Joseph had four small children qualifying for child benefit, Section 24 would be costing him a total of £10,041 in extra tax in 2026/27.

Alternatively, if Joseph were taking dividends of £81,500 in 2026/27 (instead of £31,770), Section 24 would cost him a total of £9,350 in extra tax (increasing to £9,660 in 2027/28).

Which Costs are Affected?

The Section 24 restrictions apply to interest and finance costs on any amount borrowed for the purposes of generating income from residential lettings. The restrictions therefore apply to interest and finance costs incurred by a residential landlord on all forms of borrowing, including:

- Buy-to-let mortgages
- Other mortgages and loans used to fund deposits or other business expenditure
- Personal loans or credit cards used to fund furnishings, refurbishment work, or other business expenditure
- Hire purchase agreements for the purchase of cars or other assets used in the business
- Business overdrafts

The types of cost affected include:

- Interest
- Charges equivalent to interest (e.g. on Sharia compliant mortgages)
- The finance costs listed in Section 4.6

However, as the restrictions only apply to costs related to borrowings, some items are not affected: such as bank charges on a business current account, for example.

Costs relating to non-residential property are exempt from the restrictions. Where a landlord has both residential and non-residential property, some costs may need to be apportioned.

Example 6: *Isaac borrows £1m to refinance his property portfolio. The portfolio consists of commercial property worth £800,000 and residential property worth £1.2m: a total of £2m.*

The restrictions on tax relief for interest and finance costs only apply to the element of the loan relating to Isaac's residential property. In this case, it would be reasonable to apply the restrictions to 60% of the costs arising (£1.2m/£2m = 60%).

The interest and finance costs relating to Isaac's loan amount to £75,000. Isaac can therefore deduct £30,000 (£75,000 x 40%) as a direct expense. He may also claim basic rate tax relief on the remaining £45,000 (£75,000 x 60%).

The basis for apportioning costs used by Isaac is not the only possible method. He might instead look at the borrowing history prior to the refinancing. Other alternative methods might be available: all that is required is that the apportionment is 'just and reasonable'.

If Isaac had other costs on borrowings wholly related to his residential lettings, these would be wholly subject to the restrictions on relief. Conversely, if he had other costs wholly related to his non-residential property, then none of these would be subject to those restrictions.

If performing this type of calculation for tax years up to 2024/25, remember to also exclude any element of borrowings relating to qualifying FHLs from the restrictions and claim these separately in Box 7 on Page UKP 1 of the tax return.

4.8 REPAIRS AND MAINTENANCE

Nowhere in the field of taxation is the question of 'capital or revenue' more difficult than in the area of repairs and maintenance and/or capital improvements to property. In this section, we will look at the factors that determine how expenditure of this nature should be treated and whether or not it can be claimed as a repair cost.

Generally speaking, where expenditure qualifies as a repair cost under the principles we will examine in this section, this takes precedence over any other rules. There is one exception to this, relating to integral features (see Section 4.10), which we will look at later.

Where expenditure does not qualify as a repair cost and is treated as capital expenditure, it may qualify for capital allowances (Section 4.10), or replacement of domestic items relief (Section 4.9), depending on the type of rental property involved. For those using the cash basis, capital expenditure on property will seldom qualify for any deduction at all (see Section 4.23), although a deduction may usually be claimed for any item that would otherwise qualify for replacement of domestic items relief.

Apart from that one exception regarding integral features, however, all this only becomes relevant when the expenditure is not a repair cost, so it is always important to consider this first.

Fundamental Principles

There are two fundamental principles we must consider in order to determine whether expenditure represents a repair (revenue expenditure) or a capital improvement (capital expenditure).

a) When a property is first brought into the rental business, any expenditure necessary to make it fit for use will be capital expenditure. In most cases, a property will first be brought into use when purchased, but the same rule applies when an inherited property or former home becomes a rental property.

b) Subject to (a) above, expenditure that merely restores the property to its previous condition (at a time earlier in the same ownership) will be a repair. Conversely, any expenditure that enhances the property beyond its previous condition within the same ownership will be capital improvement expenditure.

It is always important to bear these fundamental principles in mind: they lie at the heart of the whole 'capital or revenue' question for any expenditure on property. Fortunately, however, as we shall see later, they are subject to a little more leeway in practice than one might imagine!

The question of what constitutes an enhancement to the property is determined as a question of fact, not opinion. Just because you think a new extension on a building is hideous does not stop it being classed as an improvement for tax purposes.

Repairs are deductible for Income Tax purposes (as long as the property is a rental property at the time) whereas capital improvements ***may*** be deductible for CGT purposes (see Chapter 5) or, in the case of non-residential property, an allowance of just 3% per year (see Section 4.14).

The treatment of any incidental expenditure incurred as part of a building project, such as skip hire for example, will follow the treatment of the project itself. This does not extend to interest and finance costs, however, which continue to be treated as set out in Sections 4.5 to 4.7.

Some Illustrative Examples

I could write an entirely separate book covering umpteen different examples of repairs or capital improvements. Here I have tried to set out a few cases that will hopefully serve to illustrate how the principles outlined above apply in practice. Where a new principle emerges in the course of these examples, I have highlighted it as an 'Emerging Principle'.

Example 1: *Melanie buys an old farmhouse intending to rent it out as holiday accommodation. When she buys the property, it has no mains electricity, no mains sewerage and a large hole in the roof. She spends £75,000 getting the property into a fit state to let it out, including £5,000 on redecoration.*

The whole of Melanie's expenditure of £75,000 will be treated as capital expenditure and no Income Tax deduction will be available. The fact that part of the expenditure was for decorating is likely to be regarded as merely incidental to the overall capital nature of the work in this case.

> **Emerging Principle**
> Expenditure that might normally be regarded as revenue will be treated as capital where it forms an incidental part of a predominantly capital project.

Example 2: *Geri has a small townhouse in Kensington that she rents out. She decides to have a conservatory built on the back at a cost of £60,000, including £5,000 to redecorate the adjoining room. Geri's conservatory is a capital improvement and no Income Tax deduction will be available for this expenditure. Once again, the capital nature of this work extends to the cost of redecorating the adjoining room, as this was necessitated by the building work.*

Example 3: *Emma owns a row of shops she has been renting to a number of small businesses. A massive storm damages the roofs and Emma has these repaired at a cost of £50,000. Emma's expenditure represents an allowable repair cost she can claim against her rental income.*

The same storm also damaged several windows in Emma's shops. The glazier advises her it will actually be cheaper to replace the original wooden frames with new UPVC double glazing and she agrees to do this. This expenditure remains revenue expenditure despite the fact the new windows represent an improvement on the old ones.

Emerging Principle

When, due to changes in fashion, or technological advances, it becomes cheaper or more efficient to replace something with the nearest modern equivalent, the fact this represents an improvement may be disregarded and the expenditure may still be classed as a repair. Replacing single-glazed windows with equivalent double-glazing has been specifically highlighted as meeting this criterion by HMRC. Further examples are considered below.

Example 3 Continued: *At the same time, Emma also decides to have bay windows fitted in two of the shops. This element of her expenditure is a capital improvement and will have to be added to the capital value of her shops rather than claimed as a repair.*

Emerging Principle

Both capital improvements and repairs may sometimes be carried out simultaneously. In such cases, the expenditure must be apportioned between the two elements on a reasonable basis. Readers may wonder why this apportionment is allowed here, when it was denied for both Melanie and Geri above. The key difference is Melanie and Geri ***had to*** do the redecoration at the same time as the other work, whereas Emma simply ***chose*** to install the bay windows. It is the element of choice that makes the difference.

Tax Tip

Where an apportionment of expenditure is necessary, it would be wise to obtain evidence of the allocation made in support of your claim. This can be achieved by asking the builder to separately itemise the repairs and capital improvement elements of the work on their invoices.

Example 4: *Victoria has a flat she has been renting to students for several years. She decides to upgrade the flat to make it more suitable for letting to young professionals. She incurs the following expenditure:*

i) £16,000 on a new kitchen, including £4,500 on equipment
ii) £7,500 redecorating the bathroom, including £2,500 to replace existing fittings and £1,500 to install a shower (there was only a bath before)
iii) £5,000 redecorating the rest of the flat
iv) £3,000 on rewiring

New Kitchen: *The new kitchen expenditure needs to be examined on a detailed item by item basis. The treatment of each item depends on whether it is:*

a) An integral part of a fitted kitchen or a free-standing item, and
b) A direct replacement or an improvement

Any items that represent improvements cannot be claimed as repairs. Hence, for example, installing a new extractor fan within a fitted kitchen, where no such fan had existed before, would be a capital improvement.

As the fan is an integral part of a fitted kitchen, this would represent an improvement to the property as a whole and could thus be added to the cost of the property for CGT purposes (subject to the points discussed in Section 5.7).

Similarly, buying an additional chest freezer to provide extra capacity for frozen food would also be an improvement, and could not be claimed as a repair. Where the new freezer is a free-standing item, it would represent a separate asset and so could not be added to the cost of the property for CGT purposes.

Fitted Kitchen Units and Integrated Equipment: *A fitted kitchen is treated as part of the fabric of the building. The cost of a new fitted kitchen replacing a previous, broadly similar, set of units, work tops, sink, etc, would therefore be accepted as a repair expense. This treatment extends to the replacement of any equipment that is an integral part of a fitted kitchen, such as an integrated cooker or fridge. It does not, however, extend to free-standing items (which are considered below).*

Where the replacement of a fitted kitchen can be claimed as a repair, this treatment also includes the necessary additional costs of re-tiling, re-plastering, plumbing, etc.

The usual exemption for nearest modern equivalents continues to apply when considering whether items have been improved or merely replaced. If, however, Victoria's new fitted kitchen incorporates extra storage space or other extra features, then an appropriate proportion of the expenditure will need to be treated as a capital improvement. This would include any new integrated equipment that replaced an old free-standing item.

In an extreme case, where fairly standard units are replaced by expensive customised items using much higher quality materials, then the whole cost of the new kitchen will need to be regarded as a capital improvement.

Free-Standing Items: *Free-standing, moveable items are not part of the fabric of the building for tax purposes. This generally includes most free-standing 'white goods' such as fridges, dishwashers, cookers, etc; as well as other moveable items such as tables, chairs, etc.*

Victoria will be able to claim the cost of any equipment that is a direct replacement for the old equipment she previously had in the flat. She may also be able to claim part of the cost of any free-standing equipment that represents more than a simple direct replacement. See Section 4.9 for further details.

Anything that is an entirely new item of equipment will be capital expenditure and not allowable for Income Tax purposes. Since free-standing items are separate assets, they will not be added to the cost of the property for CGT purposes either.

Bathroom Fittings: *Replacing the existing bathroom fittings should usually be allowable repairs expenditure. Toilets, baths, showers, and washbasins are all regarded as part of the fabric of the building, so repairing or replacing them is generally allowable for Income Tax purposes.*

Once again, replacing the existing fittings with expensive, customised items, using much higher quality materials, will amount to a capital improvement.

Fitting the new shower will be a capital improvement if this is an extra new item in ***addition*** *to the bath. If the shower* ***replaces*** *the existing bath then it should qualify as a repair under the nearest modern equivalent principle.*

Assuming the shower is an additional item, the remaining bathroom redecoration costs need to be apportioned between the repair element and capital improvement element. Any expense arising directly due to the installation of the shower would have to be treated as part of the capital element.

Redecorating the Flat: *Most of the redecoration work, in the absence of any building work in the rooms concerned, should be fairly straightforward repairs expenditure. As usual, we need to be on the lookout for any improvement element, but a great deal of redecorating cost will always fall into the nearest modern equivalent category.*

Carpets, curtains and other similar items need to be considered separately. These are classed as furnishings and will be dealt with under the principles set out in Section 4.9. In this context, it makes no difference if you are replacing carpets or curtains that you yourself fitted previously or which you acquired when you purchased the property.

Rewiring: *The rewiring will be fully allowable if it is simply 'new for old'. If, on the other hand, Victoria took the opportunity to fit a few new sockets then there would be an improvement element and, as usual, an apportionment would be required. Such an apportionment may also necessitate an apportionment of the redecorating costs, as some of these might also be incurred due to the electrical improvements.*

Emerging Principles

The cost of replacing fixtures on a like for like basis, or with their nearest modern equivalents, is regarded as a repair to the property. This includes fitted kitchens and integrated equipment.

Moveable items, such as carpets, curtains and free-standing kitchen equipment, are not regarded as part of the fabric of the building and are therefore subject to different rules (see Section 4.9). (Carpets often cause confusion as many people see them as a 'fitting'. For tax purposes, however, they are classed as furnishings.)

In complex cases, the question of repairs or capital improvements will need to be examined room by room, or even item by item. The tax treatment of one item may have a knock-on effect on the tax treatment of another item.

Newly Acquired Properties

If we go back to the fundamental principles at the beginning of this section and take them to an extremely pedantic logical conclusion, this would mean any expenditure on a newly acquired property could not be claimed as repairs expenditure. Fortunately, this is not the case.

HMRC accept that expenditure to rectify normal wear and tear on a newly acquired rental property remains allowable as a deduction from rental income for Income Tax purposes. They take the view that there is only normal wear and tear if the property's condition does not significantly affect its purchase price.

HMRC's manuals also specifically state any expenditure on a newly acquired rental property that is not allowed for Income Tax purposes on the grounds it represents capital expenditure should be allowed for CGT purposes on a disposal of that property.

Example 5: *Danni buys a flat from an elderly couple, intending to rent it out. The elderly couple lived in the flat right up to the date of completion. Although it was a bit run down and the decor was very old-fashioned, it was perfectly habitable and met all applicable legal requirements for a rental property.*

Immediately after completion, Danni redecorates the flat in a modern style and then begins to rent it out. Danni's redecoration costs are an allowable maintenance cost for Income Tax purposes, even though she did the work straight away after buying the flat. The flat was already completely habitable and the redecoration work was purely a matter of choice or taste.

Emerging Principle

Normal routine repairs and redecoration work on newly acquired properties is usually considered allowable. Such expenditure will generally be regarded as normal if the property could have been used without it and the price of the property was not significantly affected by its condition.

Example 6: *Mel buys a rather dilapidated house in Sunderland hoping to rent it out to a family or young couple. She gets the house at a very good price owing to its current state of repair but knows safety regulations would bar her from letting it out in its present condition.*

The house desperately needs rewiring and some urgent plumbing work, which Mel carries out at a cost of £7,500. This expenditure will have to be treated as part of her capital cost.

At this point the house is basically habitable and will meet all necessary safety regulations, but it could really do with redecorating to make it attractive to the type of tenants Mel is looking for. However, if Mel redecorates at this point, this expenditure is also likely to be regarded as part of the capital cost of the property, especially since part of the redecorating will have been necessitated by the plumbing and rewiring work.

What Mel does instead, therefore, is to first let the house to a group of students for nine months. After that, she is able to redecorate the property and claim this as a revenue expense deductible for Income Tax purposes.

Tax Tip

Where there is a danger repairs or maintenance expenditure might be regarded as an incidental part of a capital project, it may be beneficial to delay this element of the work, if possible, until after an intermediate period of letting. In this way, the expenditure becomes an allowable revenue expense. Naturally, any legal requirements will have to be observed both before undertaking the initial letting period and when terminating the initial lease (including the Renters' Rights Act provisions for property in England).

Nearest Modern Equivalents

We have already seen several examples of expenditure on a property being acceptable as a repair under the nearest modern equivalent principle. The key to these claims is that something is being replaced with something else which, while it does represent an improvement from a commercial, or layperson's point of view, is really simply the modern equivalent of the old item.

HMRC's manuals refer (at BIM 46925) to whether the asset (i.e. the property) can merely perform the same function as it did before the work was carried out (making the work a repair), or whether the work means more can be done with the asset, or something new can be done that could not be done before (making the work a capital improvement).

The function of a rental property is to provide the tenant with the accommodation they need: whether that is to use as a home, holiday accommodation, shop, office, etc. Clearly something like adding an extra room is an improvement as more can then be done with the property.

But, on the basis of HMRC's manuals, I would argue the following items should be regarded as nearest modern equivalents and hence allowable as repairs expenditure:

- Replacing single-glazing with double glazing
- Replacing a bath with a shower
- Replacing battery-powered alarms with hard-wired alarms
- Replacing standard doors with fire doors
- Upgrading a heating system to a more energy-efficient one (but see further under 'Other Repairs' below)
- Replacing one-inch loft insulation with four or six-inch insulation (or whatever the metric equivalent is!)

No doubt, many readers can think of other suitable replacement expenditure, much of it driven by regulations.

This area of tax law is ever-changing and evolving (HMRC admits that). As a result, the issue is often controversial and debatable. But I feel the guidance in HMRC's manuals should generally lead them to accept claims of this nature provided that:

- A fixture, or part, of the property is being replaced,
- The replacement performs what is essentially the same function, and
- The replacement is the current industry standard for a rental property of this nature (including those required by regulation)

In the case of newly acquired properties, this must be considered in the context of the principles examined above: as ever, the property owner is in a better position where the property is an existing rental property.

Accounting Treatment

Where there are no statutory rules to the contrary, HMRC generally expects the tax treatment of an expense to mirror its treatment in the accounts. Hence, if you are using the accruals basis, and preparing a formal set of accounts, it is important to ensure valid repairs expenditure is not treated as a capital item in those accounts: as this might prevent you from claiming that expenditure for Income Tax purposes.

Conversely, however, I am afraid that treating something which is quite clearly capital expenditure as a repair in the accounts will not make it allowable. Arguably, no harm is done provided you don't try to claim it for tax purposes, although there are sometimes other reasons for preparing accounts (e.g. to obtain finance), so wrongly allocating the expenditure may disadvantage you in other ways. There is also the key point that capital improvement expenditure may be claimed for CGT purposes one day so, if you are preparing a balance sheet, it is sensible to include it in the property's value there in order to keep track of it.

For more on the interaction between the accounting and tax treatment of property expenditure, see the Taxcafe guide *Using a Property Company to Save Tax.*

Repair Cost Provisions

Under traditional accruals basis accounting, a provision is a charge made in your accounts in respect of a future cost (naturally, such provisions are not made under the cash basis). Provisions for future costs are not generally allowable until the costs have actually been incurred. There are a few exceptions to this rule, however, and a provision for repair costs may be allowed for tax purposes if:

i) There is a legal or contractual obligation to incur the expenditure,
ii) There is a specific programme of repair work to be undertaken, and
iii) The accounting provision has been computed with a reasonable degree of accuracy

Example 7: *Kylie owns three flats in Donovan Towers, a tenement block in Glasgow. In February 2027, she receives a statutory notice from the council requiring her (and the other owners in the block) to carry out some urgent roof repairs.*

The Donovan Towers Owners and Residents Association approaches Jason, a local builder, who provides them with a quotation for carrying out the work. On 4th April 2027, the association formally approves the quotation. Kylie's share of the cost will be £4,500.

Under these circumstances, Kylie may quite properly make a provision for her share of the cost in her accounts for the year ending 5th April 2027, even though the work has not even started yet. This means she will obtain relief for this cost in 2026/27.

Other Repairs

Landlords may generally claim the cost of repairs to any items of equipment, furniture, or furnishings in their rental properties. Repairs to assets classed as integral features (e.g. heating systems) within commercial property, or communal areas not within any individual dwelling, may sometimes need to be treated as capital improvements for Income Tax purposes where the accruals basis is being used. For expenditure before 6th April 2025, this also applied to FHLs. See Section 4.10 for details.

4.9 REPLACING FURNITURE, FURNISHINGS & EQUIPMENT

Under replacement of domestic items relief, residential landlords may claim the cost of replacing furnishings and other moveable items, including:

- Furniture
- Electrical equipment
- Free-standing 'white goods', such as fridges, dishwashers, etc.
- Carpets and other floor coverings
- Curtains, blinds, etc.
- Soft furnishings (cushions, lampshades, etc) and bed linen
- Cutlery, crockery, and cooking utensils

Any sale proceeds received on the disposal of the item being replaced must be deducted from the replacement cost claimed. Disposal costs may be added to the claim.

The relief does not cover the costs of the original furnishings when the property is first let out, or the cost of additional items. Landlords may, however, claim part of the cost of a replacement that performs additional functions compared to the item it replaces. Hence, for example, where a landlord replaces an old fridge with a fridge-freezer costing £300, but could have purchased a new fridge for £200, they will still be able to claim the £200 direct replacement cost.

Replacement of domestic items relief was not available on items within FHLs purchased before 6th April 2025, as these were eligible for capital allowances instead. Items within communal areas outside any individual dwelling are also subject to a different regime (see Section 4.10).

Those using the cash basis (Section 4.22) may generally claim a direct deduction for any expenditure that would otherwise qualify for replacement of domestic items relief.

Fixtures, fittings, and anything else that is part of the fabric of the building, are not classed as furnishings for tax purposes and are not eligible for replacement of domestic items relief. Replacing these items will often be claimable as a repair expense, as discussed in Section 4.8.

4.10 CAPITAL ALLOWANCES FOR LANDLORDS

Capital allowances are not available under the cash basis: except in respect of cars (Section 4.12). For the treatment of capital expenditure under the cash basis, see Section 4.23.

Landlords operating a property letting business incur a great deal of capital expenditure on property, property improvements, furniture, equipment, fixtures, and fittings. As explained in Section 3.12, capital expenditure is not directly eligible for a tax deduction under the accruals basis, but may sometimes attract capital allowances.

Many people think landlords are not eligible to claim capital allowances: that is not true. What is true, however, is that residential landlords cannot claim capital allowances on assets within a rented dwelling. Sometimes, this amounts to the same thing, but not always, because there remains scope for landlords to claim capital allowances on:

- Their own equipment, vehicles, etc.
- Their own business premises and assets within it
- Commercial rental property and assets within it
- Assets within a rented residential property, but not within an individual dwelling

Capital allowances were also available on assets purchased before 6th April 2025 for use in, or as part of, a qualifying FHL.

So, while many landlords are not able to claim any significant amounts of capital allowances, most will be able to claim at least some, and there are those who will benefit greatly: which is why it is worth us looking in detail at the capital allowances regime over the next few sections.

The more generous plant and machinery allowances described in Sections 4.11 to 4.13 are available on qualifying fixtures, fittings, furniture, equipment, and integral features. Chief among these is the annual investment allowance (AIA), which provides relief at 100% on up to £1m of qualifying expenditure each year. At the other end of the scale, the structures and buildings allowance (SBA) covered in Section 4.14, is given at the rate of just 3% per year.

We'll look at what types of asset may qualify as plant and machinery in a rental property later.

The rules for capital allowances depend on the type of property being rented, as summarised below. In some cases, this is dependent on the number of dwellings within the property and we will look at the meaning of this in more detail later. These rules cover both assets within the property and outside it. Assets outside the property include both items affixed to the exterior of the property (e.g. solar panels), or located in gardens, grounds, or outbuildings (e.g. gardening equipment).

Commercial Property (shops, offices, restaurants, etc.)
Expenditure on qualifying assets both within the property and outside it is eligible for plant and machinery allowances. Expenditure on the property that does not qualify for plant and machinery allowances may qualify for the SBA. Only non-residential property can qualify for the SBA.

Furnished Holiday Lets (Section 9.23)
Expenditure incurred before 6th April 2025 on qualifying assets both within an FHL and outside, was eligible for plant and machinery allowances. For later expenditure, FHLs are treated the same as other residential property, as detailed below.

Residential Property Incorporating More than One Dwelling (e.g. a house divided into two or more self-contained flats)
Expenditure on qualifying assets located, or stored, in communal areas not falling within any individual dwelling (see below), and serving more than one dwelling, is eligible for plant and machinery allowances.

This, for example, would include equipment in a utility room shared by the occupants of several self-contained flats in a rented building. However, assets not stored within any individual dwelling must not be for the exclusive use of the occupants of only one dwelling.

Expenditure on qualifying assets affixed to the exterior of the property and serving more than one dwelling, is eligible for plant and machinery allowances. Qualifying assets located, or stored in gardens, grounds, or outbuildings will be eligible for plant and machinery allowances provided they are not for the exclusive use of the occupants of one dwelling.

Residential Property Comprising a Single Dwelling
No capital allowances are available.

Plant and Machinery Allowances: Summary So Far
Plant and machinery allowances, including the 100% AIA (Section 4.11) are available for qualifying expenditure on, within, or outside, commercial property and, to some extent, residential property incorporating more than one dwelling. For the rest of this section, I will refer to these types of property as 'qualifying properties'.

For expenditure before 6th April 2025, FHLs were also qualifying properties. For expenditure after 5th April 2025, FHLs are treated the same as other residential property and will only be a qualifying property if they incorporate more than one dwelling.

In the case of residential property (including FHLs for expenditure after 5th April 2025), only the communal areas within the property, and the exterior, is the qualifying property, and only when the property comprises more than one dwelling. Capital allowances are not available on assets located or stored within an individual dwelling, only available to the occupants of a single dwelling, or otherwise serving only a single dwelling.

While capital allowances are not available on assets within an individual rented dwelling, the cost of replacing moveable items can be claimed under a different relief, as explained in Section 4.9.

Landlord's Own Assets

Regardless of the type of property they are renting out, landlords may claim plant and machinery allowances, as detailed in Section 4.11, on equipment purchased for their own business use, such as computers and office furniture.

Capital allowances are available on motor vehicles used in the business, as detailed in Section 4.12. If the landlord acquires their own business premises, this will be eligible for both plant and machinery allowances and the SBA in the same way as any other commercial property.

Plant & Machinery in Rental Property

Investors with qualifying properties can obtain immediate 100% tax relief on up to the maximum amount of the AIA each year, usually £1m (Section 4.11). This includes expenditure on integral features (see below).

A couple holding investment property jointly (but not as a partnership) are each entitled to their own AIA, meaning up to twice as much relief is available each year!

There are a few pitfalls to be wary of, however. Firstly, a landlord can, of course, only claim capital allowances on expenditure they have incurred themselves.

Landlords may lose the right to capital allowances on fixtures and fittings within a commercial property if they grant a lease of two years or more to a tenant and charge a lease premium. As such a premium is wholly or partly regarded as a capital sum for tax purposes (see Section 9.28), the landlord will be treated as having made a partial disposal of the property and may lose the right to claim capital allowances on assets within it.

A landlord may also lose the right to claim capital allowances on items not qualifying as 'background' plant and machinery when a property is leased for more than five years. This should not generally apply to assets on which the landlord had been able to claim capital allowances previously, before the start of the lease.

Landlords may also lose the right to capital allowances on fixtures or fittings leased to the tenant separately under a different agreement to the lease of the property itself. This problem can often be avoided by making a joint election with the tenant. This can be a useful way for the landlord to retain the right to capital allowances on assets within the property where a lease of two years or more has been granted at a premium.

Qualifying Expenditure on Rental Property

Assets in qualifying properties that qualify as plant and machinery for capital allowances purposes include:

- Integral features (see below)
- Furniture, furnishings, white goods, baths, showers, sanitary ware
- Kitchen and cleaning equipment
- Televisions, radios, music systems, and similar equipment
- Gardening tools and equipment
- Manufacturing or processing equipment
- Sound insulation and gas or sewerage systems provided to meet the special requirements of a qualifying trading activity
- Storage or display equipment, counters and checkouts, cold stores, refrigeration and cooling equipment
- Computer, telecommunication and surveillance systems, including wiring and other links
- Fire and burglar alarms, sprinklers and fire-fighting equipment
- Strong rooms and safes
- Moveable partitioning where intended to be moved in the course of a qualifying trading activity
- Decorative assets provided for public enjoyment in hotels, restaurants, and similar trades
- Advertising hoardings, signs and displays

Expenditure on the alteration of a building for the purpose of installing qualifying plant and machinery also qualifies for plant and machinery allowances itself. For example, the cost of fitting brackets to the wall of an office to instal a TV would qualify.

Qualifying assets are eligible for the same capital allowances whether they are purchased separately or as part of the purchase of a qualifying property.

Where a second-hand property is purchased, the purchaser and seller generally have to agree a value for the qualifying fixtures within the property and make a joint election (known as a Section 198 Election), which the purchaser has to submit to HMRC within two years of the date of purchase in support of their capital allowances claim. The agreed value can be anything between £1 and the original cost to the seller of the qualifying items. Sellers generally prefer a low value as this prevents or minimises balancing charges (Section 4.13), but this is a matter for negotiation.

It is not generally possible to claim capital allowances on any fixtures where the previous owner would have been entitled to make a claim, but failed to do so. Such failures to make legitimate claims are commonplace, so it is vital to check the seller's capital allowances claims history when purchasing qualifying properties second-hand.

Tax Tip

Sellers can still make retrospective capital allowances claims right up to the time they sell the property, so it will often be possible to ensure the purchaser's ability to claim capital allowances on fixtures is not diminished or lost: provided appropriate action is taken prior to the date of purchase!

Practical Pointer 1
The requirements for second-hand property detailed above only apply where the property has been in qualifying use some time after 5th April 2012. For commercial property, this will generally be the case but, for purchases of residential property, the rules can only apply where a previous owner used the property as an FHL before 6th April 2025, or where the property incorporates two or more dwellings.

Practical Pointer 2
The requirements for second-hand property only apply to expenditure on which a previous owner would have qualified for capital allowances. Where no previous owner would have qualified for capital allowances on any particular item, the rules do not apply and the purchaser may claim capital allowances based on a reasonable allocation of the property's purchase price. Most commonly, this will apply to integral features already in the property prior to 6th April 2008 and which did not qualify for capital allowances at that time. (Provided there is no subsequent owner who purchased the property after that date and had the property in qualifying use any time after 5th April 2012)

Integral Features
Expenditure on assets within a defined list of integral features falls into the special rate pool, attracting writing down allowances at the lower rate of 6% (see Section 4.11). However, these assets remain eligible for the AIA, so substantial amounts of qualifying expenditure in this category can still attract immediate 100% relief. The following items are classed as integral features:

- Electrical lighting and power systems
- Cold water systems
- Space or water heating systems, air conditioning, ventilation and air purification systems and floors or ceilings comprised in such systems
- Lifts, escalators, and moving walkways
- External solar shading

In a nutshell: All the wiring, lighting, plumbing, heating, and air conditioning in a qualifying property (or the qualifying part of a property) is eligible for capital allowances, with immediate 100% relief for up to £1m spent on these items each year.

The integral features regime applies to expenditure incurred after 5th April 2008, including qualifying items within second-hand buildings purchased after that date (subject to the requirements discussed above).

Any expenditure on integral features that is not covered by the AIA will fall into the special rate pool (see Section 4.11) and attract writing down allowances at just 6%. This includes items that might otherwise be regarded as falling under one of the other qualifying headings for plant and machinery within rental property given above.

The integral features regime does not apply to expenditure incurred before 6th April 2008 and much of this would not have qualified for capital allowances.

The following items of expenditure incurred before 6th April 2008 would, however, qualify for capital allowances:

- Electrical or cold water systems provided specifically to meet the particular requirements of a qualifying trading activity
- Heating, ventilation, air conditioning and air purification systems, including any floor or ceiling which is an integral part of the system
- Lifts, escalators and moving walkways

This remains relevant because it is possible to claim writing down allowances on qualifying expenditure incurred in earlier years, even if no allowances were claimed previously, provided the assets concerned are still used in the business. (Subject to the rules outlined above for fixtures within second-hand properties.)

In the case of a property held by the seller since before 6th April 2008, some integral features may not be subject to the rules for fixtures within second-hand properties (the beneficial implications for the purchaser were explained in 'Practical Pointer 2' above). The relevant features are electrical lighting and power systems, cold water systems, and external solar shading: except to the extent such features were provided specifically to meet the requirements of a particular trading activity.

Integral Features Benefits
Combining the integral features regime with the AIA, we can see many property investors will be able to benefit quite significantly.

Example: *In August 2026, Lulach bought an old property and converted it into office units to rent out. The conversion work was completed by December and, although the office units are really just basic shells with the minimum of fixtures and fittings, Lulach's surveyors, Macbeth & Co., nevertheless calculate he has spent £175,000 on integral features and other fixtures qualifying as plant and machinery. Lulach can therefore claim an AIA of £175,000 against his rental income in 2026/27.*

Lulach will also be able to claim the SBA on any conversion costs that do not qualify as plant and machinery.

Furthermore, as we shall see in Section 4.18, property investors may be able to claim any capital allowances in excess of their rental profits against their other income for the same tax year, or the next (although this relief is subject to certain limitations).

Remember also, a couple buying property jointly (but not as a partnership) could claim AIAs of up to ***£1m each***. Such a couple could potentially benefit from a total tax saving of up to £907,542 in 2026/27 alone: simply by buying the right property! (Based on taxable income of £100,000 each after claiming AIAs)

Replacing Integral Features
Expenditure on replacing part of an integral feature within a qualifying property is classed as a capital improvement for Income Tax purposes if, within any twelve-month period, such expenditure amounts to more than half the cost of replacing the entire feature.

This rule only applies where, and to the extent that, the integral feature qualifies for capital allowances: and those allowances, including the AIA, remain available on the expenditure. This is the one exception that overrides the general principles regarding repairs in Section 4.8. Where significant repairs are taking place, it may sometimes be worth staggering them over a longer period in order to avoid this problem.

Thermal Insulation
Expenditure on thermal insulation of an existing building used in a qualifying business also falls into the special rate pool and is eligible for the AIA. This does not generally apply to residential property, but included FHLs for expenditure up to 5th April 2025.

What is a Dwelling?
For capital allowances purposes, a dwelling is a building, or part of a building, which has all the facilities required for normal day-to-day living. Hence, where a property is made up of self-contained flats, each with their own kitchen and bathroom, the flats are the dwellings. Qualifying plant and machinery in common areas outside the flats, or on the exterior of the building, is then eligible for capital allowances.

However, where the tenants share facilities, such as a common kitchen or bathroom, the property will generally constitute a single dwelling and no capital allowances will be available.

Tax Year versus Accounting Period
Unlike trading businesses, landlords must generally claim capital allowances for the tax year, rather than their own accounting period, if this is different. As usual, however, accounts drawn up for the year ending 31st March are accepted as a good enough approximation to the tax year and, where this is the case, capital allowances will be claimed for this period instead.

4.11 PLANT AND MACHINERY ALLOWANCES

This section is not directly relevant to landlords using the cash basis.

The term 'plant and machinery' covers qualifying plant, machinery, vehicles, furniture, fixtures, fittings, computers, and other equipment used in a business. In Section 4.10, we looked at what qualifies as plant and machinery for capital allowances purposes in a property letting business. In this section, we will look at what allowances are available for expenditure on those qualifying assets.

Note that, while cars are technically included in the definition of 'plant and machinery', they are subject to their own capital allowances regime, which we will look at in Section 4.12.

The Annual Investment Allowance (AIA)

The AIA provides 100% tax relief for qualifying expenditure on plant and machinery up to the maximum amount available each year. It is available to individuals, partnerships, and companies alike. The maximum AIA available each year is currently £1m.

In the vast majority of cases, the AIA usually provides landlords with immediate 100% relief on all their qualifying capital expenditure on plant and machinery, apart from cars and assets with an element of private use (see Sections 4.12 and 4.13).

Assets do not need to be purchased new to qualify for the AIA. They must, however, be purchased from an unconnected third party on arms' length terms. Assets acquired from connected persons (Appendix B), and used assets introduced into the business by the landlord themselves, do not qualify for the AIA.

The other allowances described below are generally only relevant where the landlord is spending more than £1m on qualifying plant and machinery, has old balances of unrelieved expenditure, or is introducing used assets into the business themselves (e.g. an old van or laptop previously used privately).

The First Year Allowance

Expenditure on new, unused, qualifying plant and machinery incurred after 31st December 2025, and which is not covered by the AIA, is eligible for a first year allowance of 40%. This new allowance is not available on cars, second-hand assets, assets held for leasing overseas, or assets falling into the special rate pool (see below).

Where this first year allowance is claimed, the unrelieved 60% of the expenditure will fall into the main pool and attract writing down allowances from the following year onwards, as described below.

Writing Down Allowances

Expenditure not covered by, or not eligible for, the AIA is eligible for writing down allowances. The rate of writing down allowances on most plant and machinery is 18% up to the current, 2025/26 tax year, falling to 14% from 2026/27 onwards.

Expenditure qualifying for writing down allowances is pooled together with the unrelieved balance of qualifying expenditure brought forward from the previous year (including the 60% unrelieved balance of any expenditure on which the first year allowance described above has been claimed).

This pool of expenditure is known as the main pool. The writing down allowance is calculated on the total balance in the pool. The remaining balance of expenditure is then carried forward and the writing down allowance may be claimed on that balance in the next tax year. And so on.

However, where the balance in the main pool reduces to less than £1,000, the full balance may then be claimed immediately.

The Special Rate Pool

Certain types of expenditure must be allocated to a special rate pool instead of the main pool. These include:

- Integral features (see Section 4.10)
- Expenditure of £100,000 or more on plant and machinery with an anticipated working life of 25 years or more
- Expenditure on thermal insulation of existing buildings (Section 4.10)

Expenditure in the special rate pool qualifies for writing down allowances at just 6%. The special rate pool is particularly relevant to property investors letting out commercial property or, up to 2024/25, FHLs. However, it's worth noting that the AIA may be allocated to such spending in preference to spending qualifying for the main rate of writing down allowances: we saw some examples of the benefits of this in Section 4.10.

Where the balance on the special rate pool reduces to less than £1,000, the full balance may then be claimed immediately in the same way as for the main pool.

4.12 CAPITAL ALLOWANCES ON MOTOR VEHICLES

Capital allowances are generally available on motor vehicles used in a business. Vans and motorcycles are usually eligible for the same allowances as other plant and machinery, as described in Section 4.11 (but see Section 4.13 where there is some private use). Most cars are not eligible for the AIA or first year allowance, but do have their own system of writing down allowances.

There are effectively two different capital allowances regimes for cars. The first regime applies to: (i) cars provided to employees; (ii) cars owned by a company; and (iii) other cars that are wholly used for business purposes.

Cars falling under headings (i) and (ii) are referred to as company cars. For details of the capital allowances regime applying to company cars, see the Taxcafe guide *Using a Property Company to Save Tax*. Cars falling under heading (iii) are pretty rare as this means the car is owned and used by the owner of the business and there is absolutely no private use. In over thirty years as a tax adviser, I never encountered such a car.

For the rest of this section, I will concentrate purely on the second regime: cars owned and used by the business owner themselves, and which have some element of private use. These cars must each be put in their own individual pool for capital allowances purposes. The rate of allowances available depends on the car's CO_2 emissions, date of purchase, and whether it is purchased new or second-hand:

- New, zero emission (i.e. fully electric) cars currently attract a 100% first year allowance
- Other cars with CO_2 emissions not exceeding 50g/km attract writing down allowances at 18% up to 2025/26, falling to 14% from 2026/27 onwards
- Cars with CO_2 emissions over 50g/km attract writing down allowances at 6%

The 50g/km threshold has applied since 6th April 2021. Cars purchased before that date that qualified for writing down allowances at 18% continue to do so up to 2025/26, and will qualify for writing down allowances at 14% from 2026/27 onwards.

The 100% allowance for purchases of new electric cars will cease to apply after 5th April 2027. Purchases of new electric cars after that date will attract writing down allowances at 14%.

The allowances must be restricted to reflect the element of private use. However, the unrelieved balance of expenditure carried forward to the next year is calculated before this restriction.

Example 1: *A car purchased for £20,000 that has 115g/km of CO2 emissions and 80% private use will be eligible for an allowance of £240 (6% x £20,000 = £1,200 less 80%). The unrelieved balance carried forward to the next year is £18,800 (£20,000 – £1,200).*
Example 2: *A car purchased in March 2026 for £30,000 that has 40g/km of CO2 emissions and 75% private use will be eligible for an allowance of £1,350 in 2025/26 (18% x £30,000 = £5,400 less 75%). The unrelieved balance carried forward is £24,600 (£30,000 – £5,400). In 2026/27, this car will be eligible for an allowance of £861 (14% x £24,600 = £3,444 less 75%). The unrelieved balance carried forward to 2027/28 is £21,156 (£24,600 – £3,444).*
Example 3: *A new, fully electric car purchased in March 2027 for £60,000 that has 40% private use will be eligible for an allowance of £36,000 (100% x £60,000 less 40%). There is no unrelieved balance to be carried forward.*

Balancing Allowances and Charges
When a car with private use is disposed of, a balancing allowance, or charge, will arise, reflecting the difference between the disposal proceeds and the unrelieved balance of expenditure.

A balancing allowance, like any other capital allowance, is a deduction from taxable income. A balancing charge is added to taxable income. Balancing allowances and charges on cars with private use are subject to the same restriction in respect of private use as other capital allowances.

Summary Example: Capital Allowances, Cars with Private Use
In January 2027, Kenneth buys a car for £25,000 and uses it 40% for his property business and 60% privately. The car has 126g/km of CO2 emissions. In his accounts for the year to 5th April 2027, Kenneth claims a writing down allowance of £600 (£25,000 x 6% x 40%). The unrelieved balance carried forward is £23,500 (£25,000 – 6%).

For the year ending 5th April 2028, Kenneth is able to claim a writing down allowance of £564 (£23,500 x 6% x 40%). The unrelieved balance carried forward this time is £22,090 (£23,500 – 6%).

In February 2029, Kenneth sells the car for £15,000. This gives rise to a balancing allowance of £2,836 (£22,090 – £15,000 = £7,090 x 40%).

If Kenneth had sold the car for more than £22,090 (the unrelieved balance of expenditure) he would have been subject to a balancing charge. The charge in this case would generally have been 40% of the excess of the sale price over £22,090. However, as explained in Section 4.13, where the sale price exceeds the purchase price, the disposal proceeds used for capital allowances purposes are limited to that purchase price.

4.13 FURTHER POINTS ON CAPITAL ALLOWANCES

This section is only directly relevant to landlords using the cash basis as far as it concerns cars.

Before we move on, it is worth making a few further points regarding capital allowances on plant and machinery and motor vehicles. The points in this section relate to the allowances covered in Sections 4.11 and 4.12, and do not necessarily apply to the structures and buildings allowance, which we will cover separately in Section 4.14.

The capital allowances regime for cars examined in Section 4.12 is echoed to some extent in the case of other assets with both business and private use purchased and used by a business owner. The AIA remains available on assets (other than cars) with an element of private use. The allowance must, however, be restricted to reflect the private use.

Assets with private use must each be placed in their own capital allowances pool, or 'puddle', as I like to call them. Where the AIA is not available (e.g. in the case of existing personal assets introduced into the business), the writing down allowances on these puddles will be at 6%, 14%, or 18%, as appropriate (see Section 4.11). A suitable deduction must be made in respect of the private use of the asset. The unrelieved balance on the puddle carried forward to the next tax year is again calculated before taking account of this deduction. Balances under £1,000 in puddles cannot be written off like similar small balances in the main or special rate pools.

The great advantage/disadvantage of the puddle is that a balancing allowance/charge will arise when each asset is disposed of. These balancing allowances or charges are calculated in exactly the same way as for a car with private use, as explained in Section 4.12. Claiming the AIA on assets with private use will naturally mean a balancing charge arises whenever any proceeds are received on the disposal of those assets.

Writing down allowances may be claimed on used assets the taxpayer introduces into the business, based on their market value at the date of introduction. For example, if a landlord has an old computer they have had for many years and begins using it for business purposes, they may claim writing down allowances on the computer based on its value at that date. The usual deduction for private use continues to apply where appropriate.

Where a car is introduced into the business, the same principles apply, but the date of introduction is used to determine the rate of writing down allowances, rather than the original date of purchase. The 100% first year allowance for fully electric cars is not available on a used car.

None of the usual allowances on plant and machinery or motor vehicles are available in the tax year that a business ceases. A balancing allowance or charge will apply instead, based on the difference between the unrelieved balance of expenditure and the value of the remaining assets at the date of cessation.

Assets bought on hire purchase continue to be eligible for capital allowances as normal but must be brought into use in the business before the end of the tax year in order for full relief to be obtained in that year. In other cases, assets bought on extended credit terms of more than four months are treated as if they were purchased on the date payment is due.

For landlords with a 31st March accounting date, this date is treated as the end of their tax year for capital allowances purposes. In fact, any accounting date between 31st March and 4th April is treated as the end of the tax year, where relevant.

Subject to the above points, the full allowance due is available on any qualifying business asset purchased part-way through the tax year, even on the last day.

Any sale proceeds received for assets used wholly in the business are deducted from the balance on the main pool or special rate pool, as appropriate. Where this gives rise to a negative balance, a balancing charge will arise.

Since the advent of the AIA, most small businesses have little or no balance of unrelieved expenditure left in their main or special rate pools. Hence, there is a strong chance of a balancing charge arising whenever any asset is sold: unless it is replaced by another qualifying asset of equal or greater value within the same tax year.

Notwithstanding any of the above, where the disposal proceeds or market value of an asset that ceases to be used in the business exceeds the amount originally claimed for capital allowances purposes (before any private use deduction), the amount of proceeds or market value used in the relevant calculation is restricted to the amount originally claimed.

Where a business owner makes a gain on disposal of an asset (other than a car) that *qualified* for capital allowances, that gain is subject to CGT. This applies whether capital allowances were actually claimed or not. Where the asset has some private use, it is generally only the business use proportion of the gain that is taxable (except in the case of antiques, paintings, or other items with an anticipated life of more than fifty years).

Certain spending on new and unused plant and machinery is eligible for 100% enhanced capital allowances. This includes expenditure incurred before 6th April 2027 on installation of electric vehicle charge-points; or before 6th April 2025 on gas refuelling stations, or zero emission goods vehicles. Enhanced capital allowances claims do not use up your AIA and are not generally subject to any monetary limit.

Additional capital allowances are available to companies. As these are not available to individuals, or other business entities, they are beyond the scope of this guide. See the Taxcafe guide *Using a Property Company to Save Tax* for details.

Capital Allowance Disclaimers

Apart from balancing allowances and charges, capital allowances are not mandatory. The amount of allowance available is effectively a maximum that may be claimed. The taxpayer may claim any amount between zero and that maximum each year. But, why claim less than the maximum?

> **Tax Tip**
>
> If your total taxable income is less than your personal allowance, any capital allowances you claim may be wasted. Instead, it will generally be better to claim a lower amount of allowances in order to fully utilise your personal allowance against your income. The unrelieved balance of expenditure carried forward will then be greater, giving you higher capital allowances next year when, hopefully, they will actually save you some tax!

Some possible exceptions to the above 'Tax Tip' may arise where your property business is making losses and you are effectively able to obtain tax relief for your capital allowances in a different period: see Section 4.18.

Another reason to consider a capital allowances disclaimer is if you anticipate a balancing charge arising in the near future, and also expect to have a higher marginal tax rate at that time. For more on this area of planning, see the Taxcafe guide *Small Business Tax Saving Tactics*.

Note that if any of the allowances given at a higher rate are disclaimed, the expenditure will only attract writing down allowances at the appropriate rate in future years.

4.14 THE STRUCTURES AND BUILDINGS ALLOWANCE

This section is not directly relevant to landlords using the cash basis.

The structures and buildings allowance (SBA) applies to expenditure on the construction, renovation, improvement or conversion of qualifying non-residential property. It is available to landlords renting out non-residential property, as well as businesses using commercial property in their trade or profession. The SBA is a straight-line annual allowance on the qualifying cost, currently at 3%.

Where any contract for the construction of a property was entered into before 29th October 2018, the SBA cannot be claimed on the property itself. However, this does not prevent later projects for renovation, conversion, or improvement work from qualifying.

SBA is limited to the net direct costs relating to physically constructing the asset. Where relevant, this will include demolition costs, the costs of land alterations or preparations necessary for the construction, and other direct costs of bringing the structure or building into existence. However, the SBA does not cover:

- The cost of land, including rights over land
- SDLT and other purchase costs
- Costs of obtaining planning permission
- Other land alterations beyond what is necessary for the construction (e.g. landscaping, although landscaping that results in the creation of a separate structure does qualify)
- Land reclamation or remediation

The SBA cannot be claimed on expenditure that qualifies for plant and machinery allowances, including integral features and other qualifying fixtures (see Section 4.10).

The SBA claim generally commences on the later of the date the expenditure is incurred, and the date the building/structure is first brought into qualifying use. However, in the case of renovations or improvements to property already in qualifying use, the claim may commence on any of:

i) The last day works are carried out in relation to the project,
ii) The first day of the next tax year after (i), or
iii) The first day of the next tax year after the day the expenditure is incurred

Where a landlord prepares accounts for the year ending 31st March, this is treated as their tax year for the purposes of the SBA.

Expenditure incurred prior to the commencement of the owner's business is treated as if it were incurred on the date of commencement. Unlike the pre-trading rules for revenue expenditure (Section 3.12), there is no limit to how long prior to commencement the expenditure was incurred (provided all relevant contracts were after 28th October 2018).

The SBA is reduced on a time apportionment basis if the building or structure had not yet been brought into qualifying use at the beginning of the tax year; or where the claim commences part way through the year.

The current owner may continue to claim the SBA where a property falls into disuse, provided the property was in qualifying use immediately beforehand. However, a new owner must bring the property into qualifying use before they can claim the SBA.

For property letting businesses, a property is in qualifying use when it is being let out at full market rent. The existing owner may continue to claim the SBA during a void that follows a period of qualifying use, but a new owner must let the property out (at full market rent) before they may claim the SBA. In all cases, the property must not be in residential use (see below).

The SBA ceases when a full claim for all periods since the relevant expenditure first qualified would total 100%. At the current rate, this will take thirty-three and a third years, so the allowance is a 'long player' (if you don't understand that reference, ask your parents!) The SBA also ceases if a qualifying building or structure is demolished.

Where a qualifying property is purchased from a developer, SBA may be claimed on the purchase price, but with an appropriate exclusion for the cost of the land, integral features, and other fixtures qualifying as plant and machinery (see Section 4.10).

When a building or structure is sold, entitlement to the SBA transfers to the new owner. The SBA available for the year of sale is apportioned between the seller and purchaser, with the seller retaining entitlement for the day of transfer. There are no balancing allowances or charges at the point of sale. The price paid for the property in this situation is irrelevant: SBA is based on the original qualifying cost of the building and any subsequent improvements.

Where the person incurring qualifying expenditure is not in charge to UK tax, or not using the property in a qualifying business, subsequent owners may still claim the SBA provided the first use of the property after the qualifying expenditure is not residential use. However, the first use of the property will still determine when the period allowed for the claim comes to an end.

Residential Use
The SBA is not available when a property is in residential use. As well as normal residential dwellings, such as houses, flats, apartments, etc, this also includes residential accommodation for school pupils, students, or the armed forces. However, there is an exception for care homes providing residential accommodation together with personal care for the elderly, disabled, people with mental disorders, or alcohol or drug dependency.

Hotel rooms do not usually constitute dwellings, and a hotel will generally qualify for SBA. A guest house will not usually qualify, however.

Any structure on land in residential use, such as the garden or grounds of a house, is itself deemed to be in residential use. Additional facilities provided with serviced apartments (such as a gym or swimming pool) are also deemed to be in residential use and excluded from the SBA.

If the first use of a property following the expenditure is residential (as defined above), SBA will never be available on that expenditure. Later expenditure on the same property might qualify, however.

Example 1: *Catherine purchased a block of flats from a developer in 2019 and started to rent it out. No SBA was available as the flats were in residential use. In 2026, she spends £250,000 converting the bottom two floors of the block into shops and offices. SBA will be available on the conversion costs, giving Catherine an annual tax deduction of £7,500 (£250,000 x 3%).*

Where a building or structure has both qualifying and non-qualifying use, the costs must be apportioned and SBA may be claimed on an appropriate proportion. However, no relief is available on workplaces within a dwelling house; or where the proportion in qualifying use is insignificant (generally taken to mean 10% or less).

***Example 2:** Sofia purchases a property from the local authority for £800,000. The property was originally constructed in 2021 at a cost of £960,000. The property has six storeys, with shops on the ground floor and flats in the floors above. Sofia may claim an annual SBA of £4,800 (£960,000 x 1/6 x 3%).*

Sofia's claim is based on the original cost of the property and is unaffected by the fact the original owner was not in charge to tax. The SBA claim will, however, cease thirty-three and a third years after the local authority first brought the property into use.

The Allowance Statement

SBA claims require a written allowance statement identifying the relevant building or structure together with: (a) the date of the earliest contract relating to the relevant project; (b) the amount of qualifying expenditure; (c) the date the property was first brought into qualifying use.

The owner who incurs the qualifying expenditure makes the allowance statement. Subsequent owners must obtain a copy of the statement.

Further Points

Where the owner grants a lease for thirty-five years or more, the right to SBA on the property transfers to the tenant if the element of any premium treated as a capital disposal for tax purposes (see Section 9.28) is at least three times greater than the value of the owner's reversionary interest. A tenant will also be able to claim SBA on any qualifying expenditure they incur themselves, regardless of the length of their lease.

SBA is available on both UK and overseas property (provided the property is used in a business chargeable to UK tax). The claimant must have a relevant legal interest in the land on which the building or structure is located (e.g. a freehold or leasehold interest). Unclaimed relief is simply lost and cannot be carried forward.

The amount of qualifying expenditure for the purposes of SBA is subject to a market value cap. In other words, expenditure in excess of market value does not qualify. This rule is only likely to be relevant where work is carried out by a connected party.

Impact on Capital Gains

The amount of SBA claimed by a seller must be added to their sale proceeds to calculate the chargeable gain arising on a disposal of the property. The relief provided by SBA is therefore effectively clawed back on the sale of a property. Nonetheless, SBA claims usually remain worthwhile for individuals or partnerships, since they will generally provide Income Tax relief at higher rates than the CGT on the sale.

Where a property is transferred by way of a 'no gain/no loss' transfer, the transferee will also have to add the SBA claimed by the transferor to any future sale proceeds on disposal of the property. The most common 'no gain/no loss' transfers are those between spouses (see Section 5.5).

A holdover relief claim will have a similar, although slightly different, effect: as the SBA claimed by the transferor will effectively be deducted from the transferee's base cost for the property (see Section 5.7).

4.15 RENT ARREARS

This section is not directly relevant to landlords using the cash basis.

Under traditional accruals basis accounting, any rent you are due to receive is part of your income, even when it is in arrears. It remains part of your income, even if you *never* receive it: but, in this case, you are able to claim a bad debt expense. A bad debt is the accounting term for income you were due to receive but never got.

The difficulty, sometimes, is deciding when, exactly, the debt for the outstanding rent arrears has gone bad. When does it become reasonable to assume the cash is never going to arrive, so a claim may be made for your bad debt expense?

You need to assess the situation at the time you are preparing your accounts. Naturally, any sums you have received by this time cannot be classed as bad debts as you know you have received the money. For sums that still remain unpaid, I would generally say, unless there is a guarantor, late payment arrangements in place, or other exceptional circumstances, you may claim any amounts more than three months overdue as a bad debt.

Early Accounting

If you're preparing your accounts shortly after the end of the tax year, there may be sums that are overdue by less than three months. Here you will have to use your judgement and consider what the likelihood is that you will eventually get paid. For example, if your debtor (the tenant who owes you the rent arrears) has been made bankrupt, you may already have a good idea you are not going to get paid.

Exceptional Circumstances

The three-month cut-off suggested above is not a rule, merely a guideline. There are some circumstances where late payment may not necessarily mean the debt has gone bad. For example, if your debtor has died, but left plenty of money, the family may need to wait for probate before they can pay you. Conversely, the debtor may have died penniless, in which case you may claim a bad debt expense straight away.

Guarantors

Where there is a rent guarantor in place, this makes it more likely that you will eventually receive the relevant rent arrears, and the three-month guideline suggested above will not usually be appropriate. As usual, you need to assess the situation on a case by case basis, judging whether the guarantor is likely to pay the arrears. A bad debt provision (see below) may be appropriate under these circumstances.

Late Payment Arrangements
If you have agreed late payment arrangements with your debtor, (or they have been imposed by the court), you will need to assess the likelihood that outstanding amounts will eventually be paid. In these cases, a bad debt provision may be appropriate.

Bad Debt Provisions
Where you are not certain a debt has gone bad, but you nevertheless have doubts over whether you will eventually get paid, you may make a bad debt provision in your accounts. Specific bad debt provisions calculated on a reasonable basis are allowable for tax purposes.

Example 1: *The rent due on Angela's flat is £800 per month. Angela was a good tenant until May 2025, when she was made redundant. Since then, she has been struggling to pay and, by 5th April 2026, she owes her landlord, Greta, £6,000 in rent arrears. Angela has now managed to get a new job and has agreed with Greta she will pay off the arrears at £200 per month (on top of her current rent).*

By the time Greta is preparing her accounts for 2025/26, Angela has reduced her arrears to £4,200, but Greta is still concerned about whether the whole sum will eventually be paid. Greta feels there is a fifty-fifty chance of her getting paid, so she makes a bad debt provision of £2,100 (£4,200 x 50%) in her accounts. This is a specific provision, calculated on a reasonable basis, and is therefore allowed for Income Tax purposes.

General provisions not relating to any specific debts are not allowable for tax purposes. For example, if a landlord made a bad debt provision equal to 10% of all rent due at the end of the tax year, this could not be claimed for tax purposes.

Bad for Good
Where you have claimed bad debt relief, but eventually receive the sums in question, you will need to account for the bad debts turned good as a negative expense. In other words, the sums you eventually receive will then become taxable.

Example 1 Continued: *Despite Greta's concerns, Angela continues to pay off her rent arrears at £200 per month, reducing them to £1,800 by the time Greta is preparing her accounts for 2026/27. Greta is now cautiously optimistic that Angela will eventually pay off the arrears, but feels it prudent to maintain a provision of 50% of the amounts still unpaid, or £900. This means her bad debt provision is reduced by £1,200 (£2,100 – £900) and this sum needs to be included in her accounts as a negative expense, thus increasing her taxable profit for 2026/27.*

Long-term debts like the arrears in this example need to be kept under review on an annual basis as each set of accounts are prepared, and dealt with according to the latest information available.

Example 1 Part 3: *In March 2028, Angela quits her job to go travelling around the world. She leaves owing Greta £1,400 in arrears. Greta now has good reason to suspect this remaining debt has gone bad and claims bad debt relief of £500 for 2027/28 (the £1,400 bad debt less the £900 provision brought forward).*

A year later, Angela returns, apologises profusely and pays Greta in full. Once again, Greta has a negative expense in 2028/29: this time equal to the £1,400 of bad debt previously claimed that has now been recovered.

Debt Collection Costs

In addition to making a bad debt provision, it may sometimes also be appropriate to make a provision for legal and other costs of debt collection. Under the accruals basis, such a provision will be allowable for tax purposes provided it represents costs actually incurred, or reasonably anticipated, in respect of chasing rent that was due for the tax year (or an earlier year).

Example 2

In March 2026, Sandra's tenant absconded owing £10,000 in rent arrears. By the time Sandra is preparing her 2025/26 tax return, she has incurred £2,000 in legal fees chasing this debt and expects to incur a further £1,500 before the matter gets to court, where her lawyer estimates she has a 75% chance of recovering the debt.

In her accounts for 2025/26, Sandra makes a provision for legal costs of £3,500, as well as a bad debt provision of £2,500 (£10,000 less 75%). Both provisions relate to a specific debt outstanding at 5th April 2026 and have been calculated on a reasonable basis, and hence both are allowable for Income Tax purposes.

During 2027, Sandra's tenant offers to pay £8,000 in settlement of the arrears. She decides to accept and eventually receives the relevant sum, from which she pays her lawyer's final fees of £800. By the time she is preparing her accounts for 2026/27, she has incurred actual debt collection costs totalling £2,800 (£2,000 + £800) and suffered an actual bad debt of £2,000 (£10,000 less £8,000).

In 2026/27, Sandra will therefore have a negative bad debt expense of £500 (£2,500 – £2,000) and negative legal costs of £700 (£3,500 – £2,800): in effect, an extra £1,200 of taxable profit. But none of this alters the fact that she had £6,000 of allowable expense provisions in 2025/26 (£3,500 + £2,500), or that the original £10,000 of rent arrears had to be included in her income when the rent was due.

Accounting Treatment

Under traditional accruals basis accounting, a bad debt is an expense, and a bad debt (or debts covered by a bad debt provision) that is later recovered is a negative expense. Income should continue to be stated as the amount actually due for the tax year: this can be important for a number of reasons.

A provision for debt collection costs should be included in legal and professional fees. It should then be deducted from the actual costs as and when they are incurred in later years. Any provision that proves excessive, or is no longer required, should be released: this becomes a negative expense to be deducted from legal and professional fees.

Cash basis accounting is different. It is not possible to make provisions for costs not yet paid, and the whole issue of bad debts becomes irrelevant (although it regains greater importance than ever when a landlord leaves the cash basis: see Sections 4.22 and 9.32).

4.16 RENT-A-ROOM RELIEF

Rent-a-room relief applies to income from letting out part of your home as furnished residential accommodation. For this purpose, the property must be your main residence (see Section 5.9) for at least part of the same tax year. The letting itself must also at least partially coincide with a period when the property is your main residence.

The relief covers income from lodgers and even extends to letting a self-contained flat, provided the division of the property is only temporary, and not a permanent conversion. Live-in owners with small hotels and guest houses may also claim the relief, where appropriate.

Complete exemption is automatically provided where the gross annual rent receivable from lettings in the property does not exceed the rent-a-room relief limit of £7,500. The gross rent receivable for this purpose must include any contributions towards household expenses you receive from tenants and any balancing charges arising (Section 4.13). You can elect not to claim rent-a-room relief, for example if the letting is producing a loss that otherwise could not be claimed.

Where the gross rent receivable exceeds the rent-a-room limit, you may nevertheless elect for a form of partial exemption. You will then be taxed on the amount of gross rents receivable in excess of the rent-a-room limit, instead of under the normal basis.

Example 1: *Duncan rents out a room in his house for an annual rent of £8,000. His rental profit for 2026/27, calculated on the normal basis, is £2,800. He therefore elects to use the rent-a-room basis, thus reducing his taxable rental income to just £500.*

The partial exemption available under rent-a-room relief has become attractive to many more landlords renting out a part of their home due to the restrictions on interest relief set out in Section 4.7.

Example 2: *Linda is a higher rate taxpayer. She rents out a room in her house for an annual rent of £10,000. Computing her rental profits in the normal way would give her allowable interest of £8,000 and other deductible expenses of £400.*

Due to the Section 24 restrictions, Linda's taxable rental profit is £9,600. She will get basic rate tax relief on her £8,000 interest cost, so her tax bill for 2026/27 on an actual basis would be £2,240 (£9,600 x 40% – £8,000 x 20%).

Claiming partial exemption under rent-a-room relief would reduce Linda's taxable rental profit to £2,500 (£10,000 – £7,500) giving her a tax bill, at 40%, of £1,000. Hence, Linda is better off claiming rent-a-room relief.

Where the letting income is being shared with another person, the rent-a-room limit must be halved. Oddly, where the income is being shared with more than one other person, there is no further reduction. Hence, three or more joint owners can still each claim half the normal limit.

Where there is any letting income from the same property during the same tax year that does not qualify for the relief, none of the income from the property that year may be exempted.

Rent-a-room relief continues to apply where additional services are provided, such as cooking, cleaning, etc. Income in excess of the rent-a-room limit will generally be regarded as trading income in these circumstances.

An election to claim rent-a-room relief is deemed to remain in place for future years unless withdrawn. Where you are claiming complete exemption under rent-a-room relief, you should put an 'X' in Box 4 on page UKP 1 of your tax return.

Income eligible for rent-a-room relief is ineligible for the property income allowance (Section 4.17). Where an individual claims actual expenditure against income that would otherwise be eligible for full or partial exemption under rent-a-room relief, they cannot claim the property income allowance that year. In a few cases, this may mean it's better to claim rent-a-room relief even when allowable expenses exceed £7,500.

Example 3: *Bertie rents out a room in his house (his main residence) for an annual rent of £12,000. He has deductible expenses of £7,750 to set against this income, so he would not normally claim rent-a-room relief and would pay Income Tax on his actual profit of £4,250.*

However, in 2026/27 he also receives £1,000 from a 'one-off' rental of his holiday home. The allowable expenses deductible from this income under normal principles would only amount to £125.

If Bertie doesn't claim rent-a-room relief he can't claim the property income allowance and would be taxed on profits of £5,125 (£4,250 + £1,000 – £125).

However, by claiming rent-a-room relief on the income from his main residence, he can exempt the income from his holiday home and be taxed on profits of £4,500 (£12,000 – £7,500), thus reducing his taxable income by £625.

For the sake of illustration, I have assumed Bertie has no allowable interest or finance costs to claim against his rental income. If he did, we would also need to factor in the impact of the interest relief restrictions in Section 4.7, in a similar way to Linda in Example 2 above.

4.17 THE PROPERTY INCOME ALLOWANCE

An allowance of £1,000 per year is available to exempt small amounts of property rental income.

Income eligible for rent-a-room relief is ineligible for this allowance. See Section 4.16 for further details of the interaction between these reliefs and the implications for anyone renting out part of their own home.

Subject to this, the property income allowance applies to an individual's ***total*** property income for the tax year, both UK and overseas, not to individual properties or leases.

Where the taxpayer's total eligible property income for the tax year exceeds £1,000, they may either deduct expenses as normal, or deduct the allowance from their total gross rental income. The allowance is available to each individual and joint owners may therefore claim up to £1,000 each. Nonetheless, the allowance is unlikely to be of use to most landlords with genuine property businesses, but may be useful to anyone who:

- Ceases a property business shortly after the beginning of the tax year;
- Rents out all or part of their home under circumstances that do not qualify for rent-a-room relief (Section 4.16);
- Rents out a second home for a short period; or
- Has very few allowable costs

The allowance may also be useful to a new landlord starting a property business shortly before the end of the tax year. However, new landlords should bear in mind the ability to deduct pre-trading expenditure when the business starts (see Section 3.12). This ability would be lost if the property income allowance were claimed.

In general, any landlord with allowable costs of less than £1,000 would be better off claiming the property income allowance unless computing their results on a normal, actual, basis would lead to a loss that they might be able to utilise in future years. Any capital allowances within such a loss could also be set off against other income in the same tax year or the next.

For higher rate taxpayers with residential lettings who have total allowable costs over £1,000, but which include interest and finance costs, it is worth bearing in mind that the property income allowance will be fully deductible whereas their interest and finance costs are not (see Section 4.7).

Example: *Connor is a higher rate taxpayer with £7,000 of total gross rental income. He pays £1,000 in interest for the mortgage on his residential rental property. His other allowable costs amount to just £250. If he was to compute his rental profits for 2026/27 under normal principles, his interest cost would give him tax relief worth just £200 (£1,000 x 20%) and his other costs would give him relief worth £100 (£250 x 40%), a total of £300.*

Instead, he claims the property income allowance, giving him tax relief worth £400 (£1,000 x 40%) and an overall saving of £100 (£400 – £300).

The property income allowance cannot be claimed if you are receiving ***any*** rental income from your own company, or a partnership in which you are a partner.

These restrictions extend to income from any partnership in which a person connected with you is a partner, and any close company in which you, or a person connected with you, are a participator. See Appendix B for a list of connected persons, and see the Taxcafe guide *Using a Property Company to Save Tax* for an explanation of the other terms used here.

4.18 RENTAL LOSSES ON UK PROPERTY

All references to property or lettings in this section are to UK rental property only. Overseas rental property is treated as a separate business for tax purposes (see Section 4.19).

Up to 2024/25, it was necessary to separate UK rental property into three categories for loss relief purposes: non-commercial lettings; FHLs; and other UK rental property. From 2025/26 onwards, it is only necessary to separate out any non-commercial lettings. UK FHLs are now treated the same as other UK rental property, as described below.

For the treatment of losses arising on FHLs up to 2024/25, see Section 9.23; for the treatment of non-commercial lettings, see Section 4.20. For the rest of this section, I will be concentrating only on UK rental property that is let on an arms' length commercial basis and which, for years up to 2024/25, is not an FHL. For the sake of illustration, I will refer to this as 'normal rental property'.

Losses arising on normal rental property are automatically set off against profits on other normal rental property for the same period. Losses on normal rental property may also be set off against profits on non-commercial lettings. Any overall net losses from normal rental property remaining after this may be carried forward and set off against future profits from normal rental property or non-commercial lettings.

Losses on normal rental property consisting of capital allowances may also be set off against the landlord's other income of the same tax year or the next (subject to the tax relief cap discussed in Section 3.19).

Example: *In the tax year 2026/27, Owain has employment income of £70,000, from which he suffers deduction of tax under PAYE totalling £15,432. He also has a portfolio of rented commercial property on which he has made an overall loss of £15,000, including £10,000 of capital allowances. Owain can set his capital allowances off against his employment income, producing a tax repayment of £4,000.*

How Long Can Rental Losses Be Carried Forward?

Rental losses from normal rental property may be carried forward for as long as you continue to have a normal rental property business. There are two major pitfalls to watch out for here.

Firstly, rental losses are personal. They cannot be transferred to another person, not even your spouse, and they do not transfer with the properties. If you die with rental losses, they die with you.

Secondly, if your normal rental property business ceases, you will lose your losses. It may therefore be vital to keep your normal rental property business going. As long as you continue to have at least one normal rental property, you still have a normal rental property business.

Example: *Fergus has a large UK property portfolio. Despite having made some good profits in the past, by 2026/27 he has rental losses of £1m carried forward. Fergus decides he's had enough and begins to sell off his UK property empire. Before his rental income ceases, however, he buys one small lock-up garage in Preston and starts to rent it out. His lock-up is enough to ensure he still has a normal rental property business. It doesn't matter that it is tiny by comparison with his previous ventures; this one small garage keeps his rental losses alive, possibly saving him up to £470,000 one day (£1m at 47%).*

The only absolutely safe way to ensure you have a continuing normal rental property business is to ensure you always have at least one UK rental property let out on a commercial basis. However, HMRC will sometimes accept a cessation of all normal rental income is not necessarily the same as a cessation of your normal rental property business, especially where the rental properties are still held. They will usually accept the rental business has not ceased where:

- You can provide evidence you have been attempting unsuccessfully to let out your property, or
- Rental has only ceased temporarily for repairs or alterations

They will, however, generally regard the rental business as having ceased if there is a gap of more than three years between lettings and different properties are let before and after the gap. They may sometimes accept a gap of less than three years as not being a cessation, but not if you have clearly employed all your capital in some other type of business, or spent it for personal purposes, such as buying yourself a new home. If in doubt though, rent out that garage!

> **Wealth Warning**
> An overseas property will not preserve your normal rental property business. A non-commercial letting (e.g. to your aunt for £1 a year) will not do either. UK FHLs will work from 2025/26 onwards, however.

> **Another Wealth Warning**
> On page UKP 1 of the tax return, you are asked to put an 'X' in Box 2 if you do not expect to receive any rental income in the next tax year. Completing this box may be seen as a strong indication that your UK property business has ceased. I would recommend leaving this box blank where you have rental losses carried forward unless you are absolutely certain you will not have any UK rental income again in the future.

Unrelieved Interest

One of the consequences of the restrictions in interest relief discussed in Section 4.7 is that landlords with residential property are less likely to have allowable rental losses. They will, instead, tend to have unrelieved interest carried forward for relief at basic rate. Even those with existing rental losses are likely to see these effectively devalued and converted into unrelieved interest.

Example: *Solomon has a salary of £60,000. He also has a residential rental property portfolio and rental losses brought forward of £15,000. In 2026/27, he has rental profits before interest of £40,000 and interest costs of £45,000.*

His brought forward losses are automatically set off against his rental profits before interest, reducing them to £25,000. He can then claim basic rate relief for £25,000 of his interest, leaving £20,000 of unrelieved interest carried forward. In effect, the unrelieved interest carried forward for basic rate relief is made up of his £5,000 loss for 2026/27 ***and*** *his £15,000 of rental losses brought forward, reducing their future tax-saving value from £6,300 (42%) to just £3,300 (22%).*

4.19 OVERSEAS LETTINGS

All of a taxpayer's commercially let overseas properties (except FHLs in the EEA up to 2024/25) are treated as a single business in much the same way as, but separate from, a UK property business.

Up to 2024/25, FHLs within the EEA were subject to the same special regime as FHLs in the UK (Section 9.23). From 2025/26 onwards, these are treated the same as other overseas lettings.

A UK resident taxpayer with overseas lettings is therefore taxed on this income under exactly the same principles as UK lettings except:

- Separate accounts will be required for properties in each overseas territory where any double tax relief claims are to be made
- Recent arrivals resident in the UK for no more than four UK tax years may be exempt (see Section 9.36)
- Only FHLs in the EEA were subject to the special tax regime (covered in Section 9.23) that applied up to 2024/25

Travel expenses may be claimed when incurred wholly and exclusively for the purposes of the overseas letting business.

The UK tax treatment of losses arising from an overseas letting business is exactly the same as for a UK property business except, of course, that this is treated as a separate business from any UK lettings the taxpayer has. Hence, again, for loss relief purposes, any non-commercial overseas lettings must be separated out. FHLs within the EEA must also be separated out for tax years up to 2024/25. I will refer to other overseas rental property as 'normal overseas property' for the sake of illustration. From 2025/26 onwards, this includes FHLs within the EEA.

As before, the special rules outlined in Sections 9.23 and 4.20 apply to FHLs within the EEA up to 2024/25 and non-commercial overseas lettings respectively.

Losses arising on normal overseas property are automatically set off against profits derived from other normal overseas lettings or non-commercial overseas lettings, with the excess carried forward for set off against future normal overseas rental profits, or future profits from non-commercial overseas lettings. The same rule as set out in Section 4.18 applies to any capital allowances.

Where there are substantial normal overseas rental losses carried forward, it will be worthwhile ensuring this business continues. The same principles as set out in Section 4.18 apply here, except that, to continue the business, it is necessary to continue to have normal overseas rental property.

While the property must be let on a commercial basis, and must be outside the UK, it can be in any other part of the world and need not be in the same country as the property that gave rise to the original losses. A loss made in Albania might conceivably be set off against a profit in Zanzibar!

Non-Domiciled Individuals & Recent Arrivals
For tax years up to 2024/25, non-UK domiciled individuals may be able to claim exemption from UK Income Tax on overseas rental income that has not been remitted to the UK. For further details, see the thirtieth edition of this guide.

See also Section 9.36 for exemptions applying to individuals resident in the UK for no more than four UK tax years.

4.20 NON-COMMERCIAL LETTINGS

Where lettings are not on a commercial or 'arm's length' basis, they cannot be regarded as part of the same UK or overseas property business as any commercial lettings the taxpayer has. Profits remain taxable, but any losses arising may only be carried forward for set off against future profits from the same letting (i.e. the same property let to the same tenant).

Typically, this type of letting involves the lease of a residential property to a relative or friend at a nominal rent, considerably less than the rent the property could demand on the open market; or the lease of commercial property to a connected company or partnership.

Where the tenant of a non-commercial letting is a previous owner (e.g. a parent of the landlord) an Income Tax benefit-in-kind charge may apply. This could result in the tenant being charged Income Tax on the difference between the nominal rent they pay and full market rent. See the Taxcafe guide *How to Save Inheritance Tax* for further details.

Any plant and machinery allowances available on a property subject to a non-commercial letting (or on assets within it) will be restricted in the same way as applies to private use (Section 4.13). For example, if the rent charged is 60% of the market rate, only 60% of the available allowances may be claimed.

Furthermore, the SBA may not be available at all on a non-commercial letting, as renting the property out for less than a full market rent does not constitute qualifying use (see Section 4.14).

4.21 OTHER RECEIPTS FROM PROPERTY

Aside from rent, various other sums may be derived from land and property. In this section, I will look at how some of the most common items are treated for tax purposes.

Premiums received for granting a lease for less than two years are simply included in rental income. A premium for granting a lease for between two and fifty years is treated partly as income and partly as a capital disposal. Granting a lease for more than fifty years at a premium is a part disposal falling wholly within the CGT regime. We will take a detailed look at the benefits and pitfalls of lease premiums in Section 9.28.

Reverse premiums received for entering a lease are generally taxed as property income.

Where a tenant deposit is retained in order to cover the cost of repairs, cleaning, etc, the sum retained should be included in rental income and the full cost of the repairs, cleaning, etc, claimed as normal. In this way, the landlord effectively obtains Income Tax relief for any net cost remaining not covered by the deposit.

It is important to include tenant deposits retained within your rental income at the end of the lease, but not before. Refunded deposits should never be included in rental income.

Where a holding deposit received from a prospective tenant who does not subsequently enter into a tenancy agreement is withheld, this should be included in rental income. Such deposits may only be withheld under certain limited circumstances, however.

HMRC takes the view that any dilapidation payments received should usually be treated as rental income unless the payment is put towards the cost of repairs, when they consider it should be netted off those costs. Where repair costs exceed the payment received this treatment will be beneficial as the landlord still has on overall net expense to claim.

However, where repairs are not undertaken (perhaps because it is not practical or economical to undertake the work), HMRC's view is questionable. Some experts argue dilapidation payments then become a capital receipt: i.e. effectively a part disposal of the property, meaning the sum received falls within the CGT regime. As we will see in Section 9.27, this treatment will generally lead to significant tax savings, and there is case law to support this view: it has been held that, where the damage to a property is so severe as to lead to a permanent diminution in value, a dilapidation payment should be regarded as a capital receipt.

HMRC does accept dilapidation payments become a capital receipt if the property is not rented out again after receipt of the payment, and is subsequently sold or adopted for some other purpose (e.g. as the landlord's home or their own business premises).

Compensation payments such as for a loss of access or a 'right to light' claim should also be treated as part disposals, as explained in Section 9.27.

Some items are specifically excluded from property income, including any amounts taxable as trading income, profits from farming and market gardening, and income from mineral extraction rights. Wayleave (right of access) payments are sometimes included, however.

4.22 THE CASH BASIS FOR LANDLORDS

The cash basis of accounting is available to landlords operating as individuals or traditional partnerships, with total gross annual rental income not exceeding £150,000. It is not available to companies, trusts, LLPs, or other partnerships with one or more corporate partners.

The cash basis is the default option for all eligible landlords. In other words, if you are eligible for the cash basis, it will automatically apply unless you opt out by placing an 'X' in Box 5.2 or 20.2, as appropriate, in the UK property supplement of your tax return (see Section 3.5).

Opting out of the cash basis will ensure you are able to use traditional accruals basis accounting, which we examined in Section 3.11, and which it is generally assumed you are using throughout the rest of this guide.

For the purposes of both the £150,000 threshold and the question of whether you wish to opt out of the cash basis, your UK and overseas properties are regarded as separate businesses. Hence, you could have £100,000 of gross annual rental income from UK property and £100,000 of gross annual rental income from overseas property and still be eligible for the cash basis for both businesses. Furthermore, you could, if you wish, opt out of the cash basis for one of those businesses, but remain in the cash basis for the other.

Where you own ***any*** rental property jointly with your spouse, and you are splitting your taxable rental income equally by default (i.e. you have not made the election to split it on the basis of actual beneficial entitlement: see Section 9.6), you must both use the same basis (i.e. either the cash basis or the accruals basis) for the relevant property business (UK or overseas).

The cash basis closely reflects what many landlords actually do in practice and generally means all rent is taxable when received and allowable expenses may be claimed when paid. Subject to the points below, it does not generally alter the question of which expenses are allowable, only the timing of when they may be claimed. There are some important exceptions to this, however.

Disadvantages of the Cash Basis

The cash basis is simpler to operate than traditional accruals basis accounting, but there are a number of reasons why it will not always be beneficial, including:

i) Rent becomes fully taxable on receipt, even if it relates to a period that extends beyond the end of the tax year

ii) Expenses that have been incurred but not yet paid at the end of the tax year cannot be claimed
iii) There is a potential further restriction on interest relief in addition to the measures set out in Section 4.7: see further below
iv) Abortive expenditure relating to potential purchases of new property that are abandoned will not be allowable
v) No deductions are allowed in respect of lease premiums (see Section 9.28)
vi) Some expenditure that would normally qualify for capital allowances does not attract any relief under the cash basis
vii) Tax relief is delayed, and tax charges may even arise, where assets used in the business are being purchased under hire purchase or similar contracts
viii) Higher tax charges may arise on the disposal of assets used in the business
ix) Deductions for expenditure on assets like vans, computers, machinery, and equipment cannot be deferred to provide better tax relief, or to prevent taxable income arising in a later tax year when the landlord has a higher marginal tax rate

See Section 4.23 for details of how capital expenditure and the proceeds of asset disposals are treated under the cash basis; Section 4.13 for the tax planning opportunities available under the accruals basis referred to in point (ix); and Section 4.4 for further details on the treatment of abortive expenditure on potential property purchases.

Further Restriction on Interest Relief

The further restriction on interest relief applies where the total amount borrowed for the purposes of the property letting business (which would otherwise qualify under the principles set out in Section 4.5), is greater than the total value of the rental properties in the business when each of them was first rented out (plus other capital introduced: see Section 4.5).

When this restriction applies, the allowable interest under the cash basis is reduced by the appropriate proportion. As usual, the restriction applies equally to other finance costs.

Example 1 Part 1: *Joseph bought a rental property for £100,000 a few years ago. He also paid purchase costs of £5,500 and spent £4,500 furnishing the property. There were a further £3,000 of initial set up costs, which he was able to claim for Income Tax purposes.*

He financed his total costs of £113,000 with a buy-to-let mortgage of £85,000 and a further £28,000 obtained by re-mortgaging his home. A few years later, he carried out some urgent roof repairs on his rental property at a cost of £7,000. He financed this with a personal loan. By 2026/27, his total qualifying borrowings (under the principles set out in Section 4.5), are therefore as follows:

Buy-to-let mortgage	*£85,000*
Additional mortgage on home	*£28,000*
Personal loan	*£7,000*
Total	*£120,000*

These give rise to total allowable interest costs of £7,980, which he would be able to claim under the accruals basis (subject to the restrictions in Section 4.7). However, his total capital introduced (derived on the basis explained in Section 4.5) is as follows:

Property value when first rented	*£100,000*
Purchase costs	*£5,500*
Furnishings	*£4,500*
Total	*£110,000*

Joseph's other set up costs of £3,000 do not count for this purpose as they qualified for Income Tax relief. Hence, if Joseph adopts the cash basis in 2026/27, his allowable interest will be reduced to £110,000/£120,000 x £7,980 = £7,315. He will lose out on £665 of allowable interest. The £7,315 that is allowed will also continue to be restricted as set out in Section 4.7.

An important point to note is that only capital expenditure (see Section 3.12) counts as capital introduced for the purposes of calculating allowable interest. This seldom matters under the accruals basis, as all borrowings used to fund business expenditure qualify for relief. Under the cash basis, however, this distinction is critical.

In the example I have included the initial cost of furnishing the property as capital introduced. This is perhaps debatable since the legislation refers to expenditure 'in respect of the property' and one legal interpretation might be that furnishings are not part of the property. Such an interpretation would reduce Joseph's allowable interest cost under the cash basis to £7,016: although I would argue my interpretation is correct.

Further complications arise where the landlord is claiming interest on other borrowings not directly related to any individual rental property.

Example 1 Part 2: *Let us now assume that, under the accruals basis, Joseph would also be able to claim part of the hire purchase interest on his car and an element of the original mortgage on his home (before the re-mortgaging referred to above) within his use of home claim (see Section 3.14).*

The balance on his hire purchase agreement is £20,000, he uses the car 25% for business purposes and the interest payable during 2026/27 is £4,000.

The balance on his original mortgage (excluding the additional re-mortgaging) is £200,000, the interest payable on this balance during 2026/27 is £10,000 and the proportion of fixed costs claimed within his use of home claim is 1.5%. Hence his interest claim under the accruals basis is:

Loans and mortgages (as before)	*£7,980*
Hire purchase (£4,000 x 25%)	*£1,000*
Use of home (£10,000 x 1.5%)	*£150*
Total	*£9,130*

His total qualifying borrowings are now as follows:

Loans and mortgages (as before)	*£120,000*
Hire purchase (£20,000 x 25%)	*£5,000*
Original mortgage (£200,000 x 1.5%)	*£3,000*
Total	*£128,000*

His total capital introduced remains £110,000, so his interest claim under the cash basis would be restricted to £7,846 (£9,130 x £110,000/£128,000). Joseph is now losing £1,284 of allowable interest by using the cash basis.

Interestingly, if Joseph did not include his domestic mortgage interest within his use of home claim, his total allowable claim under the cash basis would increase to £7,902. While the difference is small in this case, it does prove landlords using the cash basis and facing this interest relief restriction might do better to exclude claims for balances with lower rates of interest.

Let's look at another example that brings together some of the cash basis issues.

Example 2 Part 1: *During 2026/27, Safiya receives rent totalling £120,000, pays interest of £70,000 and incurs other expenses of £20,000, including £2,500 paid for surveys on properties she later decided not to buy and £7,500 for roof repairs carried out in March 2027, which she pays in late April.*

For interest relief purposes, Safiya has total qualifying borrowings of £1.75m and total capital introduced of £1.65m. £12,000 of Safiya's income was received in the first five days of April 2027 and relates to the rent due for the whole of that month.

Her accountant works out her profit using traditional accruals basis accounting:

Income due for the year (£120,000 – £12,000 x 25/30)	*£110,000*
Less expenses:	
Interest	*£70,000*
Other expenses incurred	*£20,000*
Accrued accountancy fees	*£2,000*
Rental profit	*£18,000*

Safiya's interest expense will be added back to her profit for tax purposes and will instead give rise to a tax deduction at basic rate.

If Safiya does not elect to use traditional accruals basis accounting, she will fall into the cash basis by default and her profit will then be calculated as follows:

Income received in the year	*£120,000*
Less expenses paid in the year:	
Interest (£70,000 x £1.65m/£1.75m)	*£66,000*
Other (£12,500 paid less survey costs not allowed £2,500)	*£10,000*
Net rental income	*£44,000*

Safiya's allowable interest will be added to her income for tax purposes and will instead give rise to a tax deduction at basic rate. The cash basis would cause a considerable increase in Safiya's tax liability!

It must be admitted much of the difference arising in Safiya's case is only a question of timing. Nonetheless, she has permanently lost out on £6,500 worth of allowable expenses (due to the further restriction in interest relief and denial of relief for her abortive capital expenditure).

And timing is nothing to be sniffed at. Apart from the permanent loss of £6,500 of allowable expenses, a further £19,500 of taxable income has arisen at least a year earlier. For a higher rate taxpayer, that currently means paying £7,800 in tax at least a year earlier, rising to £8,190 from 2027/28 onwards: so it's not exactly unimportant.

(It's actually worse than this for Safiya, as the cash basis would give her taxable rental profits of £110,000, due to the wretched Section 24 restrictions, and she would lose some of her personal allowance.)

Advantages of the Cash Basis

In addition to being simpler to operate, the cash basis has other advantages, many relating to timing. If a landlord expects to be paying a higher tax rate in a later tax year, it could help in the following ways:

i) The cash basis may accelerate income into an earlier tax year when the landlord has a lower tax rate

ii) Expenses incurred during the year but paid after the year end may attract relief at a higher tax rate

Most landlords will, of course, be paying tax at a higher rate from 2027/28 onwards, due to the 2% 'across the board' increase in Income Tax rates on property income (Section 3.3). It is, however, debatable whether it is worth accelerating taxable income into an earlier year due to this increase alone.

Where it is more likely to be worth accelerating taxable income into an earlier year is where the landlord is currently a basic rate taxpayer but expects to be a higher or additional rate taxpayer in future. This area of tax planning is examined in detail in the Taxcafe guide *Small Business Tax Saving Tactics*.

Another potential timing advantage arises in respect of finance costs (Section 4.6). Under the cash basis, these can be claimed when paid and do not need to be spread over the useful life of the loan. However, while the question is debatable, it seems probable loan arrangement fees added to the balance of the loan can only be regarded as paid as and when the loan itself is repaid. This diminishes this potential advantage, although it will not generally affect other finance costs, as discussed in Section 4.6.

Another advantage for those leasing a car is there is no statutory 15% disallowance under the cash basis (Section 3.15).

Remember, it remains possible to amend tax returns for 2024/25 until 31st January 2027 if you now feel you would like to use the cash basis for that year; and you will have until 31st January 2028 to amend your tax return for 2025/26 (but see

Section 3.7 for issues to be taken into account when submitting an amended tax return).

Entering the Cash Basis

Transitional rules apply in the year that a landlord with an existing rental business moves from traditional accruals basis accounting to the cash basis. In effect, these rules ensure no income escapes tax; no income is taxed twice; and expenses cannot be claimed twice. Generally, the rules should also ensure allowable expenses are not omitted, but this is subject to the points listed under 'Disadvantages of the Cash Basis' above.

Example 2 Part 2: *Safiya opted out of the cash basis in 2026/27, but she decides to use it in 2027/28. This means she will be taxed on the rent she actually receives, with deductions for the allowable expenses she actually pays, but she will also have to make adjustments for:*

i) *The £10,000 (£12,000 x 25/30) of rent received in the first five days of April 2027 that was excluded from her income in 2026/27*
ii) *The £7,500 already claimed for roof repairs carried out in March 2027*
iii) *The £2,000 accrued for accountancy fees in 2026/27*

Let us also now assume Safiya paid an insurance premium of £1,500 in September 2026 but only claimed half of it in her 2026/27 accounts (under the accruals basis) as it covered the year to September 2027. This necessitates a fourth adjustment under the transitional rules, as otherwise she would be unable claim the other half of the premium.

The net effect of these adjustments is as follows:

Additional rent to be brought into account	*£10,000*
Roof repairs claimed previously	*£7,500*
Prior year accrual	*£2,000*
Prior year prepayment	*(£750)*
Net total	*£18,750*

This net total adjustment is referred to as 'adjustment income' and is added to Safiya's taxable income for 2027/28 (her first year on the cash basis).

If the net total of the adjustments required is a negative figure, this is referred to as an 'adjustment expense' and is deducted from the landlord's taxable income for their first year on the cash basis.

Long-Term Differences on a Change of Accounting Basis

The vast majority of any differences between traditional accruals basis accounting and the cash basis will be dealt with via adjustment income or an adjustment expense in the first year after the landlord changes their accounting basis, as illustrated above.

However, there is an exception for expenses already claimed on the old basis that would otherwise need to be claimed over more than one tax year after the change to the new basis. In this case, the expenses must simply be disregarded (or disallowed) in all the taxpayer's accounting periods after the change of basis.

Example 2 Part 3: *Let us now say that Safiya enters an agreement with her builder to pay for her roof repairs (carried out in March 2027) in instalments of £500 per month commencing at the end of April 2027. This means, under the basic principles of the cash basis, she would normally be able to claim payments totalling £6,000 in 2027/28 and £1,500 in 2028/29. However, she has already claimed the whole £7,500 under the accruals basis in 2026/27.*

Hence, the payments she makes in 2027/28 and 2028/29 are simply disallowed for tax purposes. The £7,500 claimed in 2026/27 is not included in her adjustment income under these circumstances (thus reducing her adjustment income to £11,250).

Leaving the Cash Basis

Similar principles apply when a landlord leaves the cash basis and adopts traditional accruals basis accounting (whether this is for the first time or represents a return to accruals basis accounting). Where an adjustment expense arises, this is deducted from the landlord's taxable income for the first year after they leave the cash basis. The same rule as before applies to any expenses already claimed which, under basic principles, would have to be claimed over more than one tax year after the landlord changes their accounting basis.

Example 2 Part 4: *After adopting the cash basis for 2027/28, Safiya re-adopts traditional accruals basis accounting for 2028/29. Once again, she received £10,000 of rent during 2027/28 that related to periods falling after 5th April 2028. However, as she was using the cash basis, this was all taxable on receipt.*

Her accountant would have made an accrual for fees of £1,500 in her 2027/28 accounts if she had been using traditional accruals basis accounting. However, as she was using the cash basis, this expense could not be claimed.

She paid an insurance premium of £1,800 in September 2027, relating to the year to September 2028. As she was using the cash basis, she claimed this in full in 2027/28.

In July 2027, she paid a total of £8,000 in loan arrangement fees and associated professional costs for a new twenty-year loan. As she was on the cash basis, she was able to claim all of this expense in 2027/28: albeit with tax relief restricted to basic rate. (For the sake of illustration, I have assumed the further restriction discussed in Part 1 of this example no longer applies in Safiya's case.)

Under traditional accruals basis accounting for 2028/29, Safiya will be taxable on the rent ***receivable*** *for the period from 6th April 2028 to 5th April 2029, including the amounts already* ***received*** *before 6th April 2028. She will be able to deduct all the expenses* ***incurred*** *in respect of the period, regardless of when they are* ***paid****. Hence, in order to prevent income being taxed twice or expenses either being relieved twice or omitted altogether, the following adjustments need to be made:*

Rent relating to period but already taxed on receipt	*(£10,000)*
Accrual that would have been made in prior year	*(£1,500)*
Prepaid expense already claimed: £1,800 x 6/12	*£900*
Net adjustment required	*(£10,600)*

Safiya can claim an adjustment expense of £10,600 in 2028/29. But remember, under accruals basis accounting, she will also have needed to include the £10,000 of rent received in advance, and the deduction for insurance premiums of £900 relating to this period, as well as excluding the accountancy fees paid in respect of the previous year, ***before*** *she includes the adjustment expense.*

The loan arrangement fees and associated costs already claimed in 2027/28 (under the cash basis) are a long-term item which, under traditional accruals basis accounting, would normally be claimed over more than one year following Safiya's change of accounting basis. Hence, these are not included in the calculation of the adjustment expense and are simply disallowed in 2028/29 and later years.

Practical Issues

If all the complexities outlined in Part 4 of the example seem like a big waste of time to you, you're right. The same overall result for 2028/29 could be achieved simply by just excluding all rental income received before 6th April 2028; claiming the accountancy fees relating to 2027/28 when they are paid; ignoring the insurance premium paid in 2027; and forgetting about any accounting adjustments for the loan arrangement fees and associated costs. Much simpler, same result!

So why did I put you through the torture of the method set out in the example? Well, because where there is an adjustment expense, you're quite right: it is all a big waste of time, BUT, where adjustment income arises when a landlord leaves the cash basis, this more complex, but technically correct, method makes a huge difference to your tax liabilities.

Spreading of Adjustment Income on Leaving the Cash Basis

Where adjustment income arises when a landlord ***leaves*** the cash basis (but not when they enter it), this is spread over the next six tax years. This provides incredible scope for landlords to defer tax on their income. But when will adjustment income arise for a landlord on leaving the cash basis and adopting (or re-adopting) traditional accruals basis accounting?

A proper interpretation of the legislation tells us one way that adjustment income may be created on leaving the cash basis is expense prepayments (such as the insurance premium Safiya paid in the example above).

However, HMRC's view is that a prepayment already claimed under the cash basis should simply mean the relevant expense is disallowed in future accounting periods (and the prepayment is excluded from adjustment income). Whether you follow the legislation or HMRC's view is up to you; but I know what I would do when the opportunity to spread this adjustment income over six years is available.

Remember though, if the prepayment represents an expense that would normally have to be claimed over more than one accounting period after leaving the cash basis (under the accruals basis) HMRC's view is correct.

Hence, the loan arrangement fees and associated professional costs Safiya paid in 2027 could not be included in adjustment income.

What is beyond doubt is the main thing that will create adjustment income on leaving the cash basis is rent arrears: rent not yet received while the landlord was using the cash basis, but which is judged to be recoverable under traditional accruals accounting (see Section 4.15).

The tax planning opportunities provided by the ability to spread adjustment income over six tax years are further enhanced by the fact a landlord may choose to accelerate their adjustment income: perhaps so more of it might fall into a year in which they have a lower marginal tax rate. We will look at these opportunities in Section 9.32.

Summary

In general, my view is the cash basis will not usually benefit most landlords for the simple reason that rent is typically received in advance and many expenses are paid in arrears. Hence, the cash basis generally accelerates taxable income into an earlier year.

It is also important to bear in mind that some expenses are ineligible for tax relief under the cash basis. As explained above, these restrictions can lead to a complete loss of relief and not merely a timing difference.

However, while most landlords will normally be better off sticking with traditional accruals basis accounting, it will always be worth considering whether the cash basis might be beneficial when eligible. Indeed, there are some expenses that can be claimed earlier if the cash basis is used. Furthermore, the cash basis does have the advantage of simplicity, which will appeal to many landlords. It can also be turned to advantage when a landlord's marginal tax rate is expected to increase in the following year.

And for those with rent arrears, the cash basis is well worth looking into, as it could provide some tremendous benefits. We'll explore these further in Section 9.32.

4.23 CAPITAL EXPENDITURE UNDER THE CASH BASIS

Landlords using the cash basis can generally claim capital expenditure as it is paid, provided it would otherwise qualify for plant and machinery allowances (Section 4.11), or replacement of domestic items relief (Section 4.9). Certain expenditure cannot be claimed, however, including:

i) Cars: Motor expenses must be claimed under one of the two alternative methods described in Section 3.15 (see further below).
ii) Land and buildings: This includes the cost of integral features (Section 4.10) and other fixtures that might normally qualify for capital allowances, where these are purchased as part of the purchase of a property. Additional fixtures added later may qualify. Replacements will usually be correctly classed as repairs and not as capital expenditure (see further below).

iii) Non-depreciating assets: Assets that have an expected useful life of 20 years or more, and which will retain at least 10% of their initial value after 20 years, do not qualify.
iv) Intangible assets: The cost of intangible assets cannot be claimed unless they have a fixed life of less than 20 years. This includes any form of intellectual property, such as patents, trademarks or copyright. Most expenditure on software is just a licence to use the software, so this would not be prevented from qualifying.

A few other items are also excluded under the cash basis legislation, but these would not qualify for relief under traditional accruals basis accounting either, so the rules are effectively the same.

Costs incurred in connection with the purchase or sale of excluded items (e.g. survey fees, legal fees, SDLT, etc) are also prohibited. This exclusion is extended to the costs of any abortive, or unsuccessful, attempts to buy or sell excluded items.

The cost of vans or motor cycles may be claimed under the cash basis, but if the purchase cost is claimed in this way, the mileage allowances explained in Section 3.15 will not be available.

Premiums paid to take out a lease on rental property (for sub-letting) or business premises, would be excluded under heading (ii). Under traditional accruals basis accounting, part of the premium could usually be claimed for Income Tax purposes (see Section 9.28). Those using the cash basis might therefore be better off negotiating a higher level of rent instead (or switching to the accruals basis).

The above restrictions only apply to capital expenditure. They do not apply to other valid business spending, such as repairs and maintenance, or software licence fees.

The rule in Section 4.10 whereby expenditure on replacing part of an integral feature may sometimes have to be classed as a capital improvement does not apply under the cash basis: such expenditure may be claimed as a repair if it meets the general criteria set out in Section 4.8.

With the exception of any expenditure relating to the excluded items listed above, brought forward balances in capital allowances pools or 'puddles' (see Sections 4.11 and 4.13) may generally be claimed in full in the year the landlord enters the cash basis. This will seldom be of any benefit, however, as most landlords will already have claimed all their qualifying expenditure under the AIA (see Section 4.11).

This apparent benefit is also subject to some important provisos. Firstly, as far as those 'puddles' are concerned, it is only the business use proportion of the brought forward balance that can be claimed.

Secondly, and more importantly, it is only expenditure that has actually been paid that can be claimed on entry into the cash basis.

Furthermore, where capital allowances have previously been claimed on unpaid expenditure (such as outstanding hire purchase payments, for example), there will be an adjustment on entry into the cash basis.

Example: *In March 2026, Charlie bought a van under hire purchase. The total cost of the van was £40,000. Charlie paid a deposit of £4,000 and is paying the rest over three years. His monthly instalments are £1,200 each, made up of capital payments of £1,000 and interest of £200 (see below).*

Charlie used traditional accruals basis accounting for 2025/26 and, since his van has 80% business use, he was able to claim capital allowances of £32,000 (£40,000 x 80%) under the AIA.

However, when Charlie joins the cash basis for 2026/27, he must make an adjustment for the amount he has claimed but not yet paid. Since all he had paid at 5th April 2026 was his £4,000 deposit, the adjustment will amount to £28,800 (£36,000 x 80%). This will be added to his taxable income for 2026/27 for Income Tax purposes.

Charlie can, of course, claim £9,600 in respect of his capital payments in 2026/27 (£1,000 x 12 x 80%), as well as interest costs of £1,920 (£200 x 12 x 80%).

How this all works out for Charlie will depend on a number of factors, including his marginal tax rates in both 2025/26 and 2026/27: so, it may, or may not, be the disaster it appears to be. If he is a residential landlord, the tax relief on his interest costs will be restricted (Section 4.7).

Note that, for the sake of illustration, I used a simple, straight line, method to allocate the interest charge within Charlie's hire purchase payments. In practice, there are better, albeit more complex, ways to do this: see the Taxcafe guide *Small Business Tax Saving Tactics* for details.

Cars Under the Cash Basis

Landlords using the cash basis should claim capital allowances on cars under the usual principles (Section 4.12): unless they are claiming the mileage allowance instead (Section 3.15). No other capital allowances may be claimed under the cash basis.

Asset Disposals Under the Cash Basis

Where an asset with business use (other than a car) is disposed of under the cash basis, the proceeds will form part of the owner's taxable income, with a suitable reduction for any private use element.

In most cases, the overall result will be similar to the balancing charge arising under traditional accruals basis accounting. Where there is a gain arising, however, the cash basis will often lead to greater tax liabilities.

Example Continued: *In 2029/30, Charlie sells his van for £45,000, making an overall gain of £5,000. If he was still using the accruals basis, he would have a balancing charge of £32,000 (£40,000 x 80%) and a taxable gain of £4,000 (£5,000 x 80%).*

If we assume Charlie is a higher rate taxpayer, and makes no other capital gains in 2029/30, he would have suffered Income Tax at 42% on his balancing charge, but would be able to set his £3,000 annual exemption against his capital gain (Section 5.19), leaving just £1,000 subject to CGT at 24%, producing a bill of £240.

Under the cash basis, however, Charlie's van sale gives him additional taxable income of £36,000 (£45,000 x 80%), all of which is subject to Income Tax at 42%. The tax suffered on the first £32,000 is the same as he would have faced under the accruals basis, but the tax suffered on the final £4,000 (the profit element) amounts to £1,680, which is £1,440 more than the CGT he would have paid if he had still been using the accruals basis.

Chapter 5

How to Save Capital Gains Tax

5.1 THE IMPORTANCE OF CAPITAL GAINS TAX

Although its impact is not as immediate as Income Tax, CGT is a highly significant tax from a property investor's perspective.

Most property investments will eventually lead to a disposal, and every property disposal presents the risk of a CGT liability arising to drastically reduce the investor's after-tax return. Paradoxically, however, CGT is also the tax that presents the greatest number and variety of tax-planning opportunities. We will be examining some of these further in Chapter 9.

In this chapter, we will be examining the current CGT regime and taking a detailed look at how it affects property investors and other people disposing of property. Before we look at the current regime, however, it is worth recalling how CGT developed.

CGT was introduced by Harold Wilson's Labour Government in 1965 in response to a growing trend for avoiding Income Tax by realising capital gains, which at that time were mostly tax free.

The high inflation of the 1970s and early 1980s led to the introduction of indexation relief, designed to exempt gains that arose purely through the effects of inflation. In 1987, CGT moved from a flat rate of 30% to a system where gains were taxed at the individual's top rate of Income Tax. In 1997, Gordon Brown introduced taper relief, designed to reward long-term investment by progressively reducing the effective rate of CGT as investments were held over a longer period.

In 2008, Alistair Darling abolished both taper relief and indexation relief and took us back to a flat rate system, this time at 18%. Two years later, the Coalition Government introduced a higher rate of 28%. In 2016, lower rates of 10% and 20% were introduced for most capital gains; but not gains on residential property. Jeremy Hunt did, however, reduce the top rate for gains on residential property to 24% in his last Budget in March 2024. Most recently, in October 2024, new Labour Chancellor Rachel Reeves increased the CGT rates on most capital gains to align them with the rates applying to residential property (and we all breathed a sigh of relief: it had been rumoured she was going to do something far worse!)

Finally then, now that every major political party has stuck their oar in, we find ourselves lumbered with a CGT regime where there is no protection against the effects of inflation and no reward for long-term investment. What the current system actually means is, when you hold property as a long-term investment, inflation alone is likely to push you into a higher tax rate. This makes understanding the tax system and the reliefs and planning opportunities available, more important than ever!

Who Pays Capital Gains Tax?
UK resident individuals and trusts pay CGT on their worldwide capital gains (subject to some exceptions for individuals resident in the UK for no more than four years: see Section 9.36; or, for gains arising prior to 6th April 2025, non-UK domiciled individuals).

Non-UK resident individuals and trusts (and those covered by the exceptions referred to above) pay CGT on disposals of UK property. For further details see Section 2.10; for a detailed look at the rules on residence, see Section 9.35.

For the rest of this guide, I will be concentrating mainly on UK resident individuals investing in property (but see Sections 9.18 to 9.20 regarding trusts and Sections 9.33 and 9.34 regarding partnerships).

5.2 CAPITAL GAINS TAX RATES

CGT is currently charged on property disposals at three rates:
- 14% where business asset disposal relief (BADR) is claimed
- 18% on other gains made by basic rate taxpayers
- 24% on other gains made by higher rate taxpayers

These rates apply to the taxable capital gain, not the total gain. As we shall see throughout this chapter, ***effective*** rates of CGT, after relevant reliefs and exemptions, can vary tremendously.

For gains on assets other than residential property arising before 30th October 2024, the main rates were 10% and 20% instead of 18% and 24%. For gains on residential property arising before 6th April 2024, the rate paid by higher rate taxpayers was 28%.

The higher rates applying to residential property before 30th October 2024 applied to any interest in land or property that had ever included a residential dwelling during the taxpayer's ownership. Contracts for off-plan purchases of residential property were also subject to these rates.

BADR is seldom available to property investors, although it can still apply to certain qualifying disposals of former FHLs (Section 9.23). The relief also remains relevant to owners of trading businesses, including those who personally own their company's business premises, or the business premises of a trading partnership in which they are a partner, so we will look at it in detail in Sections 9.24 and 9.25.

The CGT rate applying to gains on which BADR is claimed was 10% prior to 6th April 2025, rising to 14% for the current, 2025/26 tax year, and 18% from 6th April 2026.

Apart from the sections referred to above, I will assume throughout the rest of this guide that BADR is not available (unless stated to the contrary).

The Higher Rate of CGT
The higher rate of 24% applies to capital gains made by an individual to the extent their total taxable income for the year (after deducting their personal allowance), plus their total taxable capital gains arising during the year, exceeds the basic rate band (see Appendix A).

The basic rate band for each tax year from 2021/22 to (we expect) 2030/31 is normally £37,700, although this can be increased by making pension contributions or gift aid donations. This simple way to save CGT is explored further in Section 9.30.

Individuals who have sufficient taxable income to fully utilise their basic rate band pay CGT at the higher rate on all their taxable capital gains. Basic rate taxpayers pay CGT at 18% on the first part of their capital gains until their basic rate band is exhausted. Thereafter, any further gains are taxed at the higher rate.

> **Tax Tip**
> The rate of CGT you pay is linked to the amount of taxable income you have in the tax year. This means you may be able to reduce your CGT bill by ensuring your gains fall into a tax year in which you have a lower level of income. We will take a closer look at the potential savings arising in Section 9.30.

Example: *Boudica is a property investor with several buy-to-let investments. In December 2026, she sells a residential property and realises a gain of £41,000. Her taxable income for 2026/27 is £35,270. Deducting her personal allowance of £12,570 (Appendix A) means £22,700 of her basic rate band has been utilised, leaving £15,000 (£37,700 – £22,700) available for CGT purposes.*

Boudica deducts her annual exemption of £3,000 (Section 5.19) from the £41,000 gain, leaving a taxable gain of £38,000. The first £15,000 is taxed at 18% and the remainder at 24%, giving her a CGT bill of:

£15,000 x 18%	*£2,700*
£23,000 x 24%	*£5,520*
Total	*£8,220*

Allocating the Annual Exemption and Capital Losses
Taxpayers are generally free to allocate their annual exemption (Section 5.19), their basic rate band, and any capital losses they have available (Section 5.23), between their capital gains in the most beneficial manner. This remains important for cashflow purposes (see Section 5.20), although it no longer affects the overall CGT bill: unless an individual is claiming BADR (Section 9.24).

This freedom of allocation was also useful for anyone who had both gains on residential property and other gains arising during the same tax year, but before 30th October 2024.

5.3 WHAT IS A CAPITAL GAIN?

A capital gain is the profit arising on the disposal, in whole or in part, of an asset, or an interest in an asset. Put simply, the gain is the excess obtained on the sale of the asset over the price paid to buy it. (However, as we will see, matters rarely remain that simple.)

Sometimes, assets are held in such a way their disposal gives rise to an Income Tax charge instead. The same amount of gain cannot be subject to both Income Tax and CGT. The most common type of asset sale that gives rise to an Income Tax charge is a sale in the course of a trade. In other words, where the asset is, or is deemed to be, trading stock. See Sections 2.1 to 2.8 for a detailed examination of when a gain may be subject to Income Tax instead of CGT.

Just because the profit arising on a sale is a capital gain, this does not necessarily mean it is subject to CGT. A number of assets may be exempt from CGT, including motor cars, medals, and Government securities. Most importantly for property investors, the taxpayer's main residence is also exempt and we will return to this in Section 5.9.

5.4 WHEN DOES A CAPITAL GAIN ARISE?

For CGT purposes, a disposal is treated as taking place as soon as there is an unconditional contract for the sale of an asset. The effective disposal date may therefore be somewhat earlier than the date of completion. This is a vital point to remember when undertaking any CGT planning.

Example: *Aidan completes the sale of an investment property on 8th April 2027. However, the unconditional sale contract was signed on 1st April 2027. Aidan's sale therefore falls into the 2026/27 tax year.*

The deemed disposal date can have an impact on the applicable CGT rate (Section 5.2); the extent of available reliefs and exemptions; whether or not the taxpayer is UK resident (Section 9.35); and many other important factors. So, it is absolutely critical to know the relevant date.

For disposals of non-residential property or overseas property, it also determines the due date of payment for the CGT arising. If Aidan's property was ***not*** a UK residential property, the fact his disposal fell into 2026/27 means he must report this gain on his 2027 tax return and pay any CGT arising by 31st January 2028. (See Sections 5.20 and 5.21 regarding reporting deadlines and due dates for payment of CGT on disposals of UK residential property by UK residents, or any disposals of UK property by non-UK residents.)

Where the contract remains conditional on some event beyond the control of the parties to it, then the sale is not yet deemed to have taken place for CGT purposes. The most common scenarios here are for the sale to be conditional on: completion of a satisfactory survey; approval of finance arrangements; or granting of planning permission.

Many English investors who have travelled north of the border get caught out by the Scottish system where the conclusion of missives generally creates an unconditional binding contract.

What if there is no sale?
The conclusion of an unconditional contract only determines the **date** of disposal for CGT purposes. If the sale falls through, then no sale will have taken place and there will be no disposal for CGT purposes.

Anti-Forestalling Rules
Anti-forestalling rules prevent unconditional contracts being used as a means to artificially avoid an increase in CGT rates. Such an increase will apply to assets qualifying for BADR on 6th April 2026, so we will take a closer look at these rules in Section 9.24.

5.5 SPOUSES AND CIVIL PARTNERS

There are a number of cases where, although an asset is held as a capital investment, there is deemed to be no gain and no loss arising on a disposal. The most important instance of this is transfers between spouses. The effect is that these transfers are ***totally exempt*** from CGT.

The exemption comes into force on the date of marriage and applies throughout the period the couple are living together as spouses. It gives rise to many planning opportunities which we'll look at in Chapter 9.

If the couple should separate, the exemption will continue to apply for a limited period thereafter, and also in certain other circumstances. A married couple remain connected persons (see Section 5.6) throughout any period of separation and only cease to be connected if and when their divorce is finalised (usually on the grant of a decree absolute). We will look at separated and divorcing couples in Section 9.8.

For the remainder of this guide, unless expressly stated to the contrary, it is assumed any transfer between spouses is exempt from CGT.

5.6 THE AMOUNT OF THE GAIN

Having established that the profit on disposal of an asset is a capital gain, we now need to work out how much the gain is. The essence of this is the gain should be the excess obtained on the sale of the asset over the price paid to buy it. However, in practice, thanks to the many complexities introduced over more than 60 years, there are many other factors to be taken into account. Hence, one has to slightly amend the definition to: 'A capital gain is the excess of the actual or deemed proceeds arising on the disposal of an asset over that asset's base cost.' The derivation of proceeds is examined below. Base cost is covered in Section 5.7. In these two sections, we are only looking at how the capital gain is calculated, we are not yet factoring in any exemptions or reliefs that may apply.

Proceeds

In most cases, the amount of proceeds to be used in the calculation of a capital gain will be the actual sum received on disposal of the asset. From this, the taxpayer may deduct incidental disposal costs to arrive at net proceeds, which is the relevant sum for calculating the capital gain.

Incidental disposal costs that may be deducted from sales proceeds include those incurred wholly and exclusively for the purpose of the sale, such as legal fees, estate agents' commission, and advertising costs.

Professional fees incurred for the preparation of valuations or apportionments required for CGT purposes may also be included in disposal costs. As far as CGT calculations are concerned, this does not include a simple calculation of net proceeds less base cost, but covers more complex calculations, such as allocating a gain between the element that is subject to a relief, and the element that is not. There are many examples of such calculations throughout this guide.

Example: *In March 2027, George sells a house for £375,000. In order to make this sale, he spent £1,750 advertising the property, paid £5,625 in estate agents' fees, and paid £1,500 in legal fees. His net proceeds are £366,125 (£375,000 LESS £1,750, £5,625, and £1,500).*

This sounds very simple, but it is not always this easy. There are a number of cases where the proceeds used in the calculation of a capital gain are not simply the actual cash sum received. The most common exceptions are examined below.

Exception 1: Connected Persons

Where the person disposing of the asset is connected to the person acquiring it, the open market value at the time of the transfer must be used in place of the actual price paid (if any).

Example: *Mary sells a property to her son Philip for £500,000, when its market value is £800,000. She pays legal fees of £775. Mary is deemed to have received net sale proceeds of £800,000 (the market value). The legal fees she has borne are irrelevant, as this was not an arm's-length transaction.*

See Appendix B for a list of connected persons. Note, however, the exemption for transfers between spouses (Sections 5.5 and 9.8) takes precedence over the market value rule for transfers between connected persons.

Exception 2: Transactions not at Arm's-Length

Where a transaction takes place between connected persons, there is an automatic assumption the transaction is not at arm's-length and market value must be substituted for actual proceeds. There are other instances where the transaction may not be at arm's-length, such as:

- The transfer of an asset between partners in an unmarried couple
- A sale of an asset to an employee
- A transaction that is part of a larger transaction
- A transaction that is part of a series of transactions

The effect of these is much the same as before: the asset's market value must be used in place of actual proceeds, if any. The key difference from Exception 1 is it's the circumstances involved that determine whether or not it's at arm's-length, rather than there being an automatic assumption it is not at arm's-length because of the relationship between the parties.

Example: *John has a house worth £200,000. If he sold it for this amount, he would have a capital gain of £80,000. Not wishing to incur a CGT liability, John decides to sell the house to his friend Richard for £120,000. However, John only does this on condition Richard also gives him an interest-free loan of £80,000 for an indefinite period.*

The condition imposed by John means this transaction is not at arm's-length. John is deemed to have sold the house for £200,000 and still has a capital gain of £80,000.

> **Wealth Warning**
> Where a person has disposed of an asset at less than market value, whether to a connected person or not, there is a danger of Income Tax arising if the original owner later derives any benefit from the asset. IHT may also arise if the original owner dies within seven years of making the transfer. These charges do not apply to transfers between spouses.

Exception 3: Non-Cash Proceeds
Sometimes all or part of the sale consideration will take a form other than cash. The sale proceeds to be taken into account in these cases will be the market value of the assets or rights received in exchange for the asset sold.

Example: *Matilda is an elderly widow with a large house she no longer needs, so she offers it to Stephen, who lives nearby with his wife and young children. Rather than pay the whole amount in cash, Stephen offers £250,000 plus his own house, which is worth £300,000.*

Matilda incurs legal fees of £2,400 and pays SDLT of £2,500 to acquire Stephen's house. Three quarters of the legal fees are for the sale of her old house, the rest for the purchase of Stephen's.

Matilda's sale proceeds are £550,000. This is made up of the cash received plus the market value of the non-cash consideration, Stephen's house. Matilda may deduct her incidental costs of disposal from her proceeds in her CGT calculation. This is unaltered by the existence of non-cash consideration: the transaction has still taken place on arm's-length terms. However, as far as her legal fees are concerned, it is only the element relating to the disposal of her old house (£1,800) that may be deducted. The element relating to the purchase of Stephen's house will be treated as an acquisition cost for that house, as will the SDLT Matilda has paid.

Hence, the net sale proceeds to be used in Matilda's CGT calculation are £548,200 (£550,000 LESS £1,800).

Exception 4: Structures and Buildings Allowance Claims
As explained in Section 4.14, any SBA claimed by the property owner must be added to their sale proceeds.

5.7 BASE COST

The base cost is the amount deducted in the CGT calculation in respect of the cost of the asset. The higher the base cost, the less CGT payable!

The starting point is usually the actual amount paid to purchase the asset. To this you can add:

- Incidental acquisition costs (e.g. legal fees, SDLT)
- Enhancement expenditure (e.g. the cost of building an extension)
- Expenditure incurred in establishing, preserving or defending title to, or rights over, the asset (e.g. legal fees for a boundary dispute)

Interest and other costs associated with raising finance, i.e. mortgaging or re-mortgaging the property, cannot be included in the base cost. For rental property, these are dealt with as set out in Sections 4.5 to 4.7.

Survey fees will often be part of the cost of raising finance, especially if the survey was only carried out at the lender's request. A survey carried out at the purchaser's own instigation prior to making, or finalising, an offer may be claimed as an acquisition cost for CGT purposes.

Any costs claimed for Income Tax purposes cannot also be claimed for CGT. As explained in Section 4.8, expenditure on newly acquired rental properties not allowed for Income Tax purposes because it is capital in nature should be allowed for CGT purposes on a disposal of that property.

Example: *George (from Section 5.6) bought a house in 1995 for £85,000. He paid Stamp Duty of £850, legal fees of £650 and removal expenses of £1,000. Shortly after moving in, George spent £3,000 on redecorating: £1,800 of this related to one of the bedrooms, which was in such a bad state of repair it was unusable; the remainder covered repainting other rooms.*

In 1997, George's neighbour erected a new fence a foot inside George's back garden, claiming this was the correct boundary. George had to take legal advice to resolve this problem, which cost £2,500, but managed eventually to get the fence moved back to its original position.

In 1999, the house's roof was badly damaged in a storm. The repairs cost £16,000, which, unfortunately, George's insurance company refused to pay, claiming he was not covered for an 'Act of God'.

In 2005, George did a £15,000 loft conversion, putting in new windows and creating an extra bedroom. Unfortunately, he did not obtain planning permission and, when his neighbour filed a complaint with the council, George was forced to restore the loft to its original condition at a further cost of £8,000.

In 2008, George had the property extended at a cost of £80,000. He also incurred professional fees of £4,000 obtaining planning permission, etc.

When George eventually sold the property in March 2027 for £375,000, his base cost for CGT purposes was made up as follows:

- *Original cost: £85,000*
- *Incidental costs of acquisition: £1,500 (legal fees and Stamp Duty, but not removal expenses: a personal cost, not part of the cost of the property)*
- *Enhancement expenditure: £1,800 (restoration of the unusable bedroom; the remaining redecoration costs are not allowable, however, as the other rooms were already in a fit state for habitation and George's expenditure was merely due to personal taste, rather than being a capital improvement)*
- *Expenditure incurred in defending title to the property: £2,500 (the legal fees relating to his neighbour's new fence)*
- *Further enhancement expenditure: £84,000 (the cost of the new extension, including the professional fees incurred to obtain planning permission)*

Total base cost: £174,800

Notes to the Example

i) The cost of George's roof repairs does not form part of his base cost. This is not a capital improvement, but repairs expenditure of a revenue nature.

ii) Neither the cost of George's loft conversion, nor the cost of returning the loft to its original condition, form part of his base cost. This is because enhancement or improvement expenditure can only be allowed in the capital gains calculation if the relevant improvements are reflected in the state of the property at the time of sale.

Based on net proceeds of £366,125 (Section 5.6), George has a capital gain of £191,325 (£366,125 – £174,800) before any applicable reliefs. If the house was his main residence throughout his ownership, his gain would be exempt from CGT. However, we are assuming this is not the case here for the purpose of illustration.

Wealth Warning

An additional point to note under (ii) above is that enhancement or improvement expenditure is only deductible if still reflected in the state of the property at the date of ***completion*** of the sale.

Practical Pointer

George might be able to argue part of the cost of the loft conversion was still reflected in the state of the property at the date of sale. It may also be worth considering whether there was any element of improvement expenditure within the roof repairs carried out in 1999 (assuming these were not claimed for Income Tax purposes at the time). It is always worth looking at these things in detail!

As with proceeds, there are a number of exceptions where base cost is not simply determined by reference to the amount paid for the asset. Most of the exceptions relate to assets not acquired by way of a bargain at arm's length, although there are other quirks to watch out for too.

Inherited Assets

All assets are 'rebased' for CGT purposes on death. Hence, the base cost of any inherited asset is determined by reference to its market value at the date of the previous owner's death. However, while transfers on death are exempt from CGT, they are, of course, subject to IHT. See the Taxcafe guide *How to Save Inheritance Tax* for details.

Example: *Albert died on 22nd January 2001, leaving his holiday home, a cottage on the Isle of Wight, to his son Edward. The property was valued at £150,000 for probate purposes. In August 2002, Edward had a swimming pool built at the cottage at a cost of £40,000. He sold the cottage for £397,000 in March 2027. Edward's base cost is £190,000. His own improvement expenditure (£40,000) is added to the market value of the property when he inherited it. Any expenditure incurred by Albert is completely irrelevant.*

Assets Acquired from Spouses

As explained in Section 5.5, when an asset is transferred between spouses, that transfer is treated as taking place on a no gain/no loss basis. In the case of a subsequent disposal, the transferee spouse effectively takes over the transferor spouse's base cost.

Example: *Henry bought a house for £350,000 in 1999. He spent £100,000 on capital improvements then gave the house to his wife Katherine in 2008. Katherine had the house extended in 2013 at a cost of £115,000 and eventually sold it in 2026 for £950,000. Katherine's base cost for the house is £565,000. This includes both her expenditure and her husband's.*

Where a part share in a property has been transferred between spouses, the same principles apply to the part transferred.

The no gain/no loss rule does not apply in the case of a transfer on death, when the inheritance rules explained above take precedence. This creates a planning opportunity no-one ever wants to have: nevertheless, we'll take a look at it in Section 9.11.

Where the transferor spouse originally acquired the property before April 1998 and transferred it to their spouse before 6th April 2008 (but not on death), the indexation relief the transferor would have been entitled to at that time (if they had actually sold the property) is added to the transferee spouse's base cost.

Assets acquired from connected persons or by way of a transaction not at arm's length

As explained in Section 5.6, the transfer of an asset to a connected person is deemed to take place at market value. The market value rule also applies in other circumstances where an asset has not been acquired by way of a transaction at arm's length (see Exception 2 in Section 5.6). In both cases, for the person acquiring an asset by way of such a transfer, the market value at that date becomes their base cost.

Assets with held-over gains
In some cases, where a transfer is not a transaction at arm's length (and not covered by the spouse exemption), it may be possible to hold over some or all of the gain arising. The element of the gain that may be held over is the part arising due to the requirement to substitute market value for actual proceeds. In the case of an outright gift, this will be the whole gain.

Before 14th March 1989, it was possible to hold over the gain arising on a gift of any asset. Since then, however, gains can only be held over on a transfer of a qualifying business asset (broadly, either an asset used in a trade or, up to 5th April 2025, an FHL); or on transfers into, or out of, a trust (see Section 9.19 for the planning opportunities arising).

Where a gain is held over, it is deducted from the transferee's base cost. In the case of an outright gift, this generally means the transferee effectively acquires the transferor's base cost (subject to the additional points below).

Where the held over gain arose before 6th April 2008, the amount held over will be the gain arising after indexation relief. Hence, as with transfers between spouses, where the transferor originally acquired the property before April 1998, the transferee's base cost will effectively include the indexation relief the transferor would have been entitled to if they had actually sold the property.

As explained in Section 4.14, where a gain on non-residential property is held over, any structures and buildings allowance claimed by the transferor will effectively be deducted from the transferee's base cost.

Where the transferee paid something for the asset (but less than market value), their base cost will be the greater of the sum derived as above for an outright gift, or the actual price paid.

Assets acquired for non-cash consideration
Where an asset was acquired for non-cash consideration, its base cost will be determined using the market value of the consideration given.

Assets acquired before April 1982
Where an asset was acquired before April 1982, its market value at 31st March 1982 is substituted for its original cost. Enhancement or improvement expenditure may only be included where incurred after March 1982.

5.8 CAPITAL GAINS TAX RELIEFS

It is at this point in the CGT calculation, after deducting the base cost, that most reliefs and exemptions may be claimed, including:

- Private residence relief (for taxpayers selling their current or former home). This is covered in detail from Section 5.9 onwards
- Private letting relief (where a property eligible for private residence relief has also been let as private residential accommodation). See Section 5.10
- Relief for reinvestment of gains in EIS shares
- Set off of trading losses arising in the same tax year or the next

- Holdover relief on gifts of business assets. This is not generally available on investment property apart from FHLs transferred before 6th April 2025: see Section 9.23
- Holdover relief on a chargeable transfer for IHT (Section 9.19)
- Rollover relief on replacement of business assets (Section 9.26)

All these reliefs are claimed before business asset disposal relief, capital losses, and the annual exemption. We'll look at these last three later, but first we must look at the most important relief for residential property: private residence relief.

5.9 PRIVATE RESIDENCE RELIEF (PRR)

Most people are aware the sale of their home is exempt from CGT. In technical terms, this is known as private residence relief (PRR). In Chapter 9, we will look at some of the ways PRR can be used to enable a taxpayer to invest in property with little or no exposure to CGT. But first, in this section and those that follow, we will look at exactly how PRR works.

Each unmarried individual, and each legally married couple, is entitled to PRR in respect of their main residence. PRR covers the period during which the property was their main residence PLUS their last nine months of ownership.

Example: *Elizabeth bought a flat for £180,000 in October 2019 and immediately moved in, occupying it as her main residence. In January 2026, she married Philip and moved out of her flat. In October 2026, she receives an offer to sell the flat for £255,000, but is concerned about her potential tax liability. Elizabeth needn't worry. If she makes this sale, her gain on the flat will be covered by PRR. The first six years and three months of her ownership are exempt because it was then her main residence and the last nine months because it was a former main residence.*

Where the property owner is disabled or resident in a care home, the final period of exemption is three years instead of nine months.

The final period of exemption under PRR is available on any former main residence, regardless of whether the property is let out during that period. Hence, letting the property after you move out will make no difference to your CGT position (Income Tax is, of course, due on the rental profits).

Despite the general rule in Section 5.4, for PRR purposes, the owner's period of ownership starts at the date of completion of their purchase, not the date of contract.

Full Exemption

To be ***fully*** exempt under PRR, the property will generally need to become your main residence immediately on purchase; and be sold within nine months of ceasing to be your main residence. However, a delay of up to two years in initially occupying the property is permitted under certain circumstances. See Section 5.12 for details.

Proportional Relief
If you don't meet the conditions for full exemption, you won't be fully covered by PRR. However, you will still get a proportional relief based on your period of occupation of the property as your main residence, plus last nine months of ownership.

Example: *Alexander bought a house for £350,000 in December 2020 and let it out for a year. In December 2021, he sold his old home and moved into the new house. In December 2025, he moved back out of the house and started to rent it out again, until eventually selling it for £470,000 in December 2026. Alexander used the house as his main residence for four years out of six years of ownership and is also entitled to PRR for the final nine months. His total gain is £120,000, so he is entitled to PRR, as follows:*

Actual occupation as main residence: £120,000 x 4/6 =	*£80,000*
Final period exemption: £120,000/6 x 9/12 =	*£15,000*
Private residence relief:	*£95,000*

After deducting his PRR, Alexander will be left with a gain of £25,000 (£120,000 – £95,000). If his annual exemption of £3,000 (Section 5.19) is available, he will be left with a taxable gain of £22,000; giving him a CGT bill somewhere between £3,960 (at 18%) and £5,280 (at 24%), depending on how much taxable income he has for 2026/27.

Alexander was able to benefit from the additional final period of ownership exemption because he was ***not*** living in the house at the time. However, it is important to understand the extra period is not given in addition to exemption for actual occupation during the same period.

What If Part of The Property Is Unused?
PRR is not restricted merely because part of the property is left vacant and unused. Restrictions may apply, however, where part of the property is used for some purpose other than the owner's private residential occupation. The position for gardens, grounds, and outbuildings is different and is examined in Section 5.11.

Property Occupied by a Dependent Relative Before 1988
PRR is available on disposal of a property occupied rent-free by a dependent relative before 6th April 1988. There are various conditions that must be satisfied, including the fact the occupant must meet the statutory definition of a dependent relative. Nonetheless, while the dependent relative's occupation needed to start before April 1988, this additional relief continues to apply to a disposal at any time, so it's worth looking into if you think you might benefit.

5.10 PRIVATE LETTING RELIEF (PLR)

Technically, private letting relief (PLR) is an additional amount of PRR available under certain, rather restricted, circumstances. However, it is easier to refer to it as a separate relief, which is what I will do for the remainder of this guide.

PLR is now only available in respect of qualifying periods of shared occupancy. This means part of a property is being used as the owner's main residence at the same time as another part is being let out as private residential accommodation.

The part of the property being let out must not be used exclusively for the purposes of a trade (e.g. letting rooms in a guest house).

PLR is given as the lowest of:

i) The amount of gain already exempted under PRR,
ii) The gain arising as a consequence of lettings during qualifying periods of shared occupancy, and
iii) £40,000

The £40,000 limit applies on a per person basis. Hence, two joint owners may be able to claim up to £80,000 in total.

The limit also applies to every property that has been your main residence at any time during your ownership. Hence, even if you were to sell two or more former homes during the same tax year, you could conceivably still be entitled to up to £40,000 of PLR (per person) on each property.

In practice, however, the shared occupancy rule means PLR is only available on a very small proportion of residential property disposals. Nonetheless, we will take a closer look at the application of the relief in the limited circumstances where it still applies in Section 5.18.

5.11 GARDENS, GROUNDS, AND OUTBUILDINGS

There have been a great many cases before the courts over whether the grounds of a house, including subsidiary outbuildings, are covered by PRR. In the usual situation, where a house has a reasonably normal-sized garden and perhaps a shed, a garage, or other small outbuildings, there is no doubt the entire property is covered by PRR. Naturally, we are talking here only of the situation where there is no other use of any of the property apart from private residential occupation.

The general rule for grounds is these are deemed to form a normal part of the property where they do not exceed half a hectare (1.235 acres), including the area on which the house stands. Beyond this, it is necessary to argue any additional space is required 'for the reasonable enjoyment of the dwelling-house as a residence'.

What does this mean? Well, unfortunately, this is one of those rather enigmatic answers judges love to give that can only be decided on an individual case-by-case basis.

The situation changes once any part of the property is used for any other purpose. The position differs for buildings or gardens and grounds. Gardens and grounds obtain the same exemptions due on the house itself, as long as they're part of the private residence at the time of sale.

For subsidiary buildings, it is necessary to apportion any gain arising between the periods of residential occupation and the periods of non-residential use.

Example: *Lady Jane has a large house with grounds totalling half a hectare in area. For several years, she leased half her grounds to a neighbouring amusement park for use as part of their car park. Within this area there is a small outbuilding that was used as the parking attendant's hut.*

When the amusement park gave up its lease over Lady Jane's grounds, she hired a landscape gardener to restore them. The outbuilding reverted to its previous use as a storage shed for garden equipment.

In 2026 she sold the entire property. Apart from the lease of the car park, the whole property had been used as her main residence throughout her ownership.

Lady Jane's main house and her entire grounds will be fully covered by PRR. However, the element of her gain relating to the outbuilding must be apportioned between the periods of private use and the period of non-residential use. The non-residential element of the gain will be chargeable to CGT.

Lady Jane may have been better off demolishing the outbuilding prior to the sale of her house. No part of her gain would then have related to this building and her entire gain would have been covered by PRR. Naturally, it is only worth doing this if demolishing the building does not impact on the whole property's sale price by more than the potential tax saving.

Unlike the house itself, PRR does not extend to unused outbuildings or gardens and grounds and ***actual use*** for private residential purposes is required.

5.12 DELAYS IN OCCUPYING A NEW HOME

Many people buy a run-down property then embark on substantial renovation work before occupying it as their main residence. In other circumstances, a planned move may be held up by delays in selling the existing home.

The tax rules cater for this and PRR extends to cover any period of up to two years during which an individual is finalising renovation or construction work on the new property (including building a property on a vacant plot), or awaiting the sale of their existing main residence.

To qualify for this extension, the individual must actually occupy the new property as their main residence within two years of acquiring it (or the land on which it has been constructed) and ***immediately*** on completion of the renovation or building work, or sale of the previous home, as the case may be. The new property must not be used as another person's residence at any time between the date of acquisition and the date the owner first occupies it as their main residence.

During this period, it is possible for both the old and new properties to simultaneously be covered by PRR. However, where the delay in occupation of the new property is caused by a delay in selling the former home, the old property must be used as the individual's main residence immediately before its disposal and the sale of that old property must be ***completed*** (not merely 'subject to contract') within two years of the acquisition of the new property.

5.13 WHAT IS A RESIDENCE?

Before we go any further, it is worth pausing to consider what we mean when we refer to a property as an individual's residence.

In Section 5.15 we will look at individuals or married couples with more than one residence. One of these will be their main residence and will qualify for PRR. But no property can be a ***main*** residence until it is ***a*** private residence of that individual or married couple.

The question of whether a property qualifies as the owner's private residence at any given time is generally decided purely as a question of fact: based on the principles I will outline in this section. In some cases, however, those principles are subject to the additional rules in Section 5.14, which take precedence.

Having said that, it is worth pointing out the additional rules in Section 5.14 can never apply to a disposal of UK property by an individual who has been UK resident throughout their ownership of that property. Hence, most UK residents selling UK property will only need to be concerned with the basic principles covered below.

The principles below (and the rules in Section 5.14) are also subject to the rules on temporary periods of absence we will examine in Section 9.21. Generally speaking, the further rules in Section 9.21 are only likely to produce an advantage for the taxpayer, so they can be regarded as more of a planning opportunity than a cause for concern.

Residence Principles

A residence is a dwelling in which the owner habitually lives. While it needs to be habitual, occupation might be occasional and short.

Example: *Constantine owns a small cottage in Pembrokeshire but lives and works in London. Constantine bought the Pembrokeshire cottage as a holiday home, but only manages to visit it about two or three times each year, when he will typically stay for the weekend. Despite the rarity of Constantine's visits to his cottage, it nevertheless qualifies as his private residence.*

Some actual physical occupation of the property (including overnight stays) is necessary before it can be a residence. Constantine's situation is probably just about the minimum level of occupation that will qualify.

'Dwelling' means a property suitable for occupation as your home and can include a caravan or houseboat. It will not, however, include a plainly unsuitable property such as an office, shop, or factory. (Although there are flats over shops and offices that are dwellings!)

To live in a property means to adopt it as the place where you are based and where you sleep, shelter, and have your home. In principle, these guidelines apply equally to both UK and overseas property, so a foreign property could also be classed as the owner's residence: although this is subject to the additional rules in Section 5.14.

Some other use of a property at other times, when not occupied as the private residence, does not necessarily prevent it from qualifying as a residence. If such a property were treated as your main residence though, there would be a proportionate reduction in the amount of PRR.

Example: *On 1st April 2017, Bonnie bought a small cottage on Skye for £150,000. For the next ten years, she rented the cottage out as furnished holiday accommodation for 48 weeks each year and occupied it herself for the remaining four weeks. Bonnie's regular occupation of the cottage is enough to make it a residence. In this example we are also going to assume it is her main residence throughout her ownership.*

On 1st April 2027, Bonnie sells the cottage for £254,000, realising a capital gain of £104,000. For the nine years and three months from April 2015 to July 2024, Bonnie is only entitled to PRR on 4/52nds of her capital gain, reflecting her private use of the property. As usual, Bonnie is entitled to full relief for the last nine months of ownership. Bonnie's capital gain amounts to £10,400 per year of ownership (£104,000/10), so her PRR is as follows:

£10,400 x 9¼ x 4/52 =	*£7,400*
£10,400 x 9/12 =	*£7,800*
Total:	*£15,200*

Bonnie will not be entitled to any PLR as there were no periods of shared occupancy (see Section 5.10). Assuming her annual exemption of £3,000 is available, her taxable capital gain will be £85,800 (£104,000 – £15,200 – £3,000).

Bonnie is still able to treat the cottage as her private residence, even though she is renting it out as holiday accommodation. However, where a property is rented out for longer periods under a lease, it cannot be regarded as the owner's residence during the period of the let.

A residence for CGT purposes must also be a property in which the taxpayer has a legal or equitable interest. A legal interest encompasses any form of ownership, or rights over the property, sole or joint, including freehold, leasehold, or even just the tenancy of a property rented under a weekly or monthly lease.

An equitable interest is less easy to define. Generally, it must mean some sort of right over the property itself and not merely an ability to reside in it. Hence, for example, if an individual stays rent-free with family or friends, they are occupying the property under gratuitous licence and clearly have no equitable interest.

Occupation of property may also be under contractual licence, such as staying in a hotel, guest house, or private club. This again does not give the guest any legal or equitable interest in the property.

An unmarried partner in a co-habiting couple may perhaps have an equitable interest in the couple's home when it is owned wholly by the other partner, although this point has not yet been tested in court in connection with CGT.

For married couples, the principles regarding residences and main residences must be applied to the couple as a single unit. Hence, for example, if William owns a property in Brixham that he has never visited, but his wife Mary stays there regularly, then that property must be counted as a private residence of the couple.

If an individual or married couple has only one property that qualifies as a private residence, then that property must be their main residence for CGT purposes. Indeed, HMRC's capital gains manual sets out the principle that, where an individual's main home is occupied under licence, but they also own another residence, the residence the individual owns must be regarded as their main residence for CGT purposes.

Once an individual or married couple has more than one eligible private residence, we need to work out which is their main residence. We will look at this issue in Sections 5.15 to 5.17.

5.14 PRIVATE RESIDENCE RESTRICTIONS

In some cases, the principles in Section 5.13, which determine whether a property qualifies as the owner's private residence, are subject to an additional rule.

For taxpayers who are non-UK resident at the time of the disposal, the additional rule applies to any period throughout their ownership of the property. For taxpayers who are UK resident at the time of the disposal, the additional rule only applies to determine whether a property qualifies as their private residence during periods after 5th April 2015.

The Rule for UK Residents

For taxpayers who are UK resident at the time of the disposal, a property cannot be their private residence for any part of a tax year from 2015/16 onwards unless the owner:

a) Is resident for tax purposes (for at least half of that tax year) in the country in which the property is located,
b) Would be treated as resident in that country if the equivalent of the UK statutory residence test (see Section 9.35) were applied, or
c) Is physically present in the property at midnight on at least 90 days during that tax year

For the third test, days spent in the property by the owner's spouse may also be counted, as well as days spent (by either of them) in another residence the taxpayer owns in the same country (but the same day cannot be counted twice).

For years in which the property is purchased or sold, the 90-day requirement is proportionately reduced, as appropriate. For example, where a property was purchased on 1st August 2026, the test for 2026/27 under (c) above becomes 62 days (90 x 248/365 rounded up).

The Cinderella Syndrome
For the purpose of the 90-day test, you need to be present in your home at midnight in order for a day to be counted. This could mean, like Cinderella, you need to leave the ball (or party, dinner, friend's house, bar, restaurant, etc) early in order to get home by midnight.

This may seem like a really petty point (indeed it is), but I would not put it past HMRC to make use of it when your day count is exactly 90, or only just over.

Who Is Affected?
The additional restrictions affect three types of taxpayer:

i) Non-UK residents disposing of UK property
ii) UK residents disposing of overseas property, and
iii) UK residents disposing of UK property after having been non-UK resident at an earlier point in their ownership after 5th April 2015

I will take a closer look at the impact on UK residents disposing of overseas property in Section 5.16. Those falling in the third category will often benefit from the periods of absence rules in Section 9.21, which take precedence over the rules outlined in this section.

5.15 SECOND HOMES

The rules on what constitutes a private residence are set out in Sections 5.13, 5.14, and 9.21. Any reference to a residence or private residence in this section is based on the assumption the property in question qualifies as a private residence under those rules.

For CGT purposes, each unmarried individual and each legally married couple can generally only have one main residence at any given time. Many people, however, have more than one private residence.

When someone acquires a second (or subsequent) private residence they may, at any time within two years of the date they first occupy the new property as a private residence, elect which of their properties is to be regarded as their main residence for the purpose of PRR.

The election must be in writing and sent to the taxpayer's tax office. An unmarried individual must sign the election personally. A married couple must generally both sign the election (although one spouse need not sign the election if they are not affected by it: e.g. if they do not have any legal or equitable interest in any of the couple's residences).

There is no particular prescribed form for the election, although the following example wording would be suitable for inclusion:

> 'In accordance with section 222(5) Taxation of Chargeable Gains Act 1992, [I/we] hereby nominate [property] as [my/our] main residence with effect from [date*].'

* The first such election an individual or married couple makes in respect of any new combination of private residences will automatically be treated as coming into effect from the beginning of the period to which it relates: i.e. from the date on which they first occupied that new combination of residences. It is this first election for the new combination of residences to which the two-year time limit applies.

Despite HMRC's headlong rush to push everyone else into the digital age the only way to make a main residence election is still by letter!

Late elections (after the two-year limit) may be made where the individual (or married couple) did not hold interests with more than negligible market value in more than one property. This is aimed at catering for the situation where the taxpayer may be unaware of the need to make an election, for example where they have two residences, one of which is an ordinary rented property occupied under a non-transferable tenancy agreement at a weekly or monthly rent.

Typically, such elections are only made when it becomes apparent they are necessary following enquiries from HMRC after the disposal of a residence the taxpayer actually owns.

The ability to make late elections under these circumstances is useful, but it would be wise to make the election as soon as possible after you become aware of having two or more private residences (or any new combination of two or more residences).

Furthermore, it is essential to remember, if you actually ***own*** two or more residences, the strict two-year time limit will apply. For example, if you buy a second home on 1st September 2026, you will need to make your election by 31st August 2028 (yes, a day ***before*** the second anniversary).

> **Tax Tip**
> If the two-year period for making an election has expired, a new one can be opened up in a number of ways, such as:
> - Acquiring an additional private residence (renting a small flat for a short period would be sufficient)
> - Selling the main home and moving elsewhere
> - Renting out one of the properties for a short period and then re-occupying it as a private residence thereafter

Once an election is in place for any combination of residences, it may be changed, by a further written notice given to HMRC under the same procedure, at any time. A new election may be given retrospective effect, if desired, by up to two years. We will take a look at the benefit of this in Chapter 9.

Example: *Alfred lives in a small flat in Southampton. In September 2022 he also bought a house on the Isle of Wight and started spending his weekends there. In August 2024, he realised his island house had appreciated in value significantly. He therefore elected, before the expiry of the two-year time limit, that the house was his main residence.*

In March 2027 Alfred sells the Isle of Wight house at a substantial gain, which is fully exempted by PRR. Alfred's flat will not be counted as his main residence from September 2022 until the time of sale of his island house. However, should he sell the flat in the near future, his final nine months of ownership will be covered by PRR.

Tax Tip

As soon as Alfred sold his house, he should have submitted a new election nominating the Southampton flat as his main residence once more: with effect from a date nine months previously. This would give him an extra nine months of PRR on the flat, while still leaving the house fully exempt. In fact, where the annual exemption or other reliefs are available, it might be worth backdating the new election a little further (up to a maximum of two years).

Regardless of any election, a property may only be a main residence for PRR purposes if it is the taxpayer's private residence. A property cannot be covered by PRR while being let (subject to the exceptions covered in Sections 5.17 and 9.21; and the final period of ownership exemption applying to a former main residence: see Section 5.9).

If one of a taxpayer's residences ceases to be occupied by them as a private residence (e.g. because it is let out or sold), any main residence election that has been made will cease to apply: even an election in favour of a different property!

Wealth Warning

A new election is required every time an individual, or married couple, has a new combination of two or more private residences. Where a third residence is acquired, for example, a new election must be made. Remember a property may qualify as a residence whenever the taxpayer or their spouse has ***any*** legal or equitable interest in it, no matter how small.

However, a new election is not required if the new combination of residences only comes into existence because a different property to the one elected ceases to qualify as a private residence due to the rules set out in Section 5.14 or if, having previously been disqualified under those rules, it begins to qualify.

Practical Pointer

Where the number of private residences reduces to one, no new election is required, as the sole remaining residence must now be the main residence. The temporary periods of absence rules (Section 9.21) must be borne in mind, however, as these could mean the individual or married couple is still deemed to have two or more private residences and a new election is therefore required.

If the only reason the number of private residences has reduced to one is because a different property to the one elected has ceased to qualify under the rules set out in Section 5.14, the existing election will remain in force.

In Section 5.13 we considered the issue of whether a property was occupied under licence or an equitable interest existed. Where a taxpayer has only one residence in which they have a legal or equitable interest, a main residence election will not be valid.

My suggestion, however, is that whenever there is a possibility a taxpayer may have two or more eligible private residences, they should make a main residence election. If this election proves to be invalid, no harm is done and the property in which they have a legal or equitable interest will automatically be treated as their main residence.

If circumstances change so that it becomes more certain the taxpayer has a legal or equitable interest in two or more residences, it would be wise to make a fresh election in case HMRC argues the earlier one was invalid.

Former Main Residences
Under the temporary periods of absence rules (Section 9.21), a former main residence may continue to be treated as the owner's residence after they have moved out, but have not yet sold the property. In these cases, it will be wise to make a suitable main residence election. This opens up a number of planning opportunities, so we will examine this issue further in Section 9.22.

Non-Residents Disposing of UK Residential Property
Non-UK residents liable to CGT on disposal of a UK residential property may make a main residence election in favour of their UK property covering all or part of any period the property qualified as a private residence under the rules in Sections 5.13, 5.14, and 9.21 (except for any period for which another property they have previously disposed of has already been treated as their main residence for UK CGT purposes).

Such an election must be made in the non-resident CGT return at the time of disposal of the UK property and takes precedence over any previous election in favour of another property that the individual still holds. The usual two-year time limit does not apply.

Generally, it will be sensible for the election to only cover relevant qualifying periods after 5th April 2015. However, where the property has otherwise never been the non-resident's main residence at any time, an election covering a single day at some earlier time will be beneficial in order to secure PRR for the final nine months of ownership.

What if there is no election in force?
In the absence of a valid election, the question of which property is an individual's main residence has to be determined on the facts of the case. Often the answer to this will be obvious but, in borderline cases, HMRC may determine the position to the taxpayer's detriment. Clearly then, it is ***always*** wise to make the election!

The factors to be considered when determining which property was an individual's main residence for any given period not covered by an election, include:

- The address given on the individual's tax return
- The address on correspondence, utility bills, bank statements, etc.
- Where a mortgage was obtained over a property before April 2000, whether mortgage interest relief (MIRAS) was claimed
- Whether the mortgage over a property was obtained on the basis that it was the individual's main home
- The security of tenure (leasehold, freehold, etc) held over each residence
- How each residence is furnished
- Where the individual's family spend the majority of their time
- Where the individual is registered to vote
- The location of the individual's place of work
- The location of medical practices where the individual is registered
- The registered address for the individual's car

As always, a married couple have to be considered as a single unit.

Each factor is not conclusive in its own right, but will contribute to the overall picture of which property may be regarded as the main residence.

The same factors will be relevant in determining whether a property is, or was, a main residence for the purposes of SDLT or its devolved equivalents (Chapter 6), and may also be relevant in determining whether an individual is a Scottish taxpayer (see Section 3.20). It is not possible to elect for a property to be treated as a main residence for these purposes.

5.16 HOMES ABROAD

It is important to remember PRR applies to an individual's main residence, not, as some people have mistakenly thought to their cost, their main ***UK*** residence. Subject to the rules in Section 5.14, it is possible for a UK resident individual or married couple to have a private residence overseas. For periods prior to 6th April 2015, this will be determined purely under the principles in Section 5.13.

Where this means the individual or married couple had two or more private residences at some time in the past, and there was no main residence election in place at the time, the position will have to be determined under the principles set out in Section 5.15. Generally, one would expect this to lead to the conclusion the UK home was the main residence, although there will be exceptions. Naturally, where there was a main residence election in place, this will determine the position.

Where an overseas property was an individual or married couple's main residence for any period (whether by way of election or otherwise), PRR will apply in the same way as for a main residence in the UK. Private letting relief will also be available in the same way, in the rare cases where it is still applicable.

It is fairly unusual for an overseas property to qualify as a UK resident's main residence as a question of fact: although it can happen (perhaps where the overseas property is the only property in which the owner has any legal or equitable interest, as discussed in Section 5.15).

Furthermore, some overseas properties will have been a UK resident owner's main residence at some time in the past when they were resident overseas.

But, apart from these exceptions, in the vast majority of cases, the only way for a UK resident to achieve main residence status on an overseas property is to make a main residence election in favour of that property.

As we shall see in Chapter 9, such an election will almost always be beneficial, even if it is only for a short period.

Sadly, it is no longer possible to make a main residence election in favour of an overseas property unless it qualifies as a private residence under ***both*** the general principles in Section 5.13 ***and*** the rules in Section 5.14. For a UK resident, this will generally mean needing to spend at least 90 days during one or more UK tax years in the foreign holiday home: and that could have foreign tax consequences.

Example: *Abdul and Vicky, a UK resident married couple, own a holiday home in Spain. In September 2026, Vicky spends 25 nights in the property. Abdul spends 25 nights there in October. In January 2027, Vicky returns and spends another 23 nights in the property and Abdul makes a return visit of 20 nights in March.*

Between them, the couple have spent 93 nights in the property during 2026/27. They therefore pass the 90-day test, the property qualifies as their private residence, and they can make a main residence election in favour of it covering all or part of the 2026/27 UK tax year.

Furthermore, as (like most countries) Spain uses a calendar year for its tax year, neither has spent more than 25 days in Spain in any Spanish tax year (assuming the nights in their holiday home were the only nights spent in Spain). Hence, although it is always essential to take local advice, neither Abdul nor Vicky is likely to be treated as resident in Spain for tax purposes.

Assuming the Spanish property did not qualify as Abdul and Vicky's residence in 2025/26 because of the rules in Section 5.14, the position will be as follows:

- If they already have a main residence election in place in favour of another property, that election remains in force. The election could now be changed to the Spanish property and backdated by up to two years, if they wish: but not to a date earlier than 6th April 2026.
- If they had previously made an election in favour of the Spanish property, it would have ceased to be valid when the property had ceased to qualify at some earlier date, and a new election would now need to be made. The time limit for the new election will generally be 5th April 2028.
- If there is no previous election in place, they can now make an election in favour of the Spanish property (or any other residence), if desired. The time limit for the election will again be 5th April 2028.

Any election in favour of the Spanish property will cease to be valid at the beginning of any future UK tax year for which the property does not qualify as Abdul and Vicky's residence under the rules in Section 5.14. However, an election in favour of another residence would remain valid.

All of the above analysis is based on the assumption that the Spanish property qualifies as Abdul and Vicky's private residence under the general principles in Section 5.13, including the need for habitual occupation (although this can be occasional and short).

> **Tax Tip**
> Failing to meet the 90-day test in one year and then meeting it in the next would appear to be another way to create a new combination of private residences and open up a new two-year period for making a main residence election: even one in favour of an entirely different property.

> **Wealth Warning**
> Disposals of overseas property may also have foreign tax implications: even when the owner remains UK resident.

It is worth remembering the 90-day test is proportionately reduced in the years of acquisition or disposal of the property. Hence, for example, where a foreign holiday home was purchased on 1st February, it would only be necessary to occupy it for 16 nights between then and 5th April for it to qualify as a private residence and thus be eligible for a main residence election covering that period.

Where an overseas property has qualified as a private residence for more than two years, it remains possible to make a main residence election in favour of that property where there is an earlier existing election in favour of another property within the same combination of two or more residences (see Section 5.15).

5.17 JOB-RELATED ACCOMMODATION

In many occupations, it is sometimes necessary, or desirable, for an individual to live in accommodation specifically provided for the purpose. Examples include: caretakers; police officers (in some rural areas); pub landlords and landladies; members of the clergy; members of the armed services; teachers at boarding schools; the Prime Minister; and the Chancellor of the Exchequer.

For people in this situation, PRR may be extended to a property they eventually intend to adopt as their main residence. PRR will cover their property during the period they are living in job-related accommodation, despite the fact the property is not their residence at that time: even while they are letting it out. This provides an exception to the general rule that there must be some actual physical occupation of a property for it to be eligible for PRR.

This treatment can also be extended to a property owned by the spouse of a person living in job-related accommodation, which the couple eventually intend to adopt as their main residence.

If an individual in job-related accommodation has a property that might qualify as a main residence under these rules, but also has another residence, such as a holiday home, they can use a main residence election to determine which property is covered by PRR.

The election will also be appropriate where the individual has some legal or equitable interest in the job-related accommodation itself.

5.18 WHAT IF PART OF YOUR HOME IS NOT PRIVATE?

Whenever part of your home is put to some use other than your own private residential occupation, you are inevitably putting your PRR at risk.

One fundamental principle to note is that if any part of your home is used exclusively for purposes other than your own private residential occupation throughout the period when that property qualifies as your main residence, then that part will not be eligible for any PRR at all.

Hence, in order to maximise your PRR, I would generally recommend making some private use of every part of the property at some time while it is your main residence.

PLR does extend to a part of a main residence that has never been used privately by the owner; provided it remains part of the same dwelling (e.g. bedrooms within a flat the owner shares with other flatmates), and is not let out in the course of a trade (e.g. a guest house).

Taking a Lodger
HMRC generally accepts taking in one individual lodger does not necessitate any restriction to PRR. In this context, a lodger is someone who, while having their own bedroom, will otherwise live as a member of the taxpayer's household.

Other Lettings Within the Same Dwelling
Where part of the property is let out under other circumstances, PRR will be restricted. However, PLR is available to cover this restriction (except in the case of guest houses, hotels, and other lettings in the course of a trade: see Section 5.10).

Example: *Robert bought his five-storey house for £500,000 in March 2011. From June 2022 to October 2026 he let the top two floors out as a flat. He then resumed occupation of the whole house, before selling it in March 2027 for £925,000. Robert's total gain of £425,000 is covered by PRR as follows:*

Lower three floors: The gain of £255,000 (three fifths) is fully covered by PRR.
Upper two floors: The gain of £170,000 is covered by PRR from March 2011 to June 2022 AND for the last nine months of Robert's ownership, a total of 12 years out of 16. Hence, £127,500 of this gain is exempt, leaving £42,500 chargeable.

Robert can then claim PLR equal to the lowest of:

i) *The amount of PRR on the* ***whole*** *property: £382,500 (£255,000 + £127,500),*
ii) *The gain arising by reason of the qualifying letting: £42,500, or*
iii) *£40,000*

The relief is thus £40,000, leaving Robert with a gain of only £2,500. Assuming he has not used his 2026/27 annual exemption elsewhere, this will exempt the remaining part of his gain, leaving him with no CGT to pay at all!

Now, all that Robert probably did was to fit a few locks in order to separate the flat from his home. As a result, re-occupying the whole property was a simple matter and, when he came to sell it, it remained a single dwelling for tax purposes.

The situation is quite different where a property owner has carried out extensive conversion work in order to create two or more separate dwellings. We will examine the position arising in those circumstances in Section 9.14.

Adult Placement Carers

Occupation of part of your home by another person under an adult placement scheme is disregarded for PRR purposes.

Using Part of Your Home for Business

Where part of the property is used ***exclusively*** for business purposes, PRR is not available for that part of the property for the relevant period. Where the exclusive business use covers the entire period the property is the owner's main residence, the exemption for the final period of ownership will also be withdrawn for this part of the property.

Where the business use of part of the property requires extensive conversion work, that part will no longer be part of the original dwelling and PRR will not be available for the final period of ownership.

The effect on the owner's PRR is the same whether part of the property is being used exclusively in their own business, or is being rented out for use in someone else's. However, where it is their own trading business that is concerned, then this part of the property becomes business property for the purposes of a number of tax reliefs, including business asset disposal relief (Section 9.24), rollover relief (Section 9.26), and holdover relief for gifts (Section 5.7). This includes small hotels and guest houses that continue to be the owner's main residence, despite also being a business property.

Non-Exclusive Business Use (The Home Office)

Where part of the home is used non-exclusively for business purposes, there is no restriction on PRR. This is a common situation among landlords and other self-employed people who work from an office or study in their home.

To safeguard your PRR, it is wise to restrict your Income Tax claim in respect of the office's running costs to a maximum of, say, 99%, in order to reflect the room's occasional private use. For example, if an office used extensively for business purposes is one of four rooms in the house (excluding hallways, kitchen, and bathrooms), you could claim 99% of one quarter of the household running costs.

Just about any kind of private use will suffice, such as a guest bedroom, music room, library, or even just additional storage space for personal belongings. Naturally, it makes sense to adopt some form of private use that will only lead to a small reduction in the Income Tax claim.

Tax Tip

While restricting one room to, say, 99% business use, you may also be able to argue for 1% business use in another room, thus effectively reversing the effect of the restriction without affecting your CGT position.

Section 3.14 provides further details of how to claim an expense deduction for Income Tax purposes when using part of your home as an office from which to run your business. Claiming the flat rate allowances should not affect your home's CGT exemption, although it remains important to avoid exclusive business use of any part of the property.

Employees who work from home should not generally suffer any restriction in their PRR although, as always, it is important to avoid exclusive business use of any part of the property.

5.19 THE ANNUAL EXEMPTION

Each individual is entitled to an annual exemption each tax year (including minor children and non-UK residents). It exempts an amount of capital gains after all other reliefs have been claimed, including the compulsory set-off of capital losses arising in the same tax year (see Section 5.23 re capital losses brought forward). Individuals with more than one capital gain arising in the same tax year may allocate their annual exemption in the most beneficial way. Any unused annual exemption is simply lost.

Sadly, the value of the annual exemption has been dramatically slashed, from £12,300 in 2022/23, to just £6,000 in 2023/24, and then a measly £3,000 each tax year from 2024/25 onwards.

Because the annual exemption is now so pathetic, saving a maximum of £720, I am not always going to mention it in every example in this guide, and will use the term 'chargeable gain' to denote an individual's taxable gain before deducting their annual exemption. Where I do bring the annual exemption into a calculation, I am assuming it is available: in practice, it is important to remember you only get one annual exemption each tax year!

5.20 WHEN IS CAPITAL GAINS TAX PAYABLE?

For CGT arising on disposals of UK residential property, a payment on account is due 60 days after completion. The payment should usually be made together with a CGT on UK property return (see Section 5.21 for further details, including a valuable 'Practical Pointer', which has meant some people have had considerably longer to pay their CGT).

Although termed a payment on account, the amount due is actually the taxpayer's best estimate of the full amount of CGT arising on the disposal, calculated after taking account of the annual exemption and any available capital losses (see further below).

The calculation may also include reasonable estimates for:

- Valuations or apportionments required to compute the gain (where the information is not yet available), and
- The individual's taxable income for the relevant tax year

The second point is relevant if there is any possibility the individual's taxable income for the year may not exceed the higher rate tax threshold. The threshold for each tax year since 2021/22 is £50,270, and the same threshold is currently expected to apply each tax year until 2030/31. This threshold applies to all UK-resident individuals for CGT purposes, including Scottish taxpayers.

Where your total taxable income for the year is expected to be less than £50,270, you are able to anticipate the fact that some or all of your gain will be taxed at 18% instead of 24% (see Section 5.2) when making your payment on account. In many cases, this will be the most difficult part of the estimated calculation, as many individuals will not yet know their likely level of taxable income for the year, especially if the property disposal has taken place near the beginning of the tax year. Residential landlords must also bear in mind their taxable income is calculated before deduction of interest and finance costs (see Section 4.7).

Gains on other UK residential property earlier in the same tax year must be taken into account in the calculation (as these will have used up some or all of: your annual exemption, any available capital losses, and any available basic rate band). However, gains on other assets need not be taken into account. There is a presumption that the relevant reliefs, and basic rate band, will be used on UK residential property disposals in priority to other gains. This may not be the same as the final outcome: one of many flaws in this badly cobbled together system!

Any relevant claims or elections the taxpayer is likely to make may be taken into account in the estimated calculation (e.g. a main residence election, where relevant: Section 5.15). However, the relevant claims or elections must still be formally made within the usual time limits.

Taking Capital Losses into Account

Any realised capital losses may be taken into account in calculating the CGT payment on account. This means losses brought forward from an earlier tax year and losses arising on disposals earlier in the same tax year.

It is not generally possible to take account of capital losses arising later in the same tax year, except in the case of another disposal of UK residential property. In this case, the taxpayer must file a return for the loss-making sale plus an amended return for the original sale, together with a repayment claim.

Balancing Payments or Repayments

Where the payment on account proves to be less than the final amount due, a balancing payment is due by 31st January after the end of the tax year (the same date as other self-assessment tax liabilities). Interest will be charged on the underpayment for the period from the due date for the payment on account to the date of the final payment.

An overpayment is refundable and needs to be reclaimed through your CGT on UK property account (see Section 5.21). Unfortunately, HMRC's systems have proven incapable of setting these CGT refunds off against taxpayers' other self-assessment liabilities, leaving some people having to pay their Income Tax bill in full then claim their CGT refund separately: a truly inequitable situation caused by the system's poor implementation.

Other Property Disposals

For other disposals, the CGT payable for each tax year is due by the following 31st January. For example, the CGT arising on other asset disposals during 2026/27 is due by 31st January 2028. CGT is not included in the six-monthly instalment system under self-assessment (Section 3.4).

This system continues to apply to CGT arising on the disposal of all assets not falling within the report and pay regime described above, including non-residential property and overseas property.

The position is different for non-UK residents, however, as they must follow the report and pay regime for all disposals of UK property. Most non-UK residents have the same higher rate tax threshold as UK residents but, in some cases, it will only be £37,700 where they are not entitled to a personal allowance (see Section 2.10).

5.21 WHAT MUST I REPORT TO HMRC AND WHEN?

Under the report and pay regime, disposals of UK residential property must be reported to HMRC within 60 days of completion (together with the payment on account described in Section 5.20) whenever any part of the capital gain arising is chargeable to CGT.

To determine whether any part of the gain is chargeable, the taxpayer may take account of PRR (Section 5.9); PLR (Section 5.10); the annual exemption (Section 5.19); and any available capital losses (Section 5.20).

When assessing whether the annual exemption and any capital losses are available, the same criteria as those set out in Section 5.20 must be followed. No gain/no loss disposals, such as transfers to a spouse (Section 5.5), do not need to be reported.

Other claims and elections that might reduce the CGT liability to nil cannot generally be taken into account in determining whether the disposal needs to be reported, but may be taken into account when estimating the relevant payment on account (see Section 5.20).

The report and pay regime applies to individuals, partnerships, and trusts. Joint owners must each file their own return and make their own payment on account, where applicable. Non-UK residents must report all disposals of UK land and property, whether or not there is any gain chargeable to CGT.

The definition of residential property for the purposes of report and pay is broadly the same as for the structures and buildings allowance (Section 4.14), although in most cases it tends to be obvious. Where a property has mixed use (e.g. a single property with a shop on the ground floor and flats above), only the residential proportion of the capital gain falls under report and pay.

Disposals falling under report and pay should be reported by setting up an online CGT on UK property account and filing a CGT on UK property return. Each disposal must be reported on its own separate return, except where two or more properties are disposed of on the same day, when a single return for all the day's transactions should be made (or one for each joint owner, where applicable).

Practical Pointer

There have been numerous problems with the report and pay system. While it is all meant to take place online, many people have had to complete paper returns (form PPDCGT) instead.

Using form PPDCGT (which can be requested by telephoning HMRC) has the added advantage that payment of the CGT arising will not be due until after HMRC issues a demand for the tax. This has been known to take up to 16 weeks, thus producing a considerable cashflow advantage!

Where completion takes place within the last 60 days of the tax year or even afterwards (remember the gain arises on the date of unconditional contract), a similar result may sometimes be achieved through early submission of the self-assessment tax return: see further below.

Interaction with Self-Assessment

Where a disposal has been reported on a CGT on UK property return and the taxpayer has no other reportable income or gains for the tax year, there is usually no need for them to register for self-assessment. However, if the final amount of CGT due is less than is deemed to arise under the report and pay rules, a self-assessment tax return will be required.

This might happen if the taxpayer realises a capital loss on other assets (not UK residential property) later in the tax year.

For taxpayers already within self-assessment (including those subject to MTD), or who need to register for other reasons, the capital gain on disposal of a UK residential property should be reported again in their self-assessment tax return (with final figures for the CGT calculation) if they meet the criteria set out below.

Early Birds

Where a gain on disposal of UK residential property is reported on a self-assessment tax return ***before*** the 60-day deadline for reporting it under report and pay (e.g. if there was an unconditional contract shortly before the end of the tax year and you get your tax return in early), this is sufficient and the gain does not need to be reported again ***unless*** the amount of CGT that would have been due under report and pay (Section 5.20) is greater than the final amount. In the latter case, the correct final amount may be paid but the CGT on UK property return will still be required, including cases where the 60-day deadline has been missed.

The same rules apply where the gain was due to be reported on a self-assessment tax return before the 60-day deadline. This could arise in the case of a contract with a long, extended completion date.

The CGT on UK property return cannot be filed online where you have already submitted a self-assessment tax return that includes the same gain, so if the return is still required, you will have to use form PPDCGT (see 'Practical Pointer' above).

Yes, I know all this sounds like utter madness, but I am honestly not making it up: this is the mess the report and pay system has created!

Reporting Capital Gains under Self-Assessment

Where all of a taxpayer's disposals in a tax year, taken together, give rise to total proceeds exceeding £50,000, or where any of them give rise to an actual CGT liability, they will all need to be reported on the individual's self-assessment tax return using the capital gains summary (SA108). This is subject to the following exceptions:

- Disposals that are fully covered by PRR and PLR are exempted from reporting requirements. For the purposes of self-assessment, this does not include cases where the taxpayer is additionally relying on the annual exemption or any other relief to ensure full relief from CGT.
- Taxpayers not registered for self-assessment do not need to report their capital gains on a self-assessment tax return if all their capital gains for the year have already been reported on either a CGT on UK property return (and the tax deemed to arise under the report and pay system is no greater than the final CGT liability), or under the optional real time CGT service (which is available for reporting gains other than gains on UK residential property).

It is also wise to report all disposals in any tax year where an overall net capital loss arises: so the loss can be recorded and carried forward for relief in the future.

If you have a reportable property disposal under self-assessment, you will need to complete a tax return, including the capital gains summary, and attach a copy of your capital gains computation. The return is due for submission by 31st January following the end of the tax year if filed online, or by 31st October if a paper return is used.

If you are not yet in the self-assessment system, but still have a reportable gain, it is sensible to advise HMRC as soon as possible after the end of the tax year and definitely by 5th October at the latest. This is so HMRC can issue a Unique Taxpayer Reference (UTR) to enable you to submit your tax return on time.

Non-UK Residents

The report and pay system applies to ***all*** disposals of UK land and property by non-UK residents (regardless of whether any CGT is due).

5.22 JOINTLY HELD PROPERTY

Where two or more persons hold assets jointly, they must calculate CGT based on their own share of the net proceeds less their own base cost.

Example: *George and Charlotte are equal joint owners of a residential buy-to-let property they bought together for £120,000. In November 2026 they sell it for £250,000. Each person's taxable capital gain is calculated as follows:*

Net proceeds (£250,000 x ½)	*£125,000*
Less: Base cost (£120,000 x ½)	*(£60,000)*
Equals:	*£65,000*
Less: Annual exemption	*(£3,000)*
Taxable capital gain	*£62,000*

George is a higher rate taxpayer, so his CGT bill, at 24%, amounts to £14,880. Charlotte's taxable income is less than her personal allowance, so she pays CGT at 18% on the first £37,700 of her taxable gain (the basic rate band) and 24% on the remainder:

£37,700 @ 18%	*£6,786*
£24,300 @ 24%	*£5,832*
Total	*£12,618*

The couple's total CGT bill amounts to £27,498 (£14,880 + £12,618). Had the property been owned by George alone, his CGT liability would have been £30,480 (£130,000 – £3,000 = £127,000 x 24%). The couple have saved £2,982 (£30,480 – £27,498) by owning the property jointly.

This is the value of an additional annual exemption (£3,000 x 24%) plus the saving generated by using Charlotte's basic rate band (£37,700 x 6%: the difference between 18% and 24%).

The saving of £2,982 enjoyed by the couple in our example is worth noting, but is much reduced from the saving of up to £7,214 enjoyed by couples in a similar situation a few years ago. Nonetheless, there may be other good reasons for holding property jointly, including significant Income Tax savings, as we shall see in Section 9.2.

Another point to note when looking at jointly held property is the £40,000 limit for PLR (Section 5.10) applies to each individual. Hence, a total of up to £80,000 may be exempted when property is held jointly and the relief applies.

5.23 CAPITAL LOSSES

Capital losses are generally computed in the same way as capital gains. In the first instance, capital losses are automatically set off against any capital gains arising in the same tax year. Where an individual has an overall net capital loss for the year, it is carried forward and set off against gains in later years BUT only to the extent necessary to reduce future gains down to the annual exemption applying for that later year.

As explained in Section 5.2, individuals with more than one capital gain arising in the same tax year may generally allocate any available capital losses in the most beneficial way. Exceptions arise where BADR is being claimed, however: see Section 9.24.

No relief is allowed for capital losses derived from exempt assets, including the taxpayer's main residence. Relief is also denied for artificial capital losses arising as a result of transactions carried out with a main purpose of creating a tax advantage. Capital losses arising on transactions with connected persons (Appendix B) may only be set off against gains on transactions between the ***same*** parties.

Chapter 6

How to Save Stamp Taxes

6.1 STAMP DUTY LAND TAX (ENGLAND & N. IRELAND)

The rates of SDLT are generally the same regardless of what type of property business the purchaser has (or, indeed, whether the purchaser has a business at all). The rates are also mostly unaffected by whether the purchaser is an individual, a trust, or a partnership (although there are special rules for both trusts and partnerships, which we will look at in Sections 9.18 and 9.33 respectively).

SDLT is payable on all transfers of property located in England or Northern Ireland; regardless of where the vendor and purchaser are resident, and regardless of where the transfer documentation is drawn up. It is the legal responsibility of the purchaser or transferee, although the vendor/transferor will sometimes arrange to pay. SDLT no longer applies to property in Scotland or Wales: we will look at its replacements in Sections 6.10 to 6.12 and 6.13 respectively.

The thresholds given in the tables in Sections 6.2, 6.3, and 6.5 generally refer to the actual consideration paid for the purchase, whether in cash or by any other means: but see Section 6.6 for potential exceptions.

In most cases, completion of the purchase contract triggers the liability for SDLT. However, technically, the liability is triggered when a purchase is substantially performed. Generally, this occurs on the earliest of:

a) Completion of the purchase contract,
b) Payment of at least 90% of the purchase consideration,
c) Occupation of the property (including occupation under licence after the date of the contract or lease agreement),
d) Payment of the first rent (in the case of a lease), or
e) Letting or, in the case of a lease, subletting, of the property

6.2 RESIDENTIAL PROPERTY

The main rates of SDLT on residential property are currently as follows:

Up to £125,000	Nil
£125,000 to £250,000	2%
£250,000 to £925,000	5%
£925,000 to £1.5m	10%
Over £1.5m	12%

The 2% rate band did not apply between 23rd September 2022 and 31st March 2025. In all examples, etc, throughout this chapter, it is assumed the purchase or transfer is taking place after 31st March 2025.

The rates given above will seldom actually apply to purchases of property by landlords and other property business owners. Generally speaking, these basic underlying rates will only apply in the case of:

- A purchase by an unmarried individual or married couple who have no other interest in any residential property (subject to the exemption for first time buyers detailed below),
- An unmarried individual or married couple buying a new main residence to replace a former main residence sold within the previous three years, or
- A sale or transfer of a property, or an interest in a property, from one spouse to another (see Section 6.3)

In most other cases, an additional 5% charge will apply to all residential property purchases. We will look at this charge in the next section. Before that, let's look at the SDLT arising where the higher charges do not apply.

Example: *The SDLT arising on a purchase price of £1m where an individual is buying their first, or only, residential property, or replacing a main residence sold within the previous three years, is currently:*

First £125,000 @ 0%	*£0*
Next £125,000 @ 2%:	*£2,500*
Next £675,000 @ 5%:	*£33,750*
Next £75,000 @ 10%	*£7,500*
Total:	*£43,750*

First Time Buyers

There is an exemption from normal SDLT rates for first time buyers:

- The first £300,000 is fully exempt
- Purchases over £300,000 but not exceeding £500,000 are subject to a charge of 5% on the amount in excess of £300,000
- Purchases over £500,000 are subject to normal rates (as set out above)

A first time buyer is someone who has never purchased a major interest in a residential property anywhere in the world. A lease with less than 21 years left to run is not a major interest. Joint purchasers must both (or all) qualify as first-time buyers to be eligible for the exemption. Purchases under a qualifying shared ownership scheme may be eligible, however.

What is Residential Property?

For SDLT purposes, a property is classed as residential if it is used, or suitable for use, as a dwelling; or is in the process of being constructed or adapted for use as a dwelling. The gardens or grounds of any such property are also subject to the residential rates of SDLT, including any structures in those gardens or grounds.

An interest in or right over land that benefits a dwelling is also classed as residential property (e.g. a right of way needed to access a dwelling).

Residential accommodation for school pupils, students, or members of the armed forces are classed as dwellings, as well as any institution that is the sole or main residence of at least 90% of its residents.

However, these properties are subject to the following exceptions, which are instead classed as non-residential property and subject to the rates in Section 6.5:

i) Children's homes
ii) Halls of residence for students in further or higher education
iii) Care homes for the elderly, disabled, or people suffering from alcohol or drugs dependency, or mental disorder
iv) Hospitals and hospices
v) Prisons and similar institutions
vi) Hotels, inns, and similar properties

In addition to the exceptions above, property with mixed use (i.e. both residential and non-residential) is subject to SDLT at the non-residential rates. This can lead to substantial savings, as we shall see in Section 6.5. In the March 2024 Budget, it was confirmed this beneficial treatment will continue following a Government consultation on mixed use property.

6.3 HIGHER CHARGES ON RESIDENTIAL PROPERTY

Higher SDLT charges apply to most purchases of residential property by landlords, other property business owners, and those purchasing a second home. The basic rule is the higher charges apply to any purchase:

- By an individual who has any interest in more than one residential property at the end of the day of purchase, or
- By two or more persons jointly where any of them has any interest in more than one residential property at the end of the day of purchase

The higher charges are derived by adding an additional 5% surcharge to the basic charges in Section 6.2. The higher charges are thus currently:

Up to £125,000	5%
£125,000 to £250,000	7%
£250,000 to £925,000	10%
£925,000 to £1.5m	15%
Over £1.5m	17%

Purchases with total consideration of less than £40,000 are exempt from SDLT but, apart from this, the charges apply on a progressive basis. The additional surcharge was increased to a horrific 5% on Halloween 2024 (31st October), having previously been 3%.

Example: *The SDLT arising on a residential property purchased for £400,000 where the higher charges apply is currently:*

First £125,000 @ 5%	*£6,250*
Next £125,000 @ 7%:	*£8,750*
Next £150,000 @ 10%:	*£15,000*
Total:	*£30,000*

Replacement of Main Residence

There is an exemption from the higher charges where the purchaser is buying a property they intend to adopt as their main residence and is replacing a former main residence sold by them or their spouse within the previous three years. The old property must have been the purchaser's main residence at some point within that same three-year period, but not necessarily immediately before sale.

The entire interest in the former main residence must have been sold, and no part of it can have been sold to a spouse. It can, however, have been sold to another connected person, or to the owner's own company.

An investment property (e.g. a buy-to-let) purchased during the gap between selling a former main residence and purchasing a new main residence, will escape the higher charges if the purchaser does not hold any interest in other residential property. Furthermore, this would not prevent the exemption from applying to the replacement main residence.

The replacement of main residence exemption also applies where the entire interest in the purchaser's former main residence is sold by them or their spouse within three years **after** the new main residence is purchased. In this case, the higher charges will apply in the first place and a refund will have to be claimed when the former main residence is sold. The old property must again have been the purchaser's main residence at some point within the three-year period before purchase of the new property.

The deadline for selling the former main residence is extended where, due to exceptional circumstances, the taxpayer has been unable to complete the sale within the usual three-year period. The sale must be completed as soon as practicable, however.

Where all of two or more joint purchasers are either eligible for the replacement of main residence exemption, or will not have any other interest in residential property at the end of the day of purchase, then the higher charges will not apply (or can be refunded later).

In any other cases involving joint purchasers, the higher charges will apply. This includes cases where one of an unmarried couple did not own a share in the couple's former main residence (and has an interest in another residential property).

Example: *Prior to moving in together in 2020, Jack and Rose each had their own main residence. After he moved in with Rose, Jack rented out his old flat. Rose kept her flat in her own name until selling it in 2026. The couple then bought a new property jointly together for £600,000 and adopted it as their new main residence. The higher SDLT charges are payable on the new property because Jack is not replacing a former main residence that he owned and he still owns another residential property. This costs the couple an additional £30,000.*

There are a few ways of avoiding this problem, the simplest of which is to get married before either selling the former main residence or buying the replacement (whichever happens first). If this is not possible (or the couple do not wish to marry), other possible solutions include:

- Rose could buy the new property in her name alone (this may lead to difficulties in obtaining a mortgage). She might also subsequently transfer the property into joint names with Jack (but see Section 6.6 for problems arising if there is a mortgage outstanding at that time)
- They could put their existing main residence into joint names before selling it. Again, this might cause problems if there is an outstanding mortgage (see Section 6.6)
- Jack could sell his old flat before they buy the new property (this may give rise to a CGT liability: see Chapter 5 for details)

Transfers of property into joint names with an unmarried partner could also give rise to CGT liabilities if the property concerned had not always been the original owner's main residence.

See Chapter 5 for an examination of what is a main residence. It is not possible to elect which property is, or was, your main residence for the purposes of the higher SDLT charges: it will need to be determined as a question of fact (see Section 5.15 for guidance on this issue).

Other Exemptions
Exemptions from the higher charges apply to:
- Transfers of property, or an interest in property, between spouses
- A purchaser adding to their existing interest in their main residence (e.g. buying the freehold where they already own the leasehold)
- Properties bought for a child subject to the Court of Protection

The relief described in Section 6.7 is also available to reduce the charge applying on a simultaneous purchase of six or more dwellings.

Interests in Residential Property
Subject to the exceptions outlined below, any interest in residential property anywhere in the world is counted for the purpose of the higher charges. Each individual must include any interests held by their spouse or minor children (e.g. property held in trust on their behalf). An interest means any form of legal right to a share in the property for any period of time. However, there are a few exceptions:

- Interests in property worth less than £40,000
- Caravans, mobile homes, and houseboats (the definition of a 'caravan' is broader than you might think, and generally includes any dwelling that can be transported in no more than two pieces).
- Shares of 50% or less in property inherited within the last three years
- Leasehold interests for a period of less than seven years at commencement
- Superior interests where there is a leasehold interest in the property with more than 21 years left to run
- Former main residences that cannot be sold under the terms of a divorce-related court order

6.4 THE NON-RESIDENT SURCHARGE

A further SDLT surcharge of 2% applies to purchases of residential property by non-UK residents. This further surcharge is in addition to the higher charges examined in Section 6.3, creating a total 7% surcharge for most residential property purchases in England or Northern Ireland by non-UK residents, and a maximum overall rate of 19% on purchase consideration in excess of £1.5m: as an American investor once said to me, "They really don't want anyone to invest in your country, do they?"

Individuals are treated as non-UK resident for the purposes of the surcharge if they spend less than 183 days in the UK in both the calendar year ending on the date of purchase and the calendar year commencing immediately after the date of purchase.

The surcharge does not apply to: leasehold interests with a fixed term of no more than 21 years left to run; the superior interest in a property subject to a lease with a fixed term of more than 21 years left to run; or purchases for less than £40,000.

6.5 NON-RESIDENTIAL PROPERTY

The rates of SDLT on non-residential property are:

Up to £150,000	0%
£150,000 to £250,000	2%
Over £250,000	5%

For example, the SDLT payable on the purchase of a non-residential property for £850,000 is:

First £150,000 @ 0%:	£0
Next £100,000 @ 2%:	£2,000
Next £600,000 @ 5%:	£30,000
Total:	£32,000

A simple shortcut for working out SDLT on a non-residential property purchase for a consideration in excess of £250,000 is to take a flat rate of 5% then deduct £10,500 (e.g. £850,000 x 5% = £42,500 – £10,500 = £32,000, as above).

As well as commercial property, such as shops, offices, warehouses, etc, the non-residential rates apply to:

- Mixed use property, such as a shop with a flat above it, where both parts are purchased as part of the same transaction
- Properties falling into one of the exceptions listed in Section 6.2
- Property not suitable to be lived in
- Agricultural land (see further below)
- Any other land or property not part of a dwelling's garden or grounds

A farmhouse sold together with a working farm would be regarded as mixed use and hence the whole transaction will be taxed at non-residential rates.

However, residential rates will apply where land is simply sold as part of the garden or grounds of a dwelling: e.g. a cottage with fields. In borderline cases, seek professional advice.

It is important to remember the mixed-use treatment only applies where both the residential and non-residential elements are part of the same property, purchased simultaneously, as a single property title.

Comparison of Residential and Non-Residential Rates

Let's be clear about this, there is seldom any choice over whether residential or non-residential rates apply to a purchase (except in the case of a simultaneous purchase of six or more dwellings: see Section 6.7).

However, purchasers may sometimes face a choice between different, but similar properties, where one, perhaps being mixed use, would attract non-residential rates of SDLT, while the other would attract residential rates. In other cases, there may be a question of whether or not the purchaser wants to acquire the non-residential part of a property. There are also a few genuinely borderline cases where the position may not be clear. In these cases, it is worth considering what difference the non-residential rates would make.

For purchases after 31st March 2025, where the current, normal residential rates in Section 6.2 would otherwise apply, using the non-residential rates will lead to the following savings:

Purchase Consideration	**Saving**
£125,000 to £150,000	2% of consideration in excess of £125,000
£150,000 to £925,000	£500
£925,000 to £1.5m	£500 plus 5% of consideration in excess of £925,000
Over £1.5m	£29,250 plus 7% of consideration in excess of £1.5m

Where the higher charges in Section 6.3 would otherwise apply, the non-residential rates produce considerably greater savings, as follows:

Purchase Consideration	**Saving**
£40,000 to £125,000	5% of purchase consideration
£125,000 to £150,000	£6,250 plus 7% of consideration in excess of £125,000
£150,000 to £925,000	£8,000 plus 5% of consideration in excess of £150,000
£925,000 to £1.5m	£46,750 plus 10% of consideration in excess of £925,000
Over £1.5m	£104,250 plus 12% of consideration in excess of £1.5m

For example, being able to use the non-residential rates on a property purchase for £2m would save £164,250. For such high value properties, it could sometimes be worth changing your strategy accordingly.

And don't forget, non-residential rates are always available on the simultaneous purchase of six or more residential dwellings (see Section 6.7).

6.6 MARKET VALUE AND MORTGAGES

Generally speaking, there is no market value rule for SDLT and the tax is only payable on actual consideration. However, market value is used for transactions between business partners and their partnership; even changes in partnership shares: see Section 9.33. Market value also generally applies in the case of transfers to a connected company (see the Taxcafe guide *Using a Property Company to Save Tax* for details).

Although transfers between spouses are exempt from the higher charges examined in Section 6.3, there is no general exemption from SDLT at the standard rates in Sections 6.2 and 6.5. Many such transfers are gifts with no consideration, but where a property is transferred subject to a mortgage, the balance outstanding will be treated as consideration for SDLT purposes. For example, if a woman transfers a house with an outstanding mortgage of £400,000 to her husband, he would have an SDLT liability of £10,000.

Where property is being put into joint names, SDLT is payable on whatever share of the mortgage the transferee is taking on. Hence, where putting a property into equal joint names with a spouse, a mortgage of up to £250,000 should not give rise to any SDLT.

The exemption from the higher charges detailed in Section 6.3 only applies to transfers between spouses, so transfers of property, or a share in property, to anyone else will generally give rise to SDLT charges whenever the mortgage, or share of mortgage, taken over by the transferee is £40,000 or more. (Such transfers also give rise to potential CGT liabilities, as we saw in Chapter 5.)

One way to avoid SDLT charges on transfers of a share of a property subject to a mortgage, to your spouse, or other close relatives, is to use a partnership (see Section 9.33). You must be one of the partners though.

Naturally, all transfers of property subject to a mortgage will need the lender's permission, or the lender will certainly at least need to be advised. Legal advice is strongly recommended!

6.7 MULTIPLE PURCHASES

SDLT is calculated after taking account of linked transactions. Linked transactions can arise in a number of ways, including a simultaneous purchase of several properties from the same vendor, or connected vendors (see Appendix B). The basic rule is the linked transactions are treated as if they were a single purchase.

Example 1: *A property investor with at least one other residential property buys three houses from the same developer at the same time for £250,000 each. For SDLT purposes, this is treated as a single purchase for £750,000. The SDLT charge is therefore:*

£125,000 @ 5%: *£6,250*
£125,000 @ 7%: *£8,750*
£500,000 @ 10%: *£50,000*
Total: *£65,000*

For purchases of two or more dwellings before 1st June 2024, multiple dwellings relief was available to reduce the SDLT charge. This relief has now been abolished. It is, however, still worth pointing out the relief may be clawed back if one or more of the properties are sold, or otherwise disposed of, within three years.

Purchases of Six or More Dwellings

A simultaneous purchase of six or more residential dwellings (from the same vendor, or connected vendors) can be treated as a non-residential property purchase for SDLT purposes. This will always lead to savings, often quite significant savings, as we saw in Section 6.5. Only dwellings in England or Northern Ireland can be counted for this purpose.

The relief is based on the number of *dwellings* purchased, not the number of *properties*. For instance, self-contained flats within a single property each constitute a separate dwelling. This provides a major benefit for property investors buying larger properties. If, for example, an investor buys a property that has been divided into six flats, this would constitute six dwellings, so that non-residential SDLT rates can be applied, significantly reducing the amount due.

In some cases, extra purchases could be worthwhile to obtain the relief.

Example 2: *Pippa is planning to buy five properties (each a single dwelling) off-plan from a developer, for a total consideration of £1.25m. This will lead to an SDLT charge of £131,250: or a total purchase cost of £1,381,250.*

She decides to add a sixth, small residential property for an additional £150,000. This increases her purchase consideration to £1.4m, but reduces her SDLT bill to £59,500 (at non-residential rates).

In effect, the sixth property has only cost Pippa £78,250 (£1,459,500 – 1,381,250). One might view this as a discount of nearly 50%!

Annexes, Granny Flats, Etc.

There are cases where a single property is divided into more than one dwelling, such as when the property has a self-contained 'granny flat' or annex. To be classed as a separate dwelling, the annex, flat, etc, must be quite separate from the main property and have all the facilities required for normal, day-to-day living, such that it could be used by an unconnected third party as their residence.

For purchases after 31st May 2024, this will seldom make any difference for SDLT purposes, unless it pushes the total number of dwellings purchased at the same time up to six. However, this distinction is still important for property purchases in Scotland or Wales, and we will see an example of its tax saving potential in Section 6.13.

It's also worth noting that it remains possible, where you have no other residential property interests (or are replacing your main residence), to buy a property with such a flat or annex and still only pay the main rate of SDLT. This is because a flat or annex of this nature, although a separate dwelling, is still part of the same property. It is classed as a subsidiary dwelling and therefore does not, in itself, trigger the higher rates of SDLT.

6.8 LEASES

On the granting of a lease, SDLT is payable on the net present value of the rent payable under the lease over its entire term. Where the net present value does not exceed £125,000 (for residential property), or £150,000 (for non-residential property), no SDLT is payable. The threshold applying to residential leases granted between 23rd September 2022 and 31st March 2025 was £250,000.

For new leases with a net present value exceeding these limits, SDLT is payable at a rate of 1% on the excess. There are no higher charges in respect of rent on residential property: the rate remains 1% in all cases. For non-residential property, the rate increases to 2% on any amounts in excess of £5m.

VAT is excluded from the rent payable under the lease for the purposes of SDLT calculations unless the landlord has already exercised the option to tax (this applies to commercial property only: see Section 7.3).

Example: *In March 2027, Clive takes on a ten-year lease over a house in Kent at an annual rent of £48,000. The SDLT legislation provides that the net present value of a sum of money due within the next 12 months is equal to the sum due divided by a discount factor of 103.5%. Hence, the net present value of Clive's first year's rent is £46,377 (£48,000 divided by 103.5%). Similarly, the second year's rent, which is due a further 12 months later, must be discounted again by the same amount, i.e. £46,377/103.5% = £44,809.*

This process is continued for the entire life of the lease and the net present values of all the rental payments are added together to give the total net present value for the lease. In this case, this works out at £399,197. The SDLT due is therefore £2,742 (£399,197 less £125,000 = £274,197 x 1% = £2,742).

It does not matter whether the rent is payable monthly, quarterly, or annually, or in advance or arrears. Net present value is always calculated by reference to the total annual rental payable for each year of the lease. Lease **premiums** also attract SDLT at the rates in Sections 6.2 to 6.5.

Tax Tip
It is possible to grant a lease over a non-residential property with a premium of up to £150,000 **and** annual rental with a net present value of up to £150,000 with no SDLT cost whatsoever. For residential property, there will be an SDLT cost if either amount exceeds £125,000 or if the higher charges shown in Section 6.3 apply to the premium.

6.9 FIXTURES AND FITTINGS

There is a great deal of misunderstanding over the issue of SDLT on fixtures and fittings. Firstly, it must be understood that fixtures are part of the fabric of the building and are therefore subject to SDLT. This includes items such as fitted kitchens, baths, toilets, sinks, etc, and is unaffected by whether these items qualify for capital allowances (see Section 4.10).

Moveable fittings are **not** part of the fabric of the building and therefore not subject to SDLT. This includes furniture, carpets, curtains and free-standing 'white goods' such as fridges, freezers and washing machines.

It is therefore often possible to allocate a small part of a property's purchase price to the moveable fittings in the property and thus reduce the SDLT cost. For residential property purchases by landlords and other property business owners this will generally save between 5% and 10% of the amount allocated to the fittings and will often be worthwhile. For non-residential property purchases over £250,000, the saving will be 5%. Remember, however, it is only the moveable fittings that escape SDLT and there will often be very few of these in a non-residential property.

Generally, it is sensible to purchase moveable fittings by way of a side agreement (which may be no more than a handshake). The informality of such an agreement does not, however, prevent it from having to be included as part of the property's purchase price if the amount allocated to the fittings is excessive.

In summary, a small allocation of the purchase price to moveable fittings is a sensible way to reduce your SDLT bill; but be reasonable!

Remember also that the amount allocated to moveable fittings will not be deductible for CGT purposes when you sell the property. However, you and the purchaser can again agree a reasonable allocation of the sale price to any moveable fittings: saving you CGT and saving them SDLT.

6.10 LAND AND BUILDINGS TRANSACTION TAX (SCOTLAND)

SDLT has been abolished for property in Scotland and replaced by Land and Buildings Transaction Tax (LBTT).

Residential Property
The rates of LBTT on residential property are currently as follows:

Up to £145,000	Nil
£145,000 to £250,000	2%
£250,000 to £325,000	5%
£325,000 to £750,000	10%
Over £750,000	12%

Residential property purchases by landlords, other property business owners, and those purchasing second homes, are subject to the Additional Dwelling Supplement (ADS), which we will examine in Section 6.11.

Non-Residential Property

The rates of LBTT on non-residential property are currently as follows:

Up to £150,000	Nil
£150,000 to £250,000	1%
Over £250,000	5%

Similar but Different

Apart from the rates applying, LBTT operates in broadly the same way as SDLT. Many of the principles examined in Sections 6.1 to 6.9 continue to apply. Nonetheless, there are a few important differences to be aware of and we will look at some of these in Section 6.12, after we have looked at ADS.

6.11 ADDITIONAL DWELLING SUPPLEMENT (SCOTLAND)

ADS operates in a similar way to the higher SDLT charges examined in Section 6.3. It applies an additional LBTT charge to purchases of residential property in Scotland. In December 2024, this additional charge was increased to an utterly outrageous 8%!

Purchases under £40,000 are exempt but, otherwise, the basic rule is ADS applies to any purchase:

i) Made for the purposes of a property business, including property letting, etc.
ii) By an individual who has a relevant interest in more than one residential property at the end of the day of purchase, or
iii) By two or more persons jointly where any of them has a relevant interest in more than one residential property at the end of the day of purchase.

Heading (i) means ***all*** purchases of residential property in Scotland by landlords and other property business owners, for use in their business, are subject to the additional 8% charge under ADS (except purchases for less than £40,000).

Unlike the higher SDLT charges, there is no general exemption for transfers between spouses, so the issues discussed in Section 6.6 become more important for Scottish property. In effect, where an investment property in Scotland is transferred, spouses are in the same position as other transferees and ADS will be payable whenever the mortgage, or share of mortgage, taken over by the transferee is £40,000 or more.

Replacement of Main Residence

There is an exemption from ADS where the purchaser is buying a property they intend to adopt as their main residence and is replacing a previous main residence sold within the previous three years.

The exemption also applies where the purchaser's former main residence is sold within three years **after** the new main residence is purchased (eighteen months where the new main residence was purchased before 1st April 2024). In these cases, ADS applies in the first place and a refund has to be claimed later, on the sale of the former main residence.

The exemption is extended to cases where a couple (married or unmarried) are jointly purchasing a new main residence and only one of them owned their former main residence. Hence, ADS would ***not*** be payable in a scenario like 'Jack and Rose' in the example in Section 6.3.

For purchases after 31st March 2024, the exemption also applies to cases involving joint purchasers acquiring a new main residence where only one of them lived in the former main residence: provided neither (or none) of the joint purchasers retains an interest in another property.

In all cases, the old property must have been the purchaser's (or at least one of the joint purchasers') main residence at some point within the three years prior to the purchase of the new property. For new property purchases before 1st April 2024, the old property had to be the purchaser's (or *both/all* of the joint purchasers') main residence at some point within the previous eighteen months.

Relevant Interests in Residential Property

Subject to the points below, any interest in residential property anywhere in the world is a relevant interest for the purpose of ADS. Each individual must also include relevant interests in residential property held by their spouse, co-habitant (i.e. an unmarried partner), or minor children aged under 16 (e.g. property held in trust on their behalf). An interest means any form of legal right to a share in the property for any period of time.

Leases of more than 20 years are regarded as a relevant interest. Where such a lease exists, the person holding the superior interest in the property (the landlord) is not treated as having a relevant interest.

Where an individual is buying a property for use as their own home, any property to which ADS applied as a consequence of heading (i) above (or would have applied if the property had been in Scotland) can be disregarded.

> **Tax Tip**
>
> By buying a rental property in England first and then a home in Scotland, you could avoid both sets of higher charges (where you have no other residential property interests).
>
> An individual who already owns rental property, none of which was purchased before April 2016, can also avoid higher charges by buying a home in Scotland.

> **Wealth Warning**
>
> If you buy a rental property in Scotland first and then a home in England, you will pay higher charges on both properties even if you have no other residential property interests.

Caravans (see Section 6.3), mobile homes, houseboats, and interests in property worth less than £40,000, may also be disregarded for the purposes of ADS.

6.12 KEY DIFFERENCES (SCOTLAND)

The non-residential rates of LBTT apply to mixed use property, but the residential element is subject to ADS (Section 6.11), where applicable.

Example
Miranda buys a five-storey property in Edinburgh for £800,000. The property consists of a ground-floor shop and four upstairs flats. One of the flats qualifies as Miranda's replacement main residence; she intends to rent the other three out. The shop is worth £100,000; Miranda's own flat is worth £250,000; the other flats are worth £450,000 in total.

Miranda will pay LBTT at non-residential rates, which will amount to £28,500 (£100,000 x 1% + £550,000 x 5%), plus ADS of £36,000 (£450,000 x 8%). Her total LBTT/ADS bill is thus £64,500.

Multiple dwellings relief continues to be available under LBTT, but operates differently to the relief formerly available under SDLT. Where multiple dwellings relief applies, LBTT (including ADS, where applicable) is calculated based on the average price of each dwelling. This is then subject to an overall minimum of 25% of the amount that would have been due on all the residential property included in the transaction (or linked transactions) without the relief.

The LBTT deemed to arise on non-residential property included in the transaction (or linked transactions) is unaffected by multiple dwellings relief.

Example Continued
As we saw, Miranda's total LBTT/ADS bill without multiple dwellings relief was £64,500. Of this, £8,063 (£64,500 x £100,000/£800,000) is deemed to relate to the ground-floor shop and £56,437 to the flats.

If Miranda claims multiple dwellings relief, the average price of each flat is used to calculate both LBTT and ADS; and residential rates must be used. The average price per flat is £175,000 (£700,000/4), so the LBTT on each flat is £600 (£30,000 x 2%) and the ADS on each of the three rental flats is £14,000 (£175,000 x 8%). Her total LBTT/ADS bill on the flats is therefore £44,400 (£600 x 4 + £14,000 x 3).

This is more than 25% of £56,437, so the minimum charge rule does not apply and Miranda's total LBTT/ADS bill for the whole transaction with multiple dwellings relief is £52,463 (£44,400 + £8,063), saving her £12,037 in this case.

Multiple dwellings relief is optional, and will not always be beneficial, so it's important to do all the number crunching before making a claim.

As with SDLT, purchases of six or more dwellings may alternatively be taxed at non-residential rates of LBTT based on the total consideration for the transaction. ADS does not apply in this case, meaning this will always be a better option than claiming multiple dwellings relief.

For the purposes of both multiple dwellings relief and whether six or more dwellings are included in a transaction, only property in Scotland is counted for LBTT/ADS purposes.

Unlike the higher SDLT charges, subsidiary dwellings (see Section 6.7) appear to incur ADS, but this is limited to the value of the subsidiary dwelling, unless multiple dwellings relief is claimed.

Example
Hazel buys a house in Perthshire for £900,000. The house qualifies as her replacement main residence, but incorporates an annex, which is used as an FHL. The value of the annex is £180,000. Hazel will pay LBTT of £66,350 (based on the total price of £900,000: see Section 6.10 for the rates applying) plus ADS of £14,400 (£180,000 x 8%), a total of £80,750.

If Hazel were to claim multiple dwellings relief, both LBTT and ADS would be calculated on the basis of the average price for each dwelling: £450,000. Each dwelling would give rise to LBTT of £18,350; the ADS arising would be £36,000 (£450,000 x 8%). Hazel's total LBTT/ADS bill would therefore be £72,700 (£18,350 x 2 + £36,000), giving her a saving of £8,050.

There is still a saving in this case, but the increased ADS cost will often mean it's not worth claiming multiple dwellings relief when purchasing a property with a subsidiary dwelling to use as your main residence.

First time buyers purchasing a main residence in Scotland enjoy an increased threshold for the nil rate of £175,000. All other rates remain the same and, unlike the similar exemption for SDLT, the consequent saving (up to £600) is not withdrawn at any point for higher value purchases.

LBTT does not apply to rent payable under residential leases. The rates applying to rent payable under non-residential leases are the same as for SDLT (see Section 6.8), except the 2% rate applies to net present value in excess of £2m.

The non-resident surcharge (Section 6.4) does not apply for LBTT.

This is by no means an exhaustive list of all the differences between LBTT and SDLT, so it is essential to take legal advice when purchasing property in Scotland (just as it is when purchasing property anywhere else!)

Future Changes
No changes to LBTT or ADS were announced in the 2026/27 Scottish Budget on 13th January 2026. However, a comprehensive review is currently underway and may lead to changes in the near future, such as changes to the treatment of mixed-use property, first-time buyer relief, or additional ADS reliefs to apply in exceptional circumstances.

6.13 LAND TRANSACTION TAX (WALES)

SDLT has ceased to apply to property in Wales and has been replaced by Land Transaction Tax (LTT).

Residential Property
The rates of LTT on residential property are currently as follows:

Up to £225,000	0%
£225,000 to £400,000	6%
£400,000 to £750,000	7.5%
£750,000 to £1.5m	10%
Over £1.5m	12%

Higher Residential Rates
Sadly, the authorities in Cardiff appear to have the same desire to persecute landlords and other property businesses as their counterparts in London and Edinburgh. Hence, a different set of rates applies to most purchases of second or additional residential properties. These too were increased in December 2024, and are now as follows:

Up to £180,000	5%
£180,000 to £250,000	8.5%
£250,000 to £400,000	10%
£400,000 to £750,000	12.5%
£750,000 to £1.5m	15%
Over £1.5m	17%

Non-Residential Property
The rates of LTT on non-residential property are currently as follows:

Up to £225,000	0%
£225,000 to £250,000	1%
£250,000 to £1m	5%
Over £1m	6%

Important Variations
A form of multiple dwellings relief still applies in Wales. The relief operates by basing the LTT charge on the average price of each dwelling, with an overall minimum charge of 1% (increasing to 3% from 1st April 2026 as noted below).

Example
Timothy is a landlord with several residential rental properties. He is buying a large house in Pembrokeshire for £800,000 and expects to pay LTT as follows:

First £180,000 @ 5%	*£9,000*
Next £70,000 @ 8.5%	*£5,950*
Next £150,000 @ 10%	*£15,000*
Next £350,000 @ 12.5%	*£43,750*
Next £50,000 @ 15%	*£7,500*
Total:	*£81,200*

However, before completing the purchase, Timothy discovers the house has a self-contained annex used as an FHL, so he is able to claim multiple dwellings relief on the basis the property comprises two dwellings, with an average value of £400,000 each. This reduces the LTT charge as follows:

First £180,000 @ 5%	*£9,000*
Next £70,000 @ 8.5%	*£5,950*
Next £150,000 @ 10%	*£15,000*
Total for each dwelling:	*£29,950*
Total charge for two dwellings:	*£59,900*

In this case, multiple dwellings relief produces a saving of £21,300 (£81,200 – £59,900).

If Timothy did not own any other residential property, he would be able to pay LTT at normal residential rates because the annex is classed as a subsidiary dwelling (see Section 6.7). This exemption from the higher residential rates applies where the main dwelling is worth at least two-thirds of the total purchase price for the property.

For purchases after 7th February 2025, it is not possible to claim multiple dwellings relief where the normal residential rates apply under these circumstances.

As with both SDLT and LBTT, purchases of six or more dwellings may alternatively be taxed at non-residential rates, based on the total consideration for the transaction. For property in Wales, this will generally be a better option than claiming multiple dwellings relief, but exceptions may sometimes arise where the total consideration exceeds £2.225m or one of the properties qualifies for normal residential rates.

For the purposes of both multiple dwellings relief and whether six or more dwellings are included in a transaction, only property in Wales is counted for LTT purposes.

The non-resident surcharge (Section 6.4) does not apply for LTT purposes.

In other respects, LTT operates in a broadly similar way to SDLT, but there are other important variations, so professional advice is essential when purchasing property in Wales.

Proposed Changes

A number of proposed changes to LTT were announced in the Welsh Budget in October 2025. We expect these to be introduced from 1st April 2026.

- The minimum charge applying under multiple dwellings relief is to be increased from 1% to 3% (as noted above)
- A new 'equalisation' rule will be introduced for the purposes of multiple dwellings relief (an odd proposal in my view, as I thought equalisation was the whole point of the relief!)
- The higher residential charges will be refunded where a landlord buys a property and then leases it to a local authority through Leasing Scheme Wales. Normal LTT charges will still apply.

Chapter 7

How to Save VAT and Other Property Taxes

7.1 VAT PRINCIPLES

VAT, or Value Added Tax, to give it its proper name, arrived on our shores from Europe in 1973. Despite its comparative youth, VAT is one of the UK's most hated taxes and there are some nasty pitfalls for the unwary property investor.

VAT is currently charged at three different rates in the UK: a standard rate of 20%, a reduced rate of 5%, and a zero rate. All these rates may be encountered by property businesses.

For VAT purposes, a sale of a property is a supply of goods and rent on a property is a supply of services. Not all supplies of goods and services are subject to VAT, some are exempt.

The VAT treatment of goods and services in a property business depends on a number of things, including the type of property. Where a supply of goods or services is subject to VAT at any of the rates given above (including the zero rate) it is referred to as a taxable supply. Goods and services subject to VAT at the standard rate of 20% are often referred to as standard-rated.

VAT Registration
VAT is charged by VAT-registered businesses. Sadly, they do not keep it but must pay it to HMRC. They are, however, able to claim back the VAT on purchases of goods and services used to make their taxable supplies.

Where a business is making annual taxable supplies in excess of the VAT registration threshold, registration is compulsory. The threshold was increased to £90,000 from 1st April 2024 (previously £85,000).

Businesses making taxable supplies of goods or services but whose annual sales are less than the VAT registration threshold may register for VAT voluntarily. This is particularly beneficial for those making zero rated supplies, as we shall see later.

All VAT-registered businesses must now operate MTD for VAT purposes. This means keeping their records in digital format in the same way we looked at in Section 3.6 and submitting their VAT returns through HMRC's online reporting system using functional compatible software.

The Flat Rate Scheme
VAT-registered businesses with annual sales not exceeding £150,000 may join the VAT flat rate scheme.

This does not alter the amount of VAT they must charge customers or the amount of VAT they pay on their purchases. What it does alter is the amount of VAT paid over to HMRC.

Under the flat rate scheme, a special reduced rate is applied to calculate the VAT payable to HMRC on the business's sales. However, the downside is the business is unable to recover the VAT paid on most of its purchases.

> **Wealth Warning**
> Any individual, partnership, or other entity, registering for the flat rate scheme must apply the reduced VAT rate to ***all*** their business income, including any rental income that would normally be exempt from VAT.

The flat rate scheme is seldom beneficial to property businesses, with the potential exception of property investors renting out commercial property. Even in these cases, there are pros and cons to be considered.

Furthermore, the special rate for low cost traders means many of those who might have benefited in the past no longer do so. Broadly speaking, this rate applies where a business's VAT-inclusive expenditure on goods amounts to less than 2% of its VAT-inclusive sales income. Capital expenditure and certain other items are excluded for the purpose of this test. At 16.5% of the business's gross, VAT-inclusive sales income, the low cost trader rate provides little benefit. (The VAT within gross standard-rated sales income only amounts to 16.67% in any case!)

Reverse Charges in the Construction Sector
A reverse charge procedure applies to certain construction services. Under the reverse charge procedure, the customer must account for VAT on the relevant supplies, rather than the supplier. The overall VAT position is unaltered; it is simply a question of who pays the VAT over to HMRC.

The procedure only applies where the customer is making relevant taxable supplies of construction services themselves. Hence, the vast majority of property investors are unaffected by the reverse charge.

7.2 VAT ON RESIDENTIAL PROPERTY

Residential Property Letting
Generally speaking, a landlord engaged primarily in residential property letting does not need to be VAT-registered: because the letting of residential property is an exempt supply for VAT purposes. VAT is therefore not chargeable on rent, although, of course, VAT cannot be recovered on expenses and the landlord should therefore claim VAT-inclusive costs for Income Tax and CGT purposes.

Beware that the provision of ancillary services (e.g. cleaning or gardening) may sometimes be standard-rated, and hence subject to VAT at 20%, if the value of annual supplies of these services exceeds the VAT registration threshold. Some landlords making ancillary supplies of this nature prefer to register for VAT, even if they have not reached the registration threshold, to recover part of the VAT on their expenses.

The letting of holiday accommodation for up to 28 days is standard-rated for VAT purposes, meaning owners of furnished holiday lets will generally need to register for, and charge, VAT at 20% if their total rental receipts in any twelve-month period exceed the VAT registration threshold. The rate applying under the flat rate scheme (see Section 7.1) is 10.5% (but remember VAT cannot then be reclaimed on most purchases).

This is completely unaffected by the abolition of the furnished holiday letting regime that applied for Income Tax and CGT purposes up to 5th April 2025.

Residential Property Development
Sales of newly constructed residential property are zero-rated for VAT purposes. This means the developer can recover the VAT on their construction costs without having to charge VAT on the sale of the property. (In theory, VAT is charged, but at a rate of zero.)

This treatment is extended to the sale of any newly created dwellings: for example, where a barn has been converted into a house. It is important, however, that none of the new dwelling includes any part of an old dwelling existing prior to the conversion. Zero-rating is also extended to substantially reconstructed protected buildings. In essence, this means the sale of a listed building following major reconstruction work. Such activities do, of course, require approval from the authorities.

Property developers carrying out construction work under any of these headings are therefore able to register for VAT and then recover the VAT on the vast majority of their business expenses.

Other Residential Property Sales
Other sales of residential property are generally an exempt supply meaning the taxpayer making the sale is unable to recover any of the VAT on their expenses. This means VAT cannot be recovered by most residential property investors. Property developers who merely renovate or alter existing residential dwellings prior to onward sale are also generally unable to recover VAT on their costs. However, there are opportunities for both investors carrying out work on rental property, and developers making exempt supplies, to pay less VAT in the first place.

Conversions and Renovations
Whether VAT can be recovered or not, the reduced rate of 5% is available for building work carried out on a residential property where the work results in a change to the number of dwellings. This, for example, would apply to the conversion of one house into several flats; two or more flats into a single house; or two semi-detached houses into a single detached house. The reduced rate also applies to conversions of commercial property into residential use and renovation work on residential property vacant for two years or more before work commenced.

Property investors or developers carrying out projects of this nature should try to ensure they only pay the lower VAT rate from the outset, as it is difficult to recover any excess paid in error.

Energy Saving Materials

A temporary, five-year zero-rating for energy-saving materials applies until March 2027. This includes solar panels, heating pumps, and roof insulation, and extends to the installation costs for these items.

7.3 VAT ON COMMERCIAL PROPERTY

Commercial Property Letting

For commercial property, there is an option to tax. The landlord may choose, for each property and on a property-by-property basis, whether or not the rent should be a VAT exempt supply. If the option to tax is exercised, the rent becomes standard-rated for VAT purposes. The landlord may then recover VAT on expenses relating to that property. Ancillary services are again likely to be standard-rated, regardless of whether you have opted to tax the rent itself.

If the potential tenants of a commercial property are all, or mostly, likely to be VAT-registered businesses, it will generally make sense to exercise the option to tax in order to recover the VAT on expenses incurred.

If your tenants themselves have a VAT-registered, fully taxable business (for VAT purposes), then everyone's happy. The problem comes when your tenants cannot recover some or all of the VAT you are charging. And remember that (after a short cooling off period) you cannot change your option on a property for a minimum of 20 years once it has been exercised. Hence, if you opt to charge VAT to a fully taxable tenant, you will probably need to charge VAT to the next tenant in the same property, even if they cannot recover it.

Sometimes with non-taxable (for VAT) tenants, where you have not yet exercised your option to tax, you can refrain from doing so and negotiate a higher rent to compensate for loss of VAT recovery on your own costs.

Example: *Norman owns an office building and hasn't yet opted to tax the rent. He has monthly costs of £500 plus VAT (i.e. £600 gross) and expects a monthly rent of £2,500. If Norman opts to tax, he will recover £100 a month from HMRC and make a monthly profit of £2,000. However, Lenny, the prospective tenant, is not registered for VAT. If Norman opts to tax the property, Lenny's rent will effectively be 20% higher, i.e. £3,000 per month. So, as a better alternative, Norman and Lenny agree that Norman will not opt to tax the building but will, instead, charge Lenny £2,750 a month rent. Now Norman is making a monthly profit of £2,150 (£2,750 minus £600) and Lenny's rent is effectively £250 less. Norman and Lenny both win; HMRC loses.*

Commercial Property Sales & Purchases

Where the option to tax has been exercised by the owner of a commercial property, their sale of that property will be standard-rated and this has major implications for such transactions. Sales of new commercial property are also standard-rated.

Wealth Warning
Where VAT is charged on a commercial property sale, SDLT must be paid on the gross, VAT-inclusive price. This can lead to combined tax rates of up to 26%, representing a pretty hefty cost if the purchaser is not VAT-registered; possibly enough to prevent the sale taking place in some cases. Imagine an insurance company buying a new office block in central London: the combined VAT and SDLT would be astronomical! Furthermore, even when the purchaser is able to recover the VAT on the purchase, the extra SDLT paid on that VAT cannot be recovered.

Where a property investor incurs VAT purchasing a commercial property, the only way to recover it will be to exercise the option to tax on the property. Thus, the Government generally forces everyone to maintain the taxable status of the building.

If a VAT-registered business incurs VAT purchasing a commercial property for use as their own business premises, or for development purposes, they can recover the VAT in the same way as on any other purchase of goods or services for use in the business.

However, if VAT has been recovered on the purchase of a commercial property, selling it without first exercising the option to tax would be an exempt supply. If that property were trading stock held for development purposes, this would result in the loss of all the VAT initially reclaimed on purchase and on any development, renovation, or conversion work. Some VAT recovered on general overheads would probably also be repayable. The position would be different if the property is converted for residential use, as explained in Section 7.2.

When more than £250,000 is spent on the purchase or improvement of a property for use as the purchaser's own business premises, selling the property within ten years without first exercising the option to tax would also trigger VAT. The Government is planning to increase the £250,000 threshold to £600,000 at some stage, but we have no firm date for this proposed change yet.

7.4 INTERACTION BETWEEN VAT AND OTHER TAXES

A VAT-registered business should generally include only the net (excluding VAT) amounts of income and expenditure in its accounts for Income Tax purposes. Where VAT recovery is barred or restricted, the additional cost should be treated as part of the relevant expense. Expenses subject to restrictions on the recovery of VAT include:

- Business entertaining
- Purchases of motor cars
- Leasing/contract hire of motor cars
- Provision of private fuel for proprietors or staff

As we can see, many of the expenses subject to a VAT recovery restriction are also subject to some form of Income Tax restriction.

Businesses operating the flat rate scheme (see Section 7.1) should include VAT in their income and expenditure (except where it is recoverable) and then deduct the VAT they have actually paid to HMRC on their sales from their gross, VAT-inclusive income.

A non-VAT-registered business should include the VAT in its business expenditure for Income Tax purposes.

Similar principles apply for CGT purposes.

7.5 NATIONAL INSURANCE FOR PROPERTY INVESTORS

Trading income is subject to Class 4 NI at the rates given in Section 8.1 (subject to the relevant age exemptions). This includes any incidental trading income arising as part of a property investment business (but not deemed trading income: Section 2.5).

Landlords with a property letting business, including FHL owners, should never be forced to pay any class of NI on their rental profits, as this is contrary to the relevant legislation. Furthermore, NI is never payable on capital gains.

However, where a property business is being pursued in an active manner such that HMRC accepts a business exists, they may allow the landlord to pay voluntary Class 2 NI (£3.50 per week for 2025/26; £3.65 for 2026/27). This appeals to some landlords as payment of Class 2 will help to secure state pension entitlement if they are not paying any other form of NI or getting any other credit for state pension purposes.

Paying voluntary Class 2 NI in respect of a property letting business does not give rise to any liability for the rather more expensive Class 4 and is also a far cheaper way to secure state pension entitlement than paying Class 3 voluntary contributions (£17.75 per week for 2025/26; £18.40 for 2026/27).

According to HMRC, landlords may pay Class 2 NI where their property management activities extend beyond those normally associated with being a landlord. This may include, for example, cases where the landlord owns multiple properties, is looking to acquire further properties, or where the letting of properties is the landlord's main occupation.

Whether paying Class 2 NI will be beneficial in the long run depends on your personal circumstances, but landlords should never be forced to pay it on pure rental income with no trading element.

If you employ anyone to help you in your property business, their salary will be subject to both employee's and employer's Class 1 NI: currently at 8% and 15% respectively. However, employers are not required to pay employer's NI on the first £50,270 of earnings paid to employees under 21, or qualifying apprentices under 25. Employers are also generally eligible to claim exemption from the first £10,500 of employer's NI arising each tax year (£5,000 prior to 2025/26).

Any taxable benefits-in-kind you provide to employees will additionally be liable for Class 1A NI at the same rate as employer's Class 1 NI.

7.6 VISITOR LEVY

The Government plans to introduce a new Visitor Levy to be charged on short-term accommodation in England. This will cover all forms of short-term accommodation, including hotels, guest houses, hostels, campsites, and FHLs (including those let through Airbnb or similar platforms). The power to introduce the levy will be in the hands of mayors of strategic authorities (i.e. it will be a local tax).

A similar power already exists in Scotland and a 5% Visitor Levy is to be introduced in Edinburgh from July 2026.

Legislation for a Visitor Levy in Wales has been passed and sets two rates: 75p per person per night for shared accommodation such as hostels and campsites; £1.30 per person per night for other short-term accommodation. This will again be applied at a local level, possibly from as early as April 2027.

Where a Visitor Levy applies, the business owner will have to add it to the amounts charged to guests and then pay it over to the local authority. It will be neither part of the business owner's income, nor part of their deductible expenses. It comes in and goes out: like VAT and PAYE, the business owner is simply an unpaid tax collector.

7.7 MANSION TAX

A new High Value Council Tax Surcharge, popularly known as the 'Mansion Tax', will be payable from April 2028. It will be an additional Council Tax charge payable by owners of residential properties in England worth more than £2m.

Unlike most Council Tax, the Mansion Tax will be payable by the *owner* of the property, rather than the *occupier*. This means, for rental properties, the tax will have to be paid by the landlord, and not the tenant. The proposed rates of Mansion Tax for 2028/29 are as follows:

Property Value	**Tax**
£2m to £2.5m	£2,500
£2.5m to £3.5m	£3,500
£3.5m to £5m	£5,000
£5m or more	£7,500

The charges will be increased in line with CPI inflation from 2029/30 onwards.

Where a landlord suffers the charge on a rental property, they should, under basic principles, be able to deduct it from their taxable property income for Income Tax purposes: unless the Government decides otherwise!

The Valuation Office Agency will carry out a targeted valuation exercise to determine a property's value in 2026. If a property is viewed as being worth £2m or more in 2026, it will be subject to the new tax from April 2028. Revaluations will then be conducted every five years.

Scotland

The Scottish Government intends to adopt a far simpler approach, and proposes simply to adopt two new Council Tax valuation bands for properties worth in excess of £1m and £2m respectively, with higher Council Tax charges applying from April 2028. As at present, the charges will be payable by the occupier, and not necessarily the owner.

Having said that, while this approach is nice and simple, the Scottish Government is also exploring the possibility of a Scottish Wealth Tax.

Wales & Northern Ireland

At present, no announcements have been made regarding any 'Mansion Tax' style taxes in Wales or Northern Ireland.

Chapter 8

Other Property-Based Businesses

8.1 TRADING INCOME

As we saw in Chapter 2, the profits on a property disposal are sometimes treated as trading income. The profits of other property-based activities may also amount to, or be taxed as, trading income, and we will look at a few of these in this chapter.

Trading income, including deemed trading income (Section 2.5), will continue to be subject to the main rates of Income Tax from 2027/28 onwards, and will not suffer the increased rates applying to property income (Section 3.3).

Where an actual trade exists, however, trading income (but *not* deemed trading income) also suffers NI.

National Insurance (NI)
Trading profits are regarded as earnings for NI purposes and are currently subject to Class 4 NI at the following rates:

First £12,570	0%
£12,570 to £50,270	6%
Over £50,270	2%

These rates have applied since 2024/25 and are currently expected to apply each year until 2030/31.

Example: *In Section 3.4, we saw Meera was paying a total of £4,946 in Income Tax under self-assessment for 2026/27. Let us now assume Meera is a property trader and her £15,000 of property income is a trading profit. In addition to her Income Tax bill, Meera will also be liable for Class 4 NI of £146 (6% of £15,000 less £12,570), bringing her total self-assessment tax liability up to £5,092.*

Individuals with both employment income and trading income may end up paying more NI than the law demands. This may arise where each of the income sources exceeds £12,570 and the total of both exceeds £62,840 (the sum of the NI primary threshold, £12,570, and the upper earnings limit, £50,270). In such cases, the individual may apply for a refund of the excess NI paid or, if they are able to foresee this situation is likely to arise, apply for a deferment of their Class 4 liability.

Age Exemptions
Individuals over state pension age (SPA) on the first day of the relevant tax year are exempt from Class 4 NI. This includes taxpayers reaching state pension age on 6th April. The state pension age is currently 66, but rising to 67 between April 2026 and March 2028. Children under 16 on the last day of the tax year are exempt from NI.

Marginal Tax Rates on Trading Income
Factoring in NI, the overall marginal tax rates on trading income each year from 2024/25 to 2030/31 (we expect) are as follows:

Taxable Income	Under SPA	Over SPA*
Up to £12,570	0%	0%
£12,570 to £50,270	26%	20%
£50,270 to £100,000	42%	40%
£100,000 to £125,140	62%	60%
Over £125,140	47%	45%

* Also applies to deemed trading income received by any individual, or trading income received by children under 16.

The rates in the table assume the individual has no employment or pension income. See Section 3.4 regarding the impact of other sources of income.

The Trading Income Allowance
An allowance of £1,000 per year is available to exempt small amounts of trading income. Where an individual's total gross trading income for the tax year exceeds £1,000, they may either deduct expenses as normal, or deduct the allowance from the total income. The taxpayer may also deduct expenses as normal where this gives rise to a trading loss.

The trading income allowance can be used against casual income or deemed trading income (Sections 2.5 and 8.4), following the same principles. However, only a maximum of £1,000 is available to each individual in each tax year (for example, if £600 is set against casual income, only a maximum of £400 can then be set against actual or deemed trading income).

Where appropriate, a taxpayer can claim both the trading income allowance (against trading income or casual income) and the property income allowance (against rental income or anything else classed as property income: see Chapter 4) in the same tax year.

The trading income allowance is not available on partnership trading income. Furthermore, the allowance is not available at all if you receive any trading income, or casual income, from your own partnership or company. This restriction extends to income from the same partnerships and companies as for the property income allowance (Section 4.17).

State Pension Entitlement
Trading profits in excess of the small profits threshold (£6,845 for 2025/26; £7,105 for 2026/27) automatically provide a credit for state pension purposes. Those with lower profits (or with losses) who are not paying any other form of NI or getting any other credit for state pension purposes may pay voluntary Class 2 NI (£3.50 per week for 2025/26; £3.65 for 2026/27) in order to secure state pension entitlement.

Other Taxes and Tax Issues

If you have an actual trade (and not merely deemed trading income), the long-term assets of the business may be eligible for business asset disposal relief (Section 9.24), holdover relief (see Section 5.7), and rollover relief (Section 9.26) for CGT purposes.

The value of a trading business is generally eligible for business property relief for IHT purposes. However, assets held by a property trader (or property dealer) are not eligible for this relief. See the Taxcafe guide *How to Save Inheritance Tax* for further details.

Trading income may be subject to MTD (Section 3.6) where there is an actual trade. See also Chapter 7 regarding VAT.

Most trading businesses can draw up accounts under either the accruals basis or the cash basis. The cash basis for traders is broadly similar to the cash basis for landlords (Section 4.22), but there are some key differences to be aware of: see the Taxcafe guide *Small Business Tax Saving Tactics* for details.

Property held for resale in a trading business is not classed as capital expenditure, but as trading stock. This applies whether any development work is to be carried out on the property prior to sale or not. As such properties are not capital expenditure, they are not eligible for capital allowances (Sections 4.10 to 4.14).

Long-term assets of a trading business using traditional accruals basis accounting may, however, qualify for plant and machinery allowances (Sections 4.11 to 4.13) plus, for non-residential property, the SBA (Section 4.14). Those operating the cash basis may only claim capital allowances on cars (see Section 4.12), but see Section 4.23 regarding relief for other capital expenditure under the cash basis.

8.2 PROPERTY-BASED TRADES

As discussed in Chapter 2, there are a number of trades that are inextricably linked with the business's underlying property, but which are quite distinct from pure property investment businesses. Such trades include: hotels and guest houses; care homes, nursing homes, and private hospitals; serviced offices; warehousing; and holiday parks.

The key difference between these trades and the property businesses we have examined previously is the fact the property's owners actually occupy the property for use in their own trade.

The profits derived from running these business activities are treated as trading profits subject to Income Tax and NI. The only exception is any separately identifiable income purely for rental alone (and no other services): which is subject to Income Tax as property income in the usual way, but not NI. This might, for example, apply to part of the income from serviced offices.

At present, this can lead to a 6% saving for a basic rate taxpayer, or a 2% saving for a higher or additional rate taxpayer. From 2027/28 onwards, the saving for a basic rate taxpayer will be just 4% and the savings for higher or additional rate taxpayers will be eliminated.

Most of these businesses will need to be registered for VAT when their gross annual sales income exceeds £90,000.

Gains arising on disposal of the properties held by these businesses will be subject to CGT, with the full range of attendant reliefs available to business property, including business asset disposal relief, holdover relief, and rollover relief (see Sections 9.24, 5.7, and 9.26 respectively). Again, exceptions arise where there is some pure rental income, such as from serviced offices.

Most properties used in these types of business will be eligible for business property relief for IHT purposes. Dangers arise, however, where the business confers some long-term rights of occupation on its customers, as is sometimes the case with guest houses or care homes, for example; or where the facilities provided to customers are less significant than the use of the property itself, which is often a risk for holiday parks. See the Taxcafe guide *How to Save Inheritance Tax* for further details.

These trades are generally eligible for plant and machinery allowances in the same way as other property businesses (Sections 4.11 to 4.13), unless they are operating the cash basis (see Section 4.23). Furthermore, caravans and mobile homes let out as holiday accommodation qualify for plant and machinery allowances. See also Section 4.14 regarding the availability of the SBA on properties used in these trades.

8.3 RESIDENTIAL MOBILE HOME PARKS

Residential mobile home parks (sometimes referred to as caravan parks) are distinct from holiday parks in that the mobile homes are generally in long-term occupation, rather than being used for holiday lets. The park owner will also often sell the mobile homes to the occupiers, but will continue to charge ground rent, or pitch fees.

The occupiers may be occupying the mobile homes as their permanent residence, or as a holiday home, but this has no impact on the tax position for the owner of the park (other than some potential implications for Council Tax if the park is kept open all year).

This type of business is usually considered to be a trade for tax purposes. As with everything, this has advantages and disadvantages. The major disadvantage is that both Income Tax and NI will be due on all profits, including profits arising on sales of mobile homes.

A sale of all or part of the park itself would continue to be subject to CGT and would generally be eligible for rollover relief (Section 9.26). A sale of the entire business would usually qualify for business asset disposal relief (Section 9.24).

One major advantage of this type of business is that the interest relief restrictions covered in Section 4.7 will not generally apply: both because the activity is a trade and because mobile homes are not generally considered to be a dwelling house.

These businesses will not generally qualify for business property relief for IHT purposes, although the position is not always clear where the park owner provides significant additional services or facilities (see the Taxcafe guide *How to Save Inheritance Tax* for further details).

The VAT position of these businesses can be quite complex, as they will often be partially exempt. Professional advice is therefore essential whenever total gross annual income exceeds the VAT registration threshold of £90,000.

Caravans and mobile homes in long-term residential occupation do not qualify for plant and machinery allowances (they only qualify when being let out as holiday accommodation).

Mixed Parks

Finally, despite my opening comment in this section, many parks have a mixture of long-term occupiers/residents and holidaymakers. This should not generally affect the tax treatment outlined above, and indeed may even be beneficial for IHT purposes, although it will add to the complexity of the VAT position. As usual, caravans and mobile homes being let out as holiday accommodation will qualify for plant and machinery allowances.

8.4 CASUAL INCOME

In Chapter 2, we looked at whether a property business exists, and how profits or gains on disposals of property are treated when there is no business. One thing we haven't yet covered is how to deal with sundry other property-based income where there is no business.

Example: *Anne is currently on a career break while she raises her young son. Her father, a landlord with a small portfolio of rental properties is taken ill. To help him out, she takes over the property management on his portfolio and he pays her £500 per month for her help.*

This is not a business. It does not meet any of the tests set out in Section 2.4. Anne did not pursue the undertaking, it happened by chance. There may be some continuity but it only relates to a single client, Anne's father; and, because of the family relationship, it cannot be said to be conducted on sound business principles. This is just a family arrangement, not a business.

The deemed trading provisions (Section 2.5) cannot apply here, as those only relate to the profit on disposal of a property. However, it is seldom possible to obtain any kind of income tax free (unless covered by your personal allowance) and Anne's income in this scenario would be termed casual income.

Casual income is subject to Income Tax at the main rates set out in Section 8.1.

Any *direct* costs incurred in earning casual income may be deducted, but this does not usually extend to interest and finance costs or other overheads. Alternatively, the trading income allowance may be claimed against this type of income (see Section 8.1).

Underlying assets held in the course of producing casual income will not be eligible for IHT business property relief, CGT business asset disposal relief (Section 9.24), or capital allowances. Casual income does not generally give rise to VAT liabilities or an obligation to register for either VAT or MTD.

The best thing about casual income is that, since it is not an actual trade, it does not attract NI, producing a saving of up to 6%. The only drawback, of course, is that to be casual income, there must be no serious trade-like intent. In other words, once you set out to make the income in any organised manner, it inevitably ceases to be casual and you will have a property trade. For this reason, this type of income is fairly rare.

Remember that any rental income, no matter how small, will not be casual income but will be taxed as discussed in Chapter 4.

Chapter 9

Advanced Tax Planning

9.1 INTRODUCTION TO TAX PLANNING

In previous chapters we have looked at the mechanics of the UK tax system as it applies to property investors. In this chapter, we will look at some more advanced aspects of UK property taxation and some further useful planning strategies.

In many cases, the best tax-planning results will be obtained through the use of a combination of different techniques, rather than merely following any single one. Each situation is different and the optimum solution only comes through detailed analysis of all the relevant facts. Tax planning should never be undertaken without full knowledge of the facts of the case and the exact circumstances of the individuals and other legal entities involved.

For this reason, the techniques laid out in this chapter, which are by no means exhaustive, are intended only to give you some idea of the tax savings that can be achieved through careful planning. If and when you come to undertake any tax-planning of your own you should seek professional advice from someone fully acquainted with your situation.

Remember also that tax law is constantly changing. A technique that works well now may later be undermined by changes made in Parliament or decisions in Court.

For the CGT planning sections in this chapter, I have assumed there are no capital losses available unless expressly stated to the contrary. In practice, any capital losses available to an individual or their spouse should be taken into account.

Bayley's Tax Planning Law
All tax planning should be based on these guiding principles:

- Hope for the best,
- Plan for the worst,
- Review your position constantly, and
- Expect the unexpected!

The Budgets and Financial Statements we have seen over the last few years have provided some of the best arguments for these principles I have ever seen. Especially the last one!

9.2 THE BENEFITS OF JOINT OWNERSHIP

Owning property jointly with one or more other people can be highly beneficial for tax purposes.

In this section, we will look at joint ownership benefits available to anyone. In Sections 9.3 to 9.6 we will concentrate on married couples, and in Section 9.9 we will look at other joint owners.

A number of important allowances, bands, thresholds, etc, are available on a per person basis, including:

- The personal allowance
- The property income allowance
- The trading income allowance
- The annual CGT exemption
- Private letting relief
- Business asset disposal relief
- The basic rate tax band
- The £100,000 threshold for withdrawal of personal allowances
- The additional rate threshold
- The NI primary threshold
- The thresholds for introduction of MTD

Furthermore, as discussed in Section 4.10, it is also possible to structure investments so the AIA effectively operates on a per person basis.

The value of these allowances, bands, and reliefs can be doubled for properties held jointly by two people (tripled for three joint owners, etc.)

How Much Is at Stake?

Sticking with two joint owners, the maximum tax savings joint ownership can generate in 2026/27 alone are:

- £2,982 on most capital gains
- £12,582 on capital gains with PLR (although, as explained in Section 5.10, this is now only available in very limited circumstances)
- £60,720 on capital gains with business asset disposal relief (but see Sections 9.24 and 9.25 for some pitfalls to watch out for)
- £21,339 in Income Tax on rental income
- £20,082 in Income Tax and NI on trading profits
- £444,339 in Income Tax savings when claiming the AIA on commercial property or qualifying assets in a multi-dwelling property (Section 4.10)

The maximum Income Tax savings described above are based on taxpayers with high levels of income such that joint ownership can be used to reduce their taxable income to £100,000. Most higher-rate taxpayers can still achieve considerable savings, however.

Where both joint owners are over state pension age, the potential savings on trading profits are the same as on rental income. Where one joint owner is over state pension age, the potential savings may be greater (up to £23,339), or lower (up to £18,082), depending on the situation.

Note: not every tax relief or band is given on a per person basis. Exceptions include all SDLT bands, the VAT registration threshold, and rent-a-room relief.

Non-Equal Splits
When considering the benefits of joint ownership, remember it is possible to have any split of beneficial ownership you desire, as long as the correct form of joint ownership is in place (see Section 2.9). In this context, it is worth mentioning a joint tenancy can be changed fairly easily into a tenancy in common. This change is not treated as a disposal for CGT purposes unless at the same time there is also a change to a non-equal split of beneficial ownership.

Changing the Ownership Split
It is difficult to transfer a share in a property to someone other than your spouse without incurring CGT or other charges. In Section 9.9, however, we will look at how significant Income Tax savings can still be achieved at a minimal cost in CGT, and in Section 9.19, we will look at a possible way to avoid CGT on the transfer altogether. Nevertheless, for joint owners other than married couples, it is generally advisable to get your ownership structure right from the outset whenever possible.

Sales by Joint Owners or Former Joint Owners
For the purposes of calculating PRR on a property sale, the seller's period of ownership for their entire interest at the date of sale is treated as commencing on the date they first acquired any interest in the property.

9.3 USING YOUR SPOUSE TO SAVE CAPITAL GAINS TAX

Putting property into joint names with your spouse can generate considerable tax savings: just like any other joint owners, as we saw in the previous section. In some cases, an outright transfer of the whole property may even be more beneficial.

The major difference between those who have legally tied the knot and the rest of us, however, is the fact the transfer is free from tax (subject to the points in Section 6.6 regarding SDLT). Despite this, transfers to a spouse are not necessarily free of tax ***consequences***, and we will look at the impact of such transfers on PRR and PLR in Sections 9.4 and 9.5.

The example of George and Charlotte in Section 5.22 demonstrated the potential CGT savings in a simple case where PRR did not apply. In such a case (and where the couple are married), it is normally immaterial whether the property was in joint ownership throughout, or was only transferred into joint ownership at a later date, prior to the ultimate sale (often known as a pre-sale transfer). The effect on the couple's final tax liabilities usually remains the same.

As we saw in Section 5.22, the potential CGT saving on a typical investment property is up to £2,982 in 2026/27. However, the position will differ from one couple to another, so investors need to weigh up the costs of any pre-sale transfer against the saving available. At current tax rates, and with the annual exemption now just £3,000, such a transfer will no longer be worthwhile in many cases.

Two key provisos must be made for transfers to a spouse:

a) The transferee must be beneficially entitled to his/her share of the sale proceeds. Any attempt to prevent this could make the transfer invalid for tax purposes.
b) An interim transfer of property, or a share in a property, prior to sale must take place early enough to ensure the transferee genuinely has beneficial title to their share. If it is left until the ultimate sale is a contractual certainty, it may be too late to be effective for tax purposes.

Where a transfer to a spouse prior to sale is planned, the following guidelines may help make it effective for tax purposes. Bear in mind the transferee must always have beneficial ownership for the transfer to work.

- It is preferable to do the transfer as soon as possible
- Ideally, it should be before the property is put on the market
- A transfer after there is a contract for sale to a third party is likely to be ineffective in providing the transferee with beneficial ownership

Joint Ownership is Not Always Beneficial
A transfer into joint names prior to sale is not always beneficial. Sometimes, it is preferable to have the property in the sole name of one spouse at the time of sale. This may arise, for example, if:

- Some or all of one spouse's basic rate band is available but the other spouse is a higher rate taxpayer,
- Only one spouse is entitled to business asset disposal relief on the property (see Section 9.24), or
- One spouse has capital losses available to set off against the gain

As far as the annual exemption is concerned, this now has a maximum tax-saving value of just £720 (£3,000 x 24%).

If the best spouse to hold the property at the time of sale is not the one who already holds it, a pre-sale transfer could generate considerable savings. The same provisos as set out above apply equally here.

In summary, when a sale is in prospect, it is worth assessing whether a transfer into joint ownership, or to the other spouse outright, might result in a CGT saving. Always remember, however: whoever has title to the property at the time of sale must be entitled to the proceeds!

Lastly, it is worth remembering joint ownership does not have to mean equal shares and any other allocation is also possible.

9.4 SAVING MORE TAX WITH TRANSFERS TO SPOUSES

The principles outlined in this section apply only to transfers between legally married spouses or registered civil partners, but apply equally to all married couples and civil partners.

Terms like 'husband and wife' are used only for illustration: 'wife and wife', 'husband and husband', or 'civil partners' could equally be used.

As we saw in Section 5.7, a lifetime transfer of a property, or share in a property, between spouses usually results in the transferee taking over the transferor's base cost (or an appropriate share).

For transfers made after 5th April 2020, the transferee effectively also takes over the history of the property for the purposes of PPR and PLR and this can lead to some beneficial savings on the property's sale.

Example A, Part 1: *In March 2015, Babur bought a house in London for £500,000 and adopted it as his main residence for the next seven years. From 2016 to 2022, he rented out two thirds of the house as separate flats, although this did not require any structural alterations.*

In 2022 Babur married Zainab and moved out of the house into a new marital home (and main residence). He started to rent out the whole of his former home.

In September 2026, he put his old house into equal joint names with Zainab and, in March 2027, the couple sold it for £1.4m. As the transfer into joint names took place after April 2020, and while Babur and Zainab were living together as a married couple, each of them will have the same CGT calculation:

Sale proceeds (half share)	*£700,000*
Less: Cost (half share)	*(£250,000)*
Gain before reliefs	*£450,000*
Private residence relief:	
*2015 to 2016 (1/12 x £450,000)**	*(£37,500)*
*2016 to 2022 (6/12 x £450,000 x 1/3)***	*(£75,000)*
Last nine months (9/144 x £450,000)	*(£28,125)*
Private letting relief:	*(£40,000)*
Annual exemption	*(£3,000)*
Taxable gain	*£266,375*

** Babur occupied the whole property as his main residence for the first year out of his total ownership period of twelve years*
*** Only one third of the property was occupied as Babur's main residence during this period. However, the gain on the other two thirds during this qualifying period of shared occupancy is £150,000 and is eligible for PLR*

If we assume Babur is a higher rate taxpayer and Zainab's taxable income for 2026/27 is less than her personal allowance, the couple's total CGT will be:

Babur:	*£266,375 @ 24% =*	*£63,930*
Zainab:	*£37,700 @ 18% =*	*£6,786*
	£228,675 @ 24% =	*£54,882*
Total		*£125,598*

The key point is Zainab is entitled to the ***same*** PRR and PLR as Babur. It does not matter that she never lived in the house; all that matters is the transfer took place after 5th April 2020 and she and Babur were married and living together as husband and wife at the time of the transfer.

Example A, Part 2: *If, instead, Babur had still held the property in his sole name at the time of sale, his CGT calculation would have been:*

Sale proceeds	*£1,400,000*
Less: Cost	*(£500,000)*
Gain before reliefs	*£900,000*
Private residence relief:	
2015 to 2016 (1/12 x £900,000)	*(£75,000)*
2016 to 2022 (6/12 x £900,000 x 1/3)	*(£150,000)*
Last nine months (9/144 x £900,000)	*(£56,250)*
Private letting relief:	*(£40,000)*
Annual exemption	*(£3,000)*
Taxable gain	*£575,750*

Babur's CGT liability, at 24%, would then have been £138,180. The transfer has therefore saved the couple £12,582 (£138,180 – £125,598).

The saving of £12,582 achieved in this case is the maximum available through a pre-sale transfer to a spouse (unless the property is eligible for business asset disposal relief) and arises from three sources:

- A couple owning a property jointly are entitled to up to £40,000 of PLR ***each***; meaning up to £80,000 of relief may be available (where there has been a period of qualifying shared occupancy)
- Each joint owner has their own annual exemption
- The transferee's basic rate band was available to reduce the rate of CGT she paid on the first £37,700 of her gain from 24% to 18%

The maximum savings arising from each of these sources in 2026/27 are £9,600, £720, and £2,262 respectively; making the total saving of £12,582 seen above. Sadly, the largest source, the extra saving from PLR, now only arises in limited circumstances, where the property has been let out during a qualifying period of shared occupancy (see Section 5.10).

Transfers Between Spouses Before April 2020

Where a residential property, or share in a residential property, was transferred between spouses before 6th April 2020, the position depends on whether the property was the couple's main residence at the time of the transfer. If the property ***was*** the couple's main residence at the time of transfer, the position on an ultimate disposal is exactly the same as set out above.

Where the property was ***not*** the couple's main residence at the time of the transfer then, while the transferee still takes over the transferor's base cost (or an appropriate share), they are ***not*** entitled to any historic periods of PRR or PLR the transferor had built up, and are treated as acquiring their share of the property on the date of the transfer.

In some cases, this can prove highly disadvantageous. For instance, if Babur (in Example A above) had transferred the house into joint names with Zainab after moving out (but before 6th April 2020), she would not be entitled to any PRR or PLR and the couple's CGT bill would be increased to £168,948. The transfer would then have ***cost*** them £30,768 in extra tax!

The easiest way to avoid this disastrous outcome in a case like this is simply to transfer the property back into the sole ownership of the original owner prior to sale.

Alternatively, in some cases, re-adopting the property as a main residence prior to sale may provide a better opportunity to improve the position. It all depends how the maths works out.

Benefits of Earlier Transfers

As we have seen, transfers of a former main residence to a spouse before 6th April 2020, and while it was not the couple's main residence, may have disastrous consequences. However, in other circumstances, a transfer of property to a spouse before 6th April 2020, at a time when that property was not the couple's main residence, could ultimately prove highly beneficial where the property is subsequently adopted as the couple's main residence some time after the transfer.

Example B: *In March 2007, Caleb bought a property in Kensington for £750,000 and began renting it out. In March 2020, Caleb transferred the property to his husband, David. In March 2023, the couple moved into the property and adopted it as their main residence. Four years later, in March 2027, David sells the property for £1.8m. David and Caleb are both higher rate taxpayers. David's CGT calculation is as follows:*

Sale proceeds	*£1,800,000*
Less: Cost	*(£750,000)*
Gain before reliefs	*£1,050,000*
PRR (4/7 x £1.05m)	*(£600,000)*
Chargeable gain	*£450,000*

The property was the couple's main residence for four years out of David's ownership period of seven years. Caleb's ownership period is ignored because the property was not their main residence at the time of transfer and it took place before 6th April 2020.

If Caleb had held on to the property himself until sale, his CGT calculation would have been as follows:

Gain before reliefs (as above)	*£1,050,000*
PRR (4/20 x £1.05m)	*(£210,000)*
Chargeable gain	*£840,000*

The transfer to David has therefore reduced the chargeable gain by £390,000, saving the couple £93,600 in CGT (at 24%).

Although David and Caleb moved into the property soon after the transfer, this technique will still produce savings on any property you are prepared to adopt as your main residence in the future.

It is only the transfer that needs to have taken place before 6th April 2020, the period of occupation as your main residence could be much later.

Example C: *Maggie bought an investment property in Manchester for £40,000 in March 1989. Some years later, she married Peter and, in March 2020, she transferred the property to him. In March 2027, the couple adopted the property as their main residence. Peter sells the property for £256,000 in March 2029.*

The gain on the property before reliefs is £216,000. Peter will be entitled to PRR of £48,000 (two ninths) as the property was the couple's main residence for two years out of his ownership period of nine years.

If Maggie had held onto the property herself, she would only have been entitled to PRR of £10,500 (two fortieths) as the property would have been the couple's main residence for two years out of her ownership period of forty years.

The transfer in March 2020 has increased the PRR on the property by £37,500 (£48,000 – £10,500), giving the couple a CGT saving of £9,000 (at 24%).

Remember also, a second home, or other suitable property, that was transferred to a spouse before 6th April 2020 could later be adopted as the couple's main residence by way of a main residence election (see Section 5.15). The property would need to qualify as a private residence (see Sections 5.13, 5.14, and 9.21) and the election would either need to be made within the appropriate time limit, or else within a new two year 'window' created using one of the methods set out in Section 5.15. Even an overseas property might qualify, as explained in Section 5.16.

9.5 WHAT IF YOU ARE ALREADY JOINT OWNERS?

The rule explained in Section 9.2, whereby a former joint owner is treated, for the purposes of PRR, as if they had owned the whole property since the date they first acquired ***any*** beneficial ownership, takes precedence over the rules on transfers between spouses.

Hence, a transfer of jointly held property ***into*** the sole name of one spouse will sometimes have a different effect to a transfer ***from*** the sole name of one spouse into joint ownership.

Example D: *Arthur and Gwen are married. In June 2020, they bought a house together for £200,000 and adopted it as their main residence. For two years they rented out half the property as a separate flat (this did not require any structural alterations). From June 2022, they occupied the whole property until, in June 2024, they moved out of the house and started to rent all of it out.*

In June 2026, they put the house into Gwen's sole name. In June 2028, Gwen sold the house for £360,000. Her CGT calculation is as follows:

Gain before reliefs	*£160,000*
Private residence relief:	
2020 to 2022 (2/8 x £160,000 x 1/2)	*(£20,000)*
2022 to 2024 (2/8 x £160,000)	*(£40,000)*
Last nine months (9/96 x £160,000)	*(£15,000)*
Private letting relief:	
*(2/8 x £160,000 x 1/2 x 1/2)**	*(£10,000)*
Chargeable gain	*£75,000*

* *The property was let out for two years out of eight years of ownership; half the property was let out; and Gwen is only entitled to PLR in respect of her half share of the gain arising due to the letting.*

As we can see the position for Gwen, a former joint owner who became a sole owner, is different to the position for Zainab in Example A, Part 1 (Section 9.4), who went from having no previous ownership to being a joint owner. Zainab was entitled to PLR on the share of the property transferred to her, whereas Gwen is not entitled to PLR in respect of the share of the property formerly owned by her husband.

This is because PLR only extends to a transferor spouse's ownership of the property when the transferee is deemed to have owned the property from an earlier date ***due to the transfer***. This did not apply in Gwen's case because she already owned a share in the property.

Step by Step
In other cases, a property may have belonged to one spouse at the outset, then been owned jointly for a while, and then finally ended up belonging to the other spouse (not the original owner) at the time of its ultimate sale. The outcome here will depend on when each transfer took place and, if either transfer took place before 6th April 2020, whether the property was the couple's main residence at the time.

The position for each couple will be different, but it could be well worth doing the detailed number crunching to decide who is best to hold the property, and in what proportions, before the ultimate sale takes place.

9.6 HAVE YOUR CAKE AND EAT IT

Income Tax savings can be generated by transferring property into either joint names with your spouse, or into the sole name of the spouse with the lower overall income. In the right circumstances, moving income from one spouse to another in this way could save a typical higher-rate taxpayer more than £12,000 in 2026/27 alone. As we saw in Section 9.2, some taxpayers could save up to £21,339.

As explained in Section 9.3, this form of tax planning is not effective unless beneficial title in the property is genuinely transferred. But not everyone trusts their spouse enough to hand over title to their property!

For Income Tax purposes, at least, there is a way to solve this dilemma. In most cases, where property is held jointly by a married couple, there is an automatic presumption, for Income Tax purposes, that the income arises in equal shares. This 50/50 split will continue to apply unless and until the couple jointly elect for the income to be split in accordance with the true beneficial title in the property.

Hence, where a married property owner wants to save Income Tax on rental profits without giving up much of their title to the property, what they should do is:

- Transfer the property into joint names with their spouse, but
- Retain 99% of the beneficial ownership and transfer only 1%, and
- Simply never elect for the income to be split in accordance with the true beneficial title!

Conversely
Conversely, of course, there are cases where the actual beneficial ownership split is preferable. In these cases, the election to split the income on an actual basis should usually be made. Beware though, once made, this election is irreversible.

To elect for the actual basis to apply, the couple must submit a signed declaration to HMRC (known as Form 17) stating their actual beneficial interests in the property and the income arising from it. The election is only valid if their interests in the income and the property itself correspond. Each spouse should also actually receive the income to which they are entitled. HMRC states that the election only applies from the date they receive Form 17.

Exceptions
The deemed 50/50 split referred to above does not apply where the couple hold the property as a partnership (see Section 2.9); where income from the property is treated as trading income (e.g. a guest house); or, up to 2024/25, where the property was an FHL. In these cases, income is taxed according to the couple's actual beneficial entitlement.

9.7 MARRIAGE AND CIVIL PARTNERSHIPS

Getting married alters your tax status dramatically. One major aspect of this for property owners is, from that date onwards, you and your spouse can only have one main residence between you for PRR purposes.

If each of you still has your own private residence when the happy day comes, you should elect which is to be your main residence (see Section 5.15). In these circumstances, the election must be made within two years of the date of marriage. Once an election is made, you can change it at any time, as long as you still have more than one private residence between you.

Once you are married, the tax saving opportunities outlined in Sections 9.3 and 9.4 will be available. It will usually make sense to put properties into joint names in order to maximise the available reliefs on any future sale, but the points made in Section 9.3 should be taken into account and the maximum CGT saving in most cases is currently just £2,982 (at 2026/27 rates).

Nonetheless, as we saw in Section 9.2, there are also potential Income Tax savings to be made through joint ownership, and these may be even greater in some cases, including parents with young children (Section 9.31), and Scottish taxpayers (Section 3.20).

Furthermore, if you don't feel comfortable giving your spouse a joint share in your property, the potential Income Tax savings can still be achieved, at minimal risk, using the method examined in Section 9.6.

9.8 SEPARATION AND DIVORCE

If a married couple separate, their tax status begins to change again: although it doesn't all happen at once. The exemption for transfers between spouses (Section 5.5) continues until the earlier of:

a) The end of the third tax year after the tax year in which the couple separate, or
b) The date on which their divorce is finalised, their marriage or civil partnership is annulled or dissolved, or they are formally, legally separated under a separation order or judicial separation

For the purposes of (a), separated means no longer living together as a married couple and separated in circumstances that are likely to be permanent. For disposals before 6th April 2023, the period under (a) was only until the end of the tax year of separation.

For example, where a couple separate in June 2026, and none of the events under (b) above have yet occurred, the general exemption ends on 5th April 2030. If they separated in June 2021, the exemption ceased on 5th April 2022, but resumed on 6th April 2023, and then continued until the earlier of 5th April 2025 or the date of any of the events under (b).

Transfers between spouses made under a formal legal divorce or separation agreement at any time after 5th April 2023 are also exempt (it does not matter how long the couple have been separated). This exemption extends to any deferred consideration or share of sale proceeds in respect of the former marital home received at a later date under the terms of a financial settlement.

Private Residence Relief (PRR)
If you separate from your spouse, you will be able to have your own individual main residence for PRR purposes once again.

Alternatively, if you have not claimed PRR on another property in the interim, nor made any main residence election in favour of another property, your former marital home may continue to be exempt as long as your ex-spouse continues to use it as their main residence. This exemption only applies in the case of a transfer/disposal of the property, or a share in the property, under a formal legal divorce or separation agreement.

For transfers/disposals under these circumstances made after 5th April 2023, PRR can apply on a transfer to ***anyone*** other than your estranged spouse. For earlier transfers, it could only apply to a transfer to your spouse (such transfers made after 5th April 2023 are exempt anyway). The potential IHT planning benefits of the change to this rule are explored in the Taxcafe guide *How to Save Inheritance Tax*.

A PRR claim in this situation is optional. If you would prefer to maintain the main residence status of another property for the relevant period, you can decline to make the claim, even if you qualify.

9.9 PLANNING WITH OTHER JOINT OWNERS

Joint owners who are not a married couple are not subject to the deemed 50/50 split we looked at in Section 9.6. Furthermore, while such joint owners usually share rental income in proportion to their beneficial title in the property they can, alternatively, agree to share rental profits in a different proportion. Provided each joint owner genuinely receives their agreed share of profits, the Income Tax treatment will follow. The proportions used may also be varied from year to year.

It is wise to document your profit-sharing agreement and also preferable to include some commercial rationale for the proportions used (e.g. because one of the joint owners is responsible for the management of the jointly held property).

This provides an opportunity for property owners to enjoy the benefits of joint ownership without incurring significant CGT costs or other charges on a transfer of property into joint names with someone other than their spouse.

Example: *Louise has a residential rental portfolio yielding annual taxable income of £125,000, meaning she is currently subject to Income Tax at a marginal rate of 60%, rising to 63% from 2027/28 (see Section 3.10). Her son, Albert is at university and has no taxable income of his own.*

One of Louise's properties has a value of £650,000, a base cost for CGT purposes of £300,000, and yields annual rental profits of £50,000. She transfers a 5% share in the property to Albert but agrees he will be entitled to a 50% share of the profit as he is taking over the management of the property.

Louise is subject to CGT on the transfer of the 5% share. However, her capital gain is just £17,500 (£650,000 – £300,000 = £350,000 x 5%). Deducting her annual exemption of £3,000 leaves her with a taxable gain of £14,500 and a CGT bill, at 24%, of £3,480.

Meanwhile, £25,000 (£50,000 x 50%) of rental profits have effectively been transferred from Louise to Albert. This will save Louise £15,000 in Income Tax in 2026/27, rising to £15,750 every year from 2027/28 onwards.

The first £12,570 of rental profit will be tax-free in Albert's hands for as long as he has no other taxable income of his own, and the remaining £12,430 suffers Income Tax at just 20%, or £2,486 in 2026/27, rising to £2,735 (22%) each year from 2027/28 onwards. After one year, the family will already have saved a net sum of £12,514; after three years, they could have saved £38,544.

Some readers may be wondering if you could go further than this and transfer, say 1% of the beneficial title in the property, but 99% of the taxable income. In theory that might work but, personally, I do not think it would be reasonable and is likely to be attacked by HMRC. Being reasonable is the watchword here, and your position will be greatly strengthened if you have some commercial justification for the agreed profit split.

As well as an adult child, this technique would work equally well with an unmarried partner, sibling, friend, or other relative. The only people it won't work with are your spouse or your own minor child.

If the property is subject to a mortgage, the transfer will need the lender's permission. However, if you can overcome that hurdle, SDLT can be avoided as long as the share of the mortgage taken over by the transferee is less than £40,000. For example, if Louise's property in the example above was subject to a mortgage of £500,000, Albert would be deemed to take over a 5% share of that mortgage, or £25,000, and hence no SDLT would be payable.

The technique may also generate IHT savings, although the transferor will generally need to survive at least seven years.

9.10 INHERITED PROPERTY

In Section 5.7, we looked at the base cost of inherited property and saw this is generally based on the property's value at the date of the previous owner's death. In many cases, this is pretty much all there is to tell and the new owner is treated in every respect as if they had purchased the property on that date.

There are a few areas of complication, however. Firstly, there is the fact that during the period of administration the deceased's estate is treated as a separate legal person, rather like a trust.

Like trusts, estates pay CGT at the higher rate of 24% (unless business asset disposal relief is available). The estate has its own annual exemption equal to the amount given to individuals. The exemption applies for the tax year of death and the following two tax years.

If a property is sold by the deceased's estate, it is treated as if it had been acquired on the date of the deceased's death for its market value on that date. Where 75% or more of the sale proceeds are to go to one or more beneficiaries who occupied the property as their main residence at the time of the deceased's death, PRR will apply to any gain arising.

Transfers of property from the estate to the beneficiary are exempt from CGT. Once the transfer has taken place, the beneficiary is treated as if they had acquired the property (or the deceased's share) for its market value on the date of the deceased's death.

Surviving Joint Owners: Other than Widows and Widowers
Where the new owner of the whole property was already a joint owner prior to the deceased's death, the calculation of PRR is based on their whole period of ownership (see Section 9.2). However, a surviving joint owner, other than the deceased's widow or widower, cannot claim PLR on the deceased's share of an inherited property in respect of qualifying lettings made prior to the deceased's death.

Widows and Widowers: Deaths before 6th April 2020
For deaths occurring before 6th April 2020, the position applying where property passed to a surviving spouse depends on whether the property was the couple's main residence at the time of the deceased's death and on whether the survivor was already a joint owner prior to that date.

If the property was **not** the couple's main residence at the time of the deceased's death and the survivor was **not** already a joint owner then they are simply treated as having acquired the property on the date of the deceased's death.

Where the survivor was already a joint owner prior to the deceased's death, and the property was **not** the couple's main residence at that time, then they are in the same position as any other surviving joint owner, as described above.

Where the property **was** the couple's main residence at the time of the deceased's death then, for the purposes of calculating both PRR and PLR, the survivor is in the same position as for deaths occurring after 5th April 2020.

Widows and Widowers: Deaths after 5th April 2020
Where a property, or a share in a property, passes to the deceased's widow or widower following a death after 5th April 2020, the survivor is treated, for the purposes of PRR, as if they had owned the property from the earlier of the date they first acquired any interest, or the date the deceased first acquired any interest.

Where the deceased had been the sole owner of the property prior to death, the widow or widower is entitled to PLR in respect of lettings made by the deceased during qualifying periods of shared occupancy.

Where the widow or widower was already a joint owner prior to the deceased's death, they will generally only be eligible for PLR in respect of lettings during qualifying periods of shared occupancy prior to the deceased's death, on their share of the property.

However, if there had been an earlier time when the deceased was the sole owner of the property then the widow or widower will generally be eligible for PLR in respect of all lettings during qualifying periods of shared occupancy throughout the couple's ownership.

Impact on Base Costs
The rules for PRR on inherited property do not alter the basic rule regarding the property's base cost. They only act to determine what ***proportion*** of the gain is covered by PRR.

Separated Survivors
If the couple were separated at the date of the deceased's death, the survivor is treated like an unmarried partner for all CGT purposes.

9.11 TILL DEATH DO US PART

As we saw in Sections 5.7 and 9.10, the base cost of an inherited property is equal to its market value at the date of the late owner's death. In the case of property passing to the deceased's spouse, this is both exempt from IHT and subject to the increase in base cost: often known as the 'uplift on death'. Under some circumstances, this provides an opportunity to make significant CGT savings.

Example: *Freddie and Jim are a married couple and are both higher rate taxpayers. They jointly own a portfolio of residential rental properties worth £3m with a total base cost of £1m. A lifetime disposal of their properties would give rise to total CGT liabilities of up to £480,000.*

Sadly, Freddie falls terminally ill. Jim transfers his share of their property portfolio so that Freddie now owns all of it in his sole name. Freddie dies and leaves the portfolio to Jim. The transfer is exempt from IHT under the spouse exemption and Jim now has a base cost of £3m for the portfolio, thus saving him £480,000 in CGT on future sales.

It takes a tragic situation to benefit from this planning technique but, like I always say, 'If the vultures at HMRC are prepared to use death as a means to collect tax, why shouldn't we use it as a means to save it!'

If following this technique though, you do need to be confident your spouse will leave the properties to you!

9.12 SECURING PRIVATE RESIDENCE RELIEF

In any planning that places reliance on PRR, it is essential to ensure the property or properties concerned genuinely become your private residence. There is no hard and fast rule as to how long you must reside in a property to establish it as your private residence, it is the quality of occupation that counts, not the length. Hence, it is recommended you (and your spouse or partner, and/or family, if applicable):

i) Move into the property for a substantial period
ii) Ensure all relevant institutions (banks, utilities, HMRC, employers, etc) are notified
iii) Inform family/friends
iv) Furnish the property for permanent occupation
v) Register on the electoral roll for that address
vi) Do not advertise the property for sale or rent until after the expiry of a substantial period
vii) Register with medical practices local to the property

It is not possible to provide a definitive view of what constitutes a substantial period. What matters is the property genuinely becomes your permanent home. 'Permanent' means it is intended to be your residence, rather than a temporary abode. You must move into the property with no clear plans for moving out again.

As a rough guide only, you should plan your affairs on the basis you will be residing in the property for at least a year, preferably two.

You may see cases reported where taxpayers have successfully claimed PRR on a property they occupied for much shorter periods. These cases may be helpful but they are very much dependent on their own specific circumstances. They cannot be regarded as setting a minimum occupation period everyone can rely upon.

As already stated, the question will ultimately be decided on quality of occupation, rather than length. Where you are looking to use PRR on a property, you must embark upon occupying that property wholeheartedly; a mere sham occupation will not suffice.

Main Residence Elections
In some instances, you may be able to establish the desired result merely by electing for the property to be treated as your main residence (see Section 5.15). However, it can only be your ***main*** residence if it is indeed your private residence and that still necessitates following at least some of the measures set out above, albeit perhaps adapted a little. You would, for instance, still need to:

i) Use the property as a home for a substantial period (although this could be as a second home or holiday home)
ii) Furnish the property for permanent occupation
iii) Avoid advertising the property for sale or rent until after the expiry of a substantial period (although short-term lettings not subject to any enduring right of occupation, may be acceptable: see Section 9.23)

9.13 GENERAL ELECTIONS

As explained in Section 5.15, where a taxpayer has two or more private residences, it is possible to elect which is to be regarded as their main residence. In fact, it is not just possible it is ***highly recommended***, even when it seems obvious which property should be the main residence.

Example: *Diana owns a house in London purchased in 2021 for £900,000. In July 2025, she bought a cottage in Sussex for £250,000, as her weekend retreat. In early 2029, plans for a new motorway junction a mile from Diana's cottage are announced. Simultaneously, the value of her property increases dramatically, while her desire to use it rapidly diminishes. A few months later, in July, she sells it for an astonishing £750,000.*

Fortunately for Diana, her accountant insisted she make a main residence election in January 2027. At the time, she naturally nominated her London house as her main residence, since it seemed more likely to produce a significant capital gain. However, because of this earlier election, Diana was able to make a new election in January 2029, nominating her cottage as her main residence.

A week later, Diana made a third election, nominating her London house as her main residence once more. This seemed sensible as the London house still seemed likely to produce a larger capital gain and Diana wished to keep her CGT exposure to a minimum.

Nonetheless, as a result of the cottage having main residence status for a week, it is covered by PRR for the last nine months of Diana's ownership. This exempts her from CGT on £93,750 out of her total gain of £500,000 and produces a saving of £22,500 (£93,750 x 24%). Furthermore, her London house will only lose its PRR for a week.

The moral of the story: always, *always*, ***always*** make the main residence election where applicable.

Tax Tip

A property only has to be classed as your main residence for **any** period, no matter how short, for your last nine months of ownership to be covered by PRR. To minimise the impact on PRR on another property, it is only necessary to elect in favour of the new main residence for a short period. In Diana's case, she was able to preserve most of the PRR on her London house by making another revised main residence election in favour of that property a week after she made the election in favour of her Sussex cottage.

Wealth Warning

Electing for a private residence to be your main residence for just a week is fine. Do not confuse this with the need to establish the property as your private residence in the first place (as explained in Section 9.12), where a considerably longer period of occupation is generally required.

Furthermore, there are restrictions on whether an overseas property can qualify as a private residence for PRR purposes. See Section 5.16 for tips on how and when it is possible to make main residence elections in favour of homes abroad.

Practical Pointer

If the period for which a property qualifies as your main residence does not fall within the last nine months of your ownership, you will gain a little more PRR on that property without increasing the restriction on your main home. For example, if Diana had backdated each of her second and third elections by two years, the effect on her London home would have been the same, but she would have gained a further £2,404 of PRR on her cottage.

9.14 DEVELOPING YOUR HOME

Many people are able to increase the amount of tax-free capital gain on their home by making improvements to the property. However, where expenditure is incurred specifically for the purpose of realising additional profit on the sale of the property, HMRC is able to deny part of your PRR.

Example: *Harry bought his house in 1999 and has used it as his main residence ever since. In 2026, the house is worth £750,000. Harry now decides to sell the house and realises he can make more money if he has a swimming pool built. He and his family move out of the house into a new home and he has the pool built at a cost of £40,000.*

With its new swimming pool, Harry is able to sell the house for £850,000. He has therefore made an extra profit of £60,000 that will not be covered by PRR. Deducting his annual exemption of £3,000 will leave him with a taxable gain of £57,000 and a CGT liability of up to £13,680 (at 24%).

In practice, Harry might be able to argue some of the extra profit was just down to getting a good offer, or a general increase in property values over the period since work began on the pool. In other words, don't just accept the whole of the extra gain is taxable, take other factors into account.

Many readers will be horrified by this example, but let me reassure you HMRC generally only uses this power when major capital expenditure is blatantly carried out for no reason other than to make extra profit on the sale of the property.

If Harry and his family had continued using the property after the pool was built, and only sold it perhaps a year or two later, it is highly unlikely there would be any restriction to his PRR. In general, homeowners can increase the value of their property by making capital improvements and still retain full PRR: provided there's a reasonable delay between those improvements being made and the property being put up for sale.

In the more common situation where homeowners carry out minor renovation work to prepare a property for sale, there is not usually any restriction in PRR. Furthermore, in practice, HMRC will not restrict PRR simply because a homeowner has obtained planning permission for conversion or improvement work.

> **Tax Tip**
> Where part of the PRR on a property is denied as a result of expenditure incurred specifically for the purpose of realising a profit on the sale of that property, the taxable gain arising remains subject to CGT and cannot be treated as a trading profit subject to Income Tax. However, this exemption only applies to the extent the taxable gain would otherwise have qualified for PRR or PLR.

Home Conversions

Where a property undergoes extensive conversion work, it may no longer remain a single dwelling for tax purposes. This has a far wider-ranging impact than merely letting out part of your home.

Example: *David bought a large detached house for £360,000 in December 2014. He lived in the whole house for one year then converted it into two, separate, semi-detached, houses. He continued to live in one of these, but rented the other one out. The conversion work cost £60,000, bringing his total costs up to £420,000.*

In December 2026, David sold both houses for £450,000 each, making a total gain of £480,000. The gain must be apportioned between the two houses. As they each sold for the same price, the gain will be split equally (Section 9.27).

The gain on the house David retained as his home will be fully covered by PRR. However, his £240,000 gain on the other house will only be covered by PRR for one year out of his twelve years of ownership. His PRR on this house thus amounts to only £20,000, leaving a chargeable gain of £220,000.

There are two important differences here to the situation in Section 5.18 where part of the property was let out, both of which occur because the rented house is no longer part of the same dwelling: PRR is not available for the final period of ownership; and no PLR is available.

> **Tax Tip**
> David would have improved his position if he had spent time living in the other semi-detached property after the conversion.

It may sometimes be more beneficial to treat the gains arising before and after the conversion as separate gains. In David's case, this would have been preferable if the original property had already increased in value by more than £40,000 before the conversion. This gain would have been completely exempt and half of it would have related to the house that was rented out. Both approaches are equally acceptable and we will look at this alternative method in more detail later.

Conversion for Sale
David did enough conversion work to create two new dwellings and this altered the amount of PRR available. He did, however, retain both new properties long enough for them to remain capital assets in his hands.

Where conversion work is carried out as a prelude to a sale, any gain arising may be regarded as trading income (see Section 2.7). Nonetheless, there are situations where a homeowner may develop part of their property for sale and still retain the more beneficial CGT treatment. This is because HMRC cannot deem a former main residence to be trading stock unless they can show the owner has a property development trade. Again, this applies to the extent the gain arising would have been exempt under PRR or PLR had the development not taken place.

This means one-off developments homeowners carry out on their own property may continue to be subject to CGT instead of Income Tax.

Example: *Spencer inherited a large house from his uncle in March 2021 when it was worth £1.2m. Spencer adopted the house as his main residence and lived there until September 2026, at which point it was worth £1.8m. Spencer then had the house converted into five flats at a total cost of £500,000. Spencer moved into one of the flats and adopted it as his home. He sold the other flats for £650,000 each in March 2027.*

His chargeable gain is calculated as follows:

Sale proceeds (4 x £650,000)		*£2,600,000*
Less:	*Value prior to conversion (4/5 x £1.8m)*	*(£1,440,000)*
	Conversion costs (4/5 x £500,000)	*(£400,000)*
Chargeable gain:		*£760,000*

Spencer's CGT liability will thus be up to £182,400 (at 24%).

For the sake of illustration, I have taken a simplistic approach to the allocation of costs by assuming the flats are all of equal value. See Section 9.27 for details of how to calculate the gain in more complex cases.

Spencer's capital gain is based on the extra value created by the conversion. The property's previous increase in value before conversion work began continues to be exempt because the whole property was his main residence during that period.

In this particular case, Spencer does not appear to have a property development trade. His non-trading status is strengthened by the fact he inherited the property. The situation might be different if he had purchased the property within one or two years before commencing conversion work, or had carried out similar developments in the past. Furthermore, if Spencer already had a property development trade, it is likely this conversion would be seen as part of that business. In practice, each situation has to be looked at on its own merits and HMRC will frequently argue a trading activity exists.

If Spencer were deemed to have a property development trade, the gain of £760,000 would be taxed as a trading profit and could give rise to Income Tax up to £345,771 and NI up to £16,708 (the maximum Income Tax cost arises if he has other taxable income of £100,000). His total tax liability could be increased by over £180,000.

Furthermore, if Spencer were treated as a developer, HMRC might argue the development profit of £190,000 on the flat he retained should also be taxed as a trading profit, giving him a further tax bill of £89,300!

One drawback to treating the development profit as a capital gain is that Spencer cannot deduct any interest or other overheads: only direct costs. This seems a small price to pay in Spencer's case but, in some cases, it may be more beneficial if the development is treated as a trading activity. Trading treatment would also allow a developer to use other methods for allocating costs, such as floor area or, better still, calculations prepared by a surveyor.

The New Residence

The flat Spencer retained for personal use has now become his main residence and will continue to be eligible for PRR. To see how this works in practice, let's return to the example. For this purpose, I'll assume Spencer retained CGT treatment on the sale of the other flats.

Example Continued: *Spencer moves out of the flat in June 2032 and rents it out before eventually selling it in March 2035 for £1.04m. His chargeable gain is calculated as follows:*

Sale proceeds	*£1,040,000*
Less: Value when inherited (1/5 x £1.2m)	*(£240,000)*
Conversion costs (1/5 x 500,000)	*(£100,000)*
Gain before reliefs	*£700,000*
PRR (£700,000 x 12/14):*	*(£600,000)*
Chargeable gain	*£100,000*

* *March 2021 to June 2032 + last nine months =12 years out of 14*

The new flat is not the same dwelling as the original house, but both were used as Spencer's main residence. He can therefore claim PRR on the appropriate proportion of the gain both before and after the conversion.

The above calculation is not the only valid method. The law only requires it is 'just and reasonable'. An alternative might be to view the gain on the first dwelling from March 2021 to September 2026 as wholly exempt, computing the gain on the second dwelling (the flat) as follows:

Sale proceeds	*£1,040,000*
Less: Value before conversion (1/5 x £1.8m)	*(£360,000)*
Conversion costs (1/5 x 500,000)	*(£100,000)*
Gain before reliefs	*£580,000*
PRR (£580,000 x 6½/8½):*	*(£443,529)*
Chargeable gain	*£136,471*

* *September 2026 to June 2032 + last nine months = 6½ years out of 8½*

The second method produces a larger capital gain and is likely to be favoured by HMRC. Nevertheless, the first method may also be regarded as just and reasonable. I can only suggest you be aware of the alternative methods. Use the one that is best for you, but be prepared for an argument!

9.15 SOMETHING IN THE GARDEN

It's a common scenario: a homeowner has a large garden, so they sell part of it off for property development. There are the right ways to do this and there are other ways, which are very, very wrong.

Losing the Plot

DO NOT:

- Sell your house first before selling the development plot
- Fence the development plot off or otherwise separate it from the rest of your garden before selling it
- Use the development plot for any purpose other than your own private residential occupation immediately prior to the sale
- Allow the development plot to fall into disuse before sale

Each of these may result in the complete loss of PRR on the plot. Also, do not assume the plot is covered by PRR if the total area of your house and garden exceeds half a hectare (see Section 5.11 for further guidance on PRR for gardens and grounds).

Fencing off the plot alone may not necessarily lead to the loss of PRR if the plot continues to be used for your own private residential occupation up to the point of sale. Nonetheless, there remains some doubt over this issue, so it is wise to avoid any separation of the plot from the rest of the garden prior to sale.

Keeping the Faith
First, the simple way: carefully ensuring you do not commit any of the cardinal sins described above, you simply sell off the plot. This sale will now enjoy the same PRR as applies to your house (for example, if 90% of a gain on your house would have been exempt, then 90% of the gain on the plot will be exempt).

The drawback to the simple way is you do not get to participate in any of the profit on the development. There are two ways around this, one is to use a slice of the action contract (Section 9.16), the other, if you feel up to it, is to hang on to the plot and develop it yourself.

Yes, at first this looks like we've gone the wrong way, but not if you then proceed to move into the new property and adopt it as your main residence. Your old house can safely be sold any time up to nine months after the date you move out and still be covered by PRR. The new house should be fully covered by PRR as long as you move in within two years of the date development started.

> **Wealth Warning 1**
> Although the new house will be covered by PRR, there is an argument that any gain on the land comprised in the development plot arising prior to the point development commenced is not covered. For example, if the cost of the land were £20,000 (based on an allocation of the original house's purchase price) and it was worth £30,000 immediately prior to commencement of the development, there would be a gain of £10,000 that was not covered by PRR.

> **Wealth Warning 2**
> More worryingly, some commentators suggest the gain on the new house would have to be calculated on a time apportionment basis, with PRR only applying to the period of occupation. For example, if the land originally cost £20,000 in 2016; the development took place in 2026 and cost £160,000; and the house was occupied as a main residence until it was sold for £255,000 in 2031; the PRR would be restricted to just £25,000, leaving a chargeable gain of £50,000.

At present, it is not clear which of the above interpretations is correct. Personally, I would argue strongly in favour of either full PRR or the just and reasonable allocation under Wealth Warning 1, as permitted by the relevant legislation.

What is beyond doubt is if the newly developed property were sold straight away, this would give rise to deemed trading income (see Section 2.5).

Well, almost beyond doubt, as it depends on your intentions when the development commenced.

9.16 GETTING A SLICE OF THE ACTION

Another way you may benefit from the development potential of your home is to enter into a so-called 'slice of the action contract'.

Example 1: *Barraclough is having a quiet drink in his local one night when he is approached by Groutie, a local builder. "That's a big garden you've got there, Barraclough; big enough for another house. Ever thought of developing it?"*

"Well, I don't know really," replies Barraclough, "Mrs Barraclough is very fond of her garden, you know."

Groutie won't take no for an answer and eventually persuades Barraclough to give him half his garden in exchange for a quarter of the sale proceeds for the new house. The part of the garden used for the development was worth £25,000 before construction began and the new house sells for £240,000. Barraclough's share of the sale proceeds is £60,000, giving him a profit of £35,000.

Most people would prefer this profit to be treated as a capital gain, rather than income, since it would be taxed at just 18% or 24%. However, because Barraclough effectively took a share in the development profit, his profit cannot be treated as a capital gain and is treated as income.

On the other hand, Barraclough's role was totally passive. Groutie sought him out. Barraclough did not participate directly in the development or sale of the new house. Hence, there is no way he could be regarded as having a property trade. His profit is therefore deemed trading income subject to Income Tax, but not NI.

He will also have a capital gain based on the increase in value of the development land prior to entering into the contract with Groutie. For example, if the original cost of the land was £8,000, he would have a capital gain of £17,000 (£25,000 – £8,000) in addition to his deemed trading income of £35,000 (see Sections 5.11 and 9.15 for details of how such a gain would be treated).

If Barraclough had simply sold his surplus land for a fixed price of £60,000, this would have all been a capital disposal, subject to CGT. Furthermore, as we saw in Section 9.15, if he had structured the sale correctly, it may have been completely tax free. However, it is unlikely that Groutie would have been prepared to offer such a good price and take on all the risks inherent in the development himself.

Hence, we can see the slice of the action contract had the commercial advantage of yielding greater sale proceeds, but carried the disadvantage that the homeowner's share of the development profit was subject to Income Tax rather than CGT. But it is possible to get the best of both worlds.

Where a slice of the action contract includes a fixed price element, HMRC will accept the gain arising on that element is subject to CGT, with only the excess being subject to Income Tax.

Example 2: *Alex and Eddie are both higher rate taxpayers. Their jointly owned home has a large garden, but it all qualifies as part of their private residence for CGT purposes (see Section 5.11). They decide to sell off part of the garden for development. The developer is prepared to pay them 30% of the new property's eventual sale price in exchange for the development plot, which has a current value of £80,000.*

Let's say they proceed on this basis and the new property eventually sells for £380,000. Alex and Eddie's sale proceeds are therefore £114,000 (£380,000 x 30%) and they have a taxable development profit of £34,000 (£114,000 – £80,000). They will suffer Income Tax of £13,600 (£34,000 x 40%), leaving them with net proceeds of £100,400 (£114,000 – £13,600).

But, instead of this, they negotiate a different deal. At the outset, the developer believed the new property would sell for between £350,000 and £400,000. Hence, as an alternative to the simple 30% share, Alex and Eddie persuaded him to pay a fixed sum of £100,000 plus 30% of any excess of the sale price over £350,000.

Now when the property sells for £380,000, Alex and Eddie's share will be £109,000 (£100,000 + 30% x £30,000: the excess over £350,000). However, only £9,000 of this will be subject to Income Tax while the remaining gain will be covered by PRR. This reduces their Income Tax bill to just £3,600 (£9,000 x 40%), leaving them with net proceeds of £105,400 (£109,000 – £3,600). That's ***£5,000 more*** *than under the original proposed arrangement,* ***even though*** *their* ***sale proceeds were £5,000 less!***

The points in Section 9.15 regarding things to avoid prior to selling the plot apply equally here if you are hoping to get PRR on the sale. Where PRR is not available, this strategy will still yield tax savings, although those savings effectively reduce from 40% of the gain arising under the fixed price element of the contract to just 16% (the differential between CGT at 24% and Income Tax at 40%). Hence, the tax savings can only compensate for a smaller reduction in the property owner's share of sale proceeds than that given in the example above.

On the other hand, where the homeowner has a higher marginal Income Tax rate, the strategy could yield even greater tax savings (marginal Income Tax rates of 45%, 60%, or even more are possible, even higher for landlords from 2027/28 onwards: see Section 3.10).

9.17 STUDENT LOANS

Each unmarried adult is entitled to their own main residence exempt from CGT. Once your children reach the age of 18, it is therefore possible to put some tax-free capital growth into their hands. (They don't actually have to be students by the way: it works just as well if they are in employment, or even just living a life of leisure at your expense, as many teenagers seem to do!)

The basic method is straightforward: all you need to do is buy a property in their name that they move into and adopt as their main residence.

Financing can be achieved in a number of ways, but the important point is they must have beneficial ownership of the property. (Hence, this simple technique should only be used if you are prepared to pass wealth on to the children.)

The purchase of the property has possible IHT implications, but these are avoided simply by surviving seven years. You should also be careful to avoid any subsequent occupation of the property yourself as this may give rise to an Income Tax charge (see the Taxcafe guide *How to Save Inheritance Tax* for details). Alternatively, if you would prefer to keep the wealth yourself for the time being, you may want to use the trust method examined in Section 9.20.

9.18 PROPERTIES HELD IN TRUST

A trust is a separate legal entity in its own right for tax purposes. A property business held by a trust is generally taxed in the same way as a property business held by an individual. The tax rates paid by trusts differ slightly, however, and are dependent on the type of trust.

Broadly speaking, a trust is an 'interest in possession trust' where the beneficiaries have an automatic right to trust income; it is a 'discretionary trust' where the trustees have discretion over who to distribute trust income to, and how much.

Income Tax: Interest in Possession Trusts
The trust pays Income Tax at the same rates that apply to a basic rate taxpayer individual. The trust income is then allocated to the trust beneficiaries and taxed on them at their own individual tax rates, with a deduction allowed for basic rate tax already paid by the trust. The beneficiaries must account for any further tax due, or may claim a repayment of any excess.

Interest in possession trusts receiving property income from 2027/28 onwards will pay Income Tax at 22% on that income, the same as basic rate taxpayer individuals.

Income Tax: Discretionary Trusts
The trust has a basic rate band of £1,000. Income falling within this band in 2026/27 is taxed at 20%, or 10.75% for dividends. From 2027/28 onwards, the rates will be 22% for property or savings income, 10.75% for dividends, and 20% for other income.

Thereafter, the trust currently pays Income Tax at 45%, or 39.35% on dividends. From 2027/28 onwards, it will pay 47% on property or savings income, 39.35% on dividends, and 45% on other income. Further charges can arise under certain circumstances where the trust distributes a large proportion of its income to the beneficiaries.

Trust beneficiaries are subject to Income Tax at their own individual tax rates on 100/55ths of the net income distributed to them. However, they may claim a tax credit equal to 45/55ths of this net sum.

Example: *Some years ago, Edward set up the York Discretionary Trust for his sons Teddy and Richard, with his brother Dick as trustee. By 2026/27 Dick is running a successful property investment business on behalf of the trust, making a taxable rental profit of £100,000. The trust pays Income Tax of £44,750 (£1,000 x 20% + £99,000 x 45%), leaving an after-tax profit of £55,250.*

In March 2027, Dick decides to distribute a net sum of £13,750 to Teddy. This is treated as taxable income of £25,000 in Teddy's hands (£13,750 x 100/55), but he is entitled to a tax credit of £11,250 (£13,750 x 45/55). Teddy's other taxable income for 2026/27 totals £40,270, so he is due a tax repayment of £3,250, calculated as follows:

Tax due on grossed up trust income of £25,000:

First £10,000 @ 20% =	*£2,000*
Remaining £15,000 @ 40% =	*£6,000*
Total	*£8,000*
Tax credit	*£11,250*
Repayment due (£11,250 – £8,000)	*£3,250*

If, instead, Teddy had an interest in possession, giving him an automatic right to 25% of the trust income, the trust would have paid Income Tax of £5,000 on that part of the trust income (£25,000 x 20%) and Teddy would have been liable for a further £3,000 (£8,000 – £5,000). The final outcome on income distributed to beneficiaries is therefore much the same in 2026/27, but discretionary trusts also suffer a high tax charge on undistributed income.

Future Tax Position for Trust Income

From 2027/28 onwards, trusts will pay higher Income Tax rates on property or savings income, as detailed above.

Beneficiaries with an interest in possession will also pay higher Income Tax rates on property or savings income received via a trust: i.e. the same rates they would pay if they received this income directly.

Discretionary trust beneficiaries will, however, pay tax at the same rates on the income they receive from the trust as at present.

If we take the same facts as the example above, but look at 2027/28 instead, the York Discretionary Trust will pay Income Tax of £46,750 (£1,000 x 22% + £99,000 x 47%), leaving an after-tax profit of £53,250. However, Teddy's tax calculation will be exactly the same as in 2026/27.

If Teddy had a 25% interest in possession instead, the trust would pay Income Tax of £5,500 on this part of the trust income in 2027/28 (£25,000 x 22%). Teddy would have a tax bill of £8,500 on the property income received via the trust (£10,000 x 22% + £15,000 x 42%). Deducting the £5,500 paid by the trust would leave him with £3,000 to pay, the same as in 2026/27, but the net income he received in the first place will have been £500 less.

In conclusion, where a trust is receiving property income, the increase in Income Tax rates on property income from 2027/28 onwards will:

- Be suffered by the beneficiary where there is an interest in possession
- Be suffered by the trust itself where it is a discretionary trust
- Not *directly* affect discretionary trust beneficiaries

Discretionary trust beneficiaries will, of course, be *indirectly* affected, since the trust will have less money left to invest in its property business.

Further Points: Income Tax and National Insurance for Trusts
Trusts are not entitled to a personal allowance, dividend allowance, or personal savings allowance. Some partial tax relief is provided for trust management expenses. The calculation is complex and will not generally yield significant savings, especially when the trust's only activity is a property business (expenses of the property business are deductible in the usual way; trust management expenses relate to running the trust, not running the business). Trusts are not liable for NI on trading profits.

Capital Gains Tax
Subject to any available reliefs (including business asset disposal relief), trusts pay CGT at the same rate as higher rate taxpayers: 24%. Trusts have their own annual exemption. This is generally half the individual annual exemption (Section 5.19), but must be further reduced where the same person has transferred assets or funds into more than one trust.

Trusts and Private Residence Relief
PRR extends to a property held by a trust when the property is the only or main residence of one or more of the trust beneficiaries. However, PRR is not available on a property held by a trust if a hold-over relief claim was made on the transfer of that property into the trust (see Section 9.19). In some cases, this may lead to a difficult decision: decline to make a hold-over relief claim at the outset and pay some CGT immediately; or make the hold-over relief claim and risk paying more CGT on the eventual sale of the property.

In other words, where a property has already increased in value since the original owner acquired it, and is intended to be adopted as the main residence of one or more trust beneficiaries, the owner will have to weigh up their prospective current CGT bill on the transfer against the ultimate tax potentially arising on a future sale.

Properties with held over gains already held in trust before 10th December 2003 are still eligible for PRR in respect of periods of occupation by a beneficiary as their main residence prior to that date. The additional nine months exemption at the end of the period of ownership does not apply.

Similar restrictions apply where a hold over relief claim is made on a transfer of property out of a trust. Once again, PRR cannot be claimed on a subsequent disposal of that property by the transferee.

Despite these restrictions, trusts can be used to obtain PRR on properties occupied by adult children or other friends and relatives. We will examine this tax-saving opportunity further in Section 9.20.

Stamp Taxes for Trusts

Trusts pay SDLT on purchases of non-residential property in the same way, and at the same rates, as other purchasers. For purchases of residential property by a trust, these are treated as if they were a purchase by the beneficiary for SDLT purposes if:

- The beneficiary will have the right to live in the property for life, or
- The beneficiary will have an interest in possession in the income from the property

Broadly speaking, this means the 5% SDLT surcharge will not apply if the beneficiary has no other interest in residential property, if the new property is replacing the beneficiary's previous main residence, or if the property is purchased from the beneficiary's spouse. The trust remains liable for SDLT at normal rates as set out in Section 6.2.

All other residential property purchases made by trusts will be subject to the 5% SDLT surcharge unless they fall within one of the general exemptions applicable to all purchasers.

As explained in Chapter 6, different taxes apply to purchases of property in Scotland or Wales. While many of the principles are much the same, there are important differences. Local professional advice is essential.

Inheritance Tax and Trusts

Using a trust has significant IHT implications. Problems can usually be avoided, however, where:

- The value of property, funds, or other assets transferred into the trust does not exceed the nil rate band (currently £325,000). A couple can effectively double this amount as long as they structure their investments carefully,
- The ultimate transfers out of the trust to the beneficiary, or beneficiaries, take place within less than ten years, and
- The original transferor survives at least seven years after making transfers into the trust

See the Taxcafe guide *How to Save Inheritance Tax* for a more detailed explanation of the different types of trust, the IHT consequences of using them, and the effect of transferring property or funds into a trust; including full details of the IHT implications and tax-saving potential of the planning techniques set out in Sections 9.19 and 9.20.

9.19 TAX-FREE PROPERTY TRANSFERS

As we have already seen, married couples are able to transfer property from one spouse to the other free from CGT. However, transfers of property, or shares in property, to other people, such as an unmarried partner or adult child, present a problem.

In principle, such transfers must be treated as if the property, or property share, had been sold for open market value.

In many cases, this would produce a significant CGT liability, but there are important exceptions, including the transferor's main residence and property used in the transferor's trading business.

Where a property owner makes a lifetime transfer into a trust, they may elect to hold over the capital gain arising. At a later date, the trust can then transfer the property to the intended recipient, and the trustees may again elect to hold over the gain. In this way, CGT can be avoided on both transfers and the end result is the transferee is treated as if they had purchased the property for the same price as the transferor. However, they are *not* treated as if they acquired the property at the same *time* as the transferor. For all other CGT purposes, the transferee's date of acquisition is the date the property is finally transferred out of the trust.

This technique does not work where the trust is a settlor-interested trust: a trust that includes the transferor, their spouse, or a dependent minor child of the transferor, as one of its beneficiaries. Furthermore, it should not generally be used where PRR is available (see Section 9.18). Also, hold over relief is only available for CGT purposes and would not apply to property classed as trading stock!

9.20 USING A TRUST TO GET EXTRA PRIVATE RESIDENCE RELIEF

As explained in Section 9.18, a trust is generally eligible for PRR on a property occupied as a main residence by one or more trust beneficiaries. Although the relief does not apply where a capital gain on a property has been held over on transfer into the trust, there is no problem where the property is purchased by the trust in the first place (or is transferred to the trust with no hold over claim). Hence, it is possible to obtain PRR on an additional property using the following method:

i) Set up a trust with another person (or persons) as the beneficiary (but not your spouse)
ii) Purchase a residential property through the trust
iii) The beneficiary adopts the property as their main residence (remember, like everyone else, they can only have one main residence and the usual rules apply if they are married)

You retain the reversionary interest in the trust. This means the trust assets will ultimately revert to you. As explained in Section 9.19, this means the trust is a settlor-interested trust and hold over relief is not available on a transfer of property into the trust. This is not a problem: you don't want hold over relief anyway!

Some years later, but within nine months of when the property ceases to be the beneficiary's main residence, the trust can either sell the property or transfer it to you. Either way, the gain arising up to this point will be exempt from CGT and you can either retain the property (with a base cost equal to its current market value) or enjoy the tax-free sale proceeds.

9.21 TEMPORARY PERIODS OF ABSENCE

A former main residence is deemed to be an individual's private residence for CGT purposes during certain temporary periods of absence, as follows:

i) Any single period of up to three years, or shorter periods totalling no more than three years, regardless of the reason,
ii) A period of up to four years when the individual or their spouse is required to work elsewhere by reason of their employment or their place of work, and
iii) A period of any length when the individual or their spouse is working in an office or employment whose duties are all performed outside the UK

The individual must occupy the property as their main residence for a period ***before*** the absence period, ***and*** one of the following conditions must also be met:

a) The individual occupies the property as their main residence for a period ***after*** the absence period, or
b) In the case of absences under headings (ii) or (iii) above, the individual or their spouse are prevented from resuming occupation of the property following their absence by reason of their place of work, or a condition imposed by their contract of employment that requires them to reside elsewhere (such a condition needs to be a reasonable requirement to secure the effective performance of their duties)

These rules only apply where the property is not occupied as a residence by the individual during the absence period. Hence, for example, they do not apply where the property is retained as a second home to use at weekends (in such cases, a main residence election should be used: see Section 5.15).

Where the absence period rules apply, they take precedence over the normal rules on whether a property qualifies as a private residence during the relevant period (Sections 5.13 and 5.14): unless the property undergoes a significant change of use (such as being converted into a shop or office, or into multiple dwellings).

Barring a change of use, there is nothing to prevent the taxpayer from renting out the property during a qualifying absence period and still having it qualify as their private residence.

The periods under headings (i) to (iii) can run consecutively, or be divided into shorter periods. Where the period of absence under (i) or (ii) exceeds the permitted period, it is only the excess that ceases to qualify.

It is important to understand the qualifying absence periods only mean the property qualifies as the individual's ***private residence***. Whether it qualifies as their ***main residence*** depends on the rules set out in Section 5.15. To summarise, in most cases, the position will be as follows:

- Where they had no legal or equitable interest in any other private residence, the property will automatically be their main residence
- Where their only legal or equitable interest in another private residence had negligible capital value (e.g. a non-transferable monthly lease at full market rent), they can establish the property as their main residence through a late main residence election
- Where they are non-UK resident at the time of disposal of the property, they can establish it as their main residence through an election on their Non-Resident CGT Return
- Where they are UK resident at the time of disposal and had a legal or equitable interest in another private residence with more than negligible value (i.e. they owned another home), they would only be able to establish the property as their main residence through an election within the normal two-year time limit

Married couples must be considered as a single unit for these purposes.

Example: *In March 2002, Linda bought a flat in Edinburgh and adopted it as her main residence. In April 2004, she moved back in with her parents and start renting out the flat. In October 2005, she got a job in London and moved down there. For the first six months she stayed with friends then, in April 2006, she rented a flat of her own. In June 2010, she got a job in Italy and moved there. For the first four years she rented a house on the outskirts of Milan then, in June 2014, her employer relocated her to Rome. She rented an apartment in Rome for just over a year then, in August 2015, she bought an apartment of her own.*

In May 2020, Linda sold her apartment in Rome and returned to the UK. She set up her own business in Manchester and moved in with her unmarried partner. Sadly, in November 2025, both her business and relationship failed. She left Manchester and moved back in with her parents. In August 2026, she moved back into her Edinburgh flat, adopting it as her main residence again, until she sold it in March 2027. Her periods of absence are dealt with as follows:

April 2004 to October 2005: Qualifies as her private residence under heading (i); also qualifies as her main residence as she had no legal or equitable interest in any other residence
October 2005 to April 2006: Qualifies as her private residence under heading (ii); also qualifies as her main residence as she had no legal or equitable interest in any other residence
April 2006 to October 2009: Qualifies as her private residence under heading (ii); could be nominated as her main residence by way of a late election, as her only other legal or equitable interest in a residence had negligible capital value
October 2009 to June 2010: Cannot qualify under heading (ii) as the maximum four-year period has been used, but qualifies under heading (i); could be nominated as her main residence by way of a late election
June 2010 to August 2015: Qualifies as her private residence under heading (iii); could be nominated as her main residence by way of a late election
August 2015 to May 2020: Qualifies as her private residence under heading (iii); BUT could only be nominated as her main residence by way of an election made by August 2017 (we will assume Linda made no such election)

May 2020 to March 2021: Cannot qualify under heading (ii) as the maximum four-year period has been used, but qualifies under heading (i) and uses up the last ten months of the maximum three-year period under this heading; qualifies as her main residence as she had no legal or equitable interest in any other residence
March 2021 to August 2026: Does not qualify as her private residence

In summary, providing Linda makes the relevant late main residence election (as permitted by legislation), she will be entitled to PRR for the periods from when she bought her Edinburgh flat in March 2002 to when she bought her apartment in Rome in August 2015; from when she sold her apartment in May 2020 to the expiry of the three-year period permitted under heading (i) in March 2021; and for her final nine months of ownership (June 2026 to March 2027).

This gives Linda a total of 15 years' worth of PRR out of her total ownership period of 25 years. On a gain of, let's say £300,000, this will provide relief of £180,000, saving her £43,200 in CGT (at 24%).

The position here is clear because Linda resumed occupation of the flat as her main residence before selling it. In other words, condition (a) above was met. Where the individual is relying on condition (b), the position is less clear, as there is some debate over whether the condition is met when the individual changes jobs. In essence the question is this: can the individual be regarded as 'prevented from resuming occupation of the property following their absence by reason of their place of work' when they have chosen to change jobs (or set up their own business). My suspicion is HMRC's answer to this would be 'no'.

Based on this, harsher, interpretation, Linda would not have had any qualifying periods of absence if she had not resumed occupation of the property as her main residence before sale. This would have left her with PRR for just the period of actual occupation (March 2002 to April 2004) and her final nine months of ownership: a total of just 34 months out of 25 years (300 months). This would reduce her PRR to £34,000 (£300,000 x 34/300), increasing her taxable gain by £146,000 (£180,000 – £34,000).

Moving back into her property before sale has therefore saved Linda £35,040 in CGT (£146,000 x 24%).

A more liberal interpretation of the rules might allow Linda to treat the property as her private residence for some additional periods, but the position is far from clear. In short, the sensible thing is to re-adopt the property as your main residence for a period before sale in order to put matters beyond doubt and maximise your PRR.

9.22 PLANNING WITH ABSENCE PERIODS

In Section 9.21, we saw some periods of absence from a main residence may be included as a period of occupation as a private residence for the purposes of PRR where certain conditions are met. In particular, a property investor could generate the following additional periods of PRR on a former main residence:

i) Up to three years in any case
ii) Up to seven years if they move elsewhere in the UK for work for at least four years during that period
iii) Indefinitely if they move abroad to work

As explained in Section 9.21, where the investor purchases another private residence during their absence, they will need to make a main residence election in order to obtain PRR on the former main residence. This election should be made within two years of moving out of the former main residence.

For the reasons explained in Section 9.21, it is also essential or, in some cases, at least highly advisable, that the former main residence is re-occupied as a main residence prior to sale.

Example: *Jimmy is a self-employed property developer and part-time residential landlord. In October 2026, he bought a house in Kent for £1.5m and occupied it as his main residence for two years. In October 2028, he relocated his property development business to Devon, where he bought a small cottage for £200,000. He moved out of the house in Kent and started to rent it out. Within the permitted two-year time limit (see Section 5.15), he nominated the house in Kent as his main residence.*

In March 2036, Jimmy retired. He moved back into the house in Kent and adopted it as his main residence again before selling it for £3m in July 2036.

Jimmy's house is treated as his private residence, and thus also his main residence (because of his election) for: the four years from October 2028 to October 2032 (under heading (ii) in Section 9.21); and the three years from October 2032 to October 2035 (under heading (i) in Section 9.21). The house also attracts PRR for his actual period of occupation from October 2026 to October 2028, and his last nine months of ownership. In summary, his entire gain of £1.5m is completely exempt from CGT.

Jimmy will have some exposure to CGT on his Devon cottage, although this will be eligible for PRR from October 2035 to March 2036, any later periods of occupation as his main residence, and the last nine months of his ownership (unless he nominates another property as his main residence for these periods). However, even without this, he is unlikely to suffer anywhere near as much CGT on the cottage as the £360,000 (£1.5m x 24%) he has saved on his house in Kent.

9.23 FURNISHED HOLIDAY LETS: THE AFTERMATH

The special, and highly beneficial, tax regime for furnished holiday lets (FHLs) was abolished on 6th April 2025. From that date onwards, FHLs are generally treated the same as other residential property lettings for both Income Tax and CGT purposes. There are, however, still a few lingering tax-saving opportunities that should not be overlooked.

In this section, we will look at what qualified as an FHL before 6th April 2025 and some of the issues to consider for those properties in the aftermath of the regime's abolition.

First though, it is important to remember the letting of short-term holiday accommodation is a standard-rated taxable supply for VAT purposes (see Sections 7.1 and 7.2). Many holiday lettings may also, in future, be subject to the Visitor Levy (Section 7.6).

Qualifying Conditions

To qualify as an FHL, the property had to meet the qualifying conditions for the relevant period. The relevant period was normally the tax year, but when the property began or ceased to be let out fully furnished, it was the first or last twelve months for which it is so let (see further below).

The qualifying conditions were that the property must have been:

i) Situated in the UK or the EEA (see Section 3.5)
ii) Fully furnished
iii) Let out on a commercial basis with a view to making profits
iv) Available for letting as holiday accommodation to the public generally for at least 210 days
v) Actually let as holiday accommodation to members of the public for at least 105 days (strictly speaking, the lettings had to be to holidaymakers and tourists in order to qualify)
vi) Not in longer term occupation for more than 155 days

Longer term occupation meant any period of more than 31 consecutive days during which the property was in the same occupation, unless this arose due to exceptional circumstances (e.g. the tenant fell ill, or their flight home was delayed). Periods of longer-term occupation could not be counted towards the 105 days required under condition (v).

A taxpayer with more than one FHL could use a system of averaging to determine whether they met condition (v).

Landlords could elect for properties that qualified in the previous year (including those qualifying by using averaging) to stay within the regime for up to two further tax years (up to 2024/25), despite failing to meet condition (v). The property had to meet the other qualifying conditions.

The Special Tax Regime and Its Aftermath

Properties qualifying as FHLs before 6th April 2025 were, and in some cases, still are, eligible for a number of CGT reliefs, as well as additional Income Tax deductions and allowances.

A general point to note is that any property rented out as a furnished let before 6th April 2025 can still qualify as an FHL up to 5th April 2025 if it meets the qualifying conditions above for the first twelve months of furnished letting. This includes properties rented out furnished for the first time during 2024/25.

Another general point is that tax returns for the last year of the FHL regime, 2024/25, can be amended any time up to 31st January 2027. The guidance below therefore caters for this possibility, but please bear in mind the potential consequences of amending a tax return, as discussed in Section 3.7.

Interest and Finance Costs

From 6th April 2025, FHL owners are subject to the same despicable restriction on relief for interest and finance costs as other residential landlords (Section 4.7), with relief restricted to basic rate only.

For a higher or additional rate taxpayer, it may be worth considering taking steps to maximise the claim for finance costs relating to FHLs in 2024/25, such as reassessing the useful life of underlying loans (see Section 4.6), or joining the cash basis (Section 4.22).

There are some possible ways to avoid the interest relief restriction, all of which will usually come at a cost and carry many complex implications that need to be considered. The first possible method is to transfer FHLs to a company. Even now, it may be possible to hold over the capital gains arising on the transfer and thus avoid any immediate CGT charge. This relief is available where a property business is substantial, generally involving the owner spending an average of more than twenty hours per week on the business. However, there will usually still be a significant SDLT cost, unless the FHLs are currently run by a partnership. These issues are considered in detail in the Taxcafe guide *Using a Property Company to Save Tax*.

The second possible method for retaining proper, full Income Tax relief for interest and finance costs is to establish that the FHL business can properly be classed as a trade. This will not always be possible, however, as it needs to involve the provision of significant additional services for tenants, such as housekeeping, meals and refreshments, or concierge services. Furthermore, HMRC are extremely resistant to this approach. For those under state pension age, trading status also carries the disadvantage that profits will be subject to Class 4 NI (see Section 8.1). For more information on when it may be possible, or desirable, for an FHL business to be treated as a trade, see the Taxcafe guide *Furnished Holiday Lets: Big Tax Changes Ahead*.

A third possibility is to convert the property into commercial use, such as a shop, for example. This will not always be possible or commercially viable though.

The one thing that definitely won't work is changing to long-term residential lets. So how, exactly, the Government thinks persecuting FHL owners is going to solve the housing crisis defies understanding!

Capital Allowances

From 6th April 2025, FHLs are subject to the same restrictions on capital allowances as other residential rental property (see Section 4.10).

Expenditure on replacement assets incurred after 5th April 2025 will generally be eligible for a deduction as repairs expenditure (Section 4.8: this applies equally to earlier expenditure) or, for moveable assets, under replacement of domestic items relief (Section 4.9: this does not apply to earlier expenditure in an FHL). It is only purchases of new, additional assets, or improvements, within rented dwellings that will cease to enjoy any tax relief.

Capital allowances claimed on expenditure incurred before 6th April 2025 will not be clawed back on the abolition of the FHL tax regime, provided the relevant assets remain in business use. Furthermore, any unrelieved balances transfer to the landlord's 'normal' property letting business (UK or overseas, as the case may be) and continue to attract writing down allowances in future years (see Section 4.11).

It is therefore worth reviewing your capital allowances claim for 2024/25 to ensure nothing has been missed. Remember, all the items listed as 'Qualifying Expenditure on Rental Property' in Section 4.10 will qualify for the allowances in Section 4.11, including the AIA.

It is also worth reviewing past expenditure in earlier years for possible claims that have been overlooked. Claims can be made in your 2024/25 tax return for qualifying expenditure incurred in earlier years, provided the assets were still in business use that year. While only writing down allowances are available on late claims, these may still provide valuable relief, which will continue after the abolition of the FHL tax regime.

Example: *In 2019, Anne bought a house in Dorset for £250,000 and started renting it out as an FHL. While she claimed capital allowances on the furniture and equipment she purchased, she did not know she could also claim for the integral features (Section 4.10) and other qualifying fixtures within the property.*

While reviewing her 2024/25 tax return, Anne realises (perhaps with the help of a surveyor) that her purchase in 2019 included £40,000 worth of integral features and £15,000 worth of other qualifying fixtures. She is therefore able to claim writing down allowances as follows:

	Integral Features	***Other Fixtures***	***Total***
2024/25	*£2,400 (6%)*	*£2,700 (18%)*	*£5,100*
2025/26	*£2,256 (6%)*	*£2,214 (18%)*	*£4,470*
2026/27	*£2,121 (6%)*	*£1,412 (14%)*	*£3,533*
2027/28	*£1,993 (6%)*	*£1,214 (14%)*	*£3,207*

Anne's writing down allowances will continue thereafter, slowly diminishing each year, for as long as she is renting out the property. Assuming she is a higher rate taxpayer and is making rental profits on her FHL, she will already have saved £6,588 by 2027/28, and will save more in the future (at 42%).

If this particular property is not yielding a rental profit, Anne can set the allowances claimed in 2024/25 against profits from any other UK FHLs she has, with any excess carried forward as a rental loss (see below). The allowances claimed in 2025/26 and later years can effectively be set against any of her taxable income (see Section 4.18).

Losses

Up to 2024/25, losses arising in an FHL business could only be carried forward for set off against future profits from the same business. For this purpose, all a landlord's UK FHLs were regarded as one business, but FHLs in the EEA were regarded as a different business. (All FHLs within the EEA were regarded as the same business.)

Losses arising in an FHL business and not yet relieved by 2024/25 will transfer and will be carried forward as normal UK or overseas rental losses as the case may be (Sections 4.18 and 4.19). This will include losses arising as a result of capital allowances claims, or interest and finance costs incurred before 6th April 2025.

Private Use and Capital Gains Tax Reliefs
Where a property qualified as an FHL, but was also used privately by the owner or their family (e.g. as a holiday home during the 'off season'), the available CGT reliefs were restricted accordingly. As we will see below, this remains relevant in a few cases.

Private use at any time during the seller or transferor's ownership led to a restriction in rollover relief on replacement of the property, or holdover relief on a gift. In the case of BADR, however, it is only private use in the last two years of the FHL business that leads to a restriction.

Business Asset Disposal Relief (BADR)
As explained in Section 9.24, BADR is available when a qualifying business, or part of a qualifying business, is sold; or when assets used in a qualifying business are sold within three years of that business's cessation. As also explained in Section 9.24, a part of a qualifying business must be capable of being run as a going concern in its own right in order to qualify.

Up to 5th April 2025, FHLs constituted a qualifying business for the purposes of BADR, thus providing the opportunity to save up to £140,000 in CGT, or even £280,000 for a couple owning property jointly. For a detailed examination of when BADR may have been available on disposal of an FHL before 6th April 2025, see the previous edition of this guide.

Where an FHL business ceased ***before*** 6th April 2025 (i.e. before, and not as a consequence of, the abolition of the FHL tax regime), a disposal of any property formerly used in that business within three years after the cessation will qualify for BADR. Ceasing an FHL business before 6th April 2025 generally necessitated ceasing all furnished lettings of the relevant properties. Some FHL businesses may also have ceased as a consequence of not meeting the qualifying conditions in 2024/25 or earlier years: however, there is some debate over whether this alone counts as a cessation for the purposes of BADR when the owner continued to rent the property out (HMRC have made it clear they *do not* think it counts).

Example: *In March 2007, Camilla bought a cottage in Sussex. For eighteen years, she rented it out as an FHL for nine months each year and occupied it herself as a holiday home for the remaining three months. She stopped all lettings of the property after 5th January 2025 (the last day of her final booking) and then began to use the property exclusively as a holiday home. She had no other FHLs.*

Camilla sells the property, making a capital gain of £400,000. If this sale takes place by 5th January 2028, she will be entitled to BADR on £300,000 (£400,000 x 9/12). In this case, the relief is restricted by the proportion of private use during the period from 6th January 2023 to 5th January 2025: the last two years of Camilla's FHL business. If there had been no private use during this period, there would be no restriction.

If Camilla's sale takes place during 2025/26, she will pay CGT at 14% on the gain eligible for BADR, saving her £30,000. If her sale takes place between 6th April 2026 and 5th January 2028, she will pay CGT at 18% on the gain eligible for BADR, saving her £18,000. If her sale takes place after 5th January 2028, she will ***not*** *be entitled to BADR.*

As we saw in Section 5.13, Camilla may have been able to elect for her cottage to be treated as her main residence for CGT purposes (generally she would have needed to elect within two years of first occupying the property as her private residence: but see Section 5.15 for further details). If this was the case, she would be able to claim PRR to exempt some of her gain. For example, if the main residence election covered her entire period of ownership (or the entire period apart from her last nine months of ownership), and she sells the property in March 2027 (twenty years after her purchase), her PRR would be:

£400,000 x 18/20 x 3/12 =	£90,000
£400,000 x 2/20 =	£40,000
Total	£130,000

The remaining gain of £270,000 would then be eligible for BADR. Assuming her annual exemption of £3,000 is available, this would leave her with a CGT bill of £48,060 (£267,000 x 18%). That compares with a CGT bill of up to £95,280 (£397,000 x 24%) for a sale after 5th January 2028 with no main residence election.

Holdover Relief

A gift, or sale at below market value, of an FHL before 6th April 2025 was eligible for holdover relief, meaning that an immediate CGT charge could either be avoided (on a gift, or a sale for a price not exceeding the transferor's base cost) or effectively fixed at a lower, more acceptable level (on a sale for a price exceeding the transferor's base cost but less than market value). This is no longer possible for gifts or sales after 5th April 2025, but claims may still be possible in respect of earlier transfers.

As discussed above, holdover relief may continue to be available on transfers of a substantial FHL business to a company after 5th April 2025.

Holdover relief on the transfer of property into a trust (Section 9.19) is also unaffected by the abolition of the FHL tax regime.

Rollover Relief

Prior to 6th April 2025, FHLs were qualifying assets for the purposes of rollover relief on replacement of business assets (Section 9.26). Where an FHL was sold before 6th April 2025, the gain arising can still be rolled over into the purchase of qualifying trading premises within three years after the date of sale.

Gains rolled over on the purchase of an FHL before 6th April 2025 did not become taxable when the FHL regime was abolished, but will be deducted from the property's base cost on a future sale.

Pension Contributions

FHL profits ceased to be qualifying earnings for the purposes of pension contributions after 5th April 2025. FHL owners may wish to check whether their FHL profits (and other qualifying earnings) for 2024/25 were sufficient to cover any gross pension contributions in excess of £3,600 that they made. If such earnings are insufficient, one possible solution may be to consider a capital allowances disclaimer (Section 4.13). It remains important to 'pool' the relevant expenditure (Section 4.11).

Business Premises

The reliefs described above extended to any property used in an FHL business before 6th April 2025. This included not only the holiday accommodation itself, but also any office premises from which the business was run.

From 6th April 2025, office premises used to run an FHL business have ceased to qualify for the CGT reliefs described above (subject to the same provisos as the FHL properties themselves). Interest and finance costs relating to such properties are also now subject to the Section 24 restrictions (Section 4.7). Capital allowances continue to be available on these business premises in the same way as other commercial property (Sections 4.10 to 4.14).

9.24 BUSINESS ASSET DISPOSAL RELIEF

Business asset disposal relief (BADR) provides a reduced CGT rate. This reduced rate is 14% for 2025/26, rising to 18% from 6th April 2026. The rate was 10% prior to 6th April 2025. Gains on which BADR is claimed use up the individual's basic rate tax band first, in priority to other gains.

Sadly, BADR is not generally available to property investors, except in the case of some former FHLs, as detailed in Section 9.23, or individuals who own the trading premises used by their company or partnership (see Section 9.25).

Broadly speaking, BADR is available on the disposal of:

i) The whole or part of a trading business
ii) Assets previously used in a trading business that has ceased
iii) Shares or securities in a personal company (see Section 9.25)
iv) Property or other assets held personally and used in a qualifying business carried on by the owner's personal company, or a partnership in which they are a partner

The last category is referred to as an 'associated disposal'. We will look at associated disposals in detail in Section 9.25.

A part of a business can only be counted for these purposes if it is capable of operating as a going concern in its own right, but an interest in a business, such as a partnership share, may qualify.

A disposal of assets previously used in a qualifying business must take place within three years after the business ceases.

The individual making the disposal must have owned the business for at least two years prior to its disposal or cessation.

Each individual may claim BADR on a maximum cumulative lifetime total of £1m of capital gains. This maximum applies to all claims made on gains arising after 5th April 2008 (including claims made when the relief was called entrepreneur's relief). Thereafter, the CGT rate on further business asset disposals will revert to normal rates (Section 6.2).

Where a taxpayer is claiming BADR, any capital losses arising on those disposals must be set off against capital gains on assets used in the same business. BADR is then claimed on the overall net gain.

Any other capital losses set off against gains subject to BADR are set off after the relief has been claimed, meaning relief for those losses is effectively given at a lower rate and more of the taxpayer's lifetime maximum will have been used. Now that the lifetime limit is only £1m, this is an important point to bear in mind.

However, BADR is not mandatory and taxpayers may choose whether to claim it. This avoids the need to waste any of the cumulative lifetime maximum on gains that would mostly be covered by capital losses (Section 5.23), the annual exemption, or, for gains arising after 5th April 2026, the basic rate band (there will be no saving after 5th April 2026).

Planning with Business Asset Disposal Relief

The £1m cumulative lifetime limit for BADR applies on a per person basis. Hence, it may be possible to obtain additional relief on qualifying business assets by putting them into joint ownership with another individual. Since most assets that qualify for BADR will also qualify for holdover relief (see Section 5.7), this can usually be done without any CGT cost. Transfers to your spouse are exempt in any case.

It is important not just to transfer the assets, but also to ensure the transferee has a qualifying stake in the business. To qualify for BADR, the individual making the disposal must have owned a share in the business for at least two years prior to cessation or sale. A pre-sale transfer of property to a spouse, partner, or other family member might result in the loss of relief if the transferee did not also own a share of the business for at least the qualifying period.

In many cases, this effectively means making the transferee a business partner and this has numerous tax and legal implications that should be considered (although some of these can be beneficial). One issue that may need to be considered is SDLT: this can be a problem where either (a) there is a mortgage over the property (see Section 6.6); or (b) the transferee is not your spouse or another close relative *and* the partnership business is property development or property trading (see Section 9.33).

See Section 9.25 for additional points that need to be considered where the ultimate disposal of the property will be an associated disposal.

Turning Investment Property into Qualifying Property
Associated disposals (see Section 9.25) are subject to a number of restrictions, but there are no similar restrictions on other BADR claims and a property used in the owner's own qualifying business will be eligible for full relief as long as it was used in that business immediately prior to the disposal or cessation of the business.

Example: *Abdul is a higher rate taxpayer. In 1992, he bought a shop as an investment property for £75,000. It is now worth £475,000 and he would like to sell it. Before selling the property, Abdul adopts it as his own trading premises for just over two years. He then ceases trading and sells the property in 2028, making a gain of £400,000.*

Because Abdul used the property in his own trade, he is entitled to business asset disposal relief, reducing the CGT due on his sale from £96,000 (24%) to £72,000 (18%). He still gets the relief despite the fact the entire gain arose before he adopted the property as his trading premises!

Abdul would need to use the property in his own qualifying trade: e.g. as a shop with him as sole proprietor. Using it as the office for his investment business will not suffice. He can, however, employ a manager to run the shop for him if he wishes.

Anti-Forestalling Rule: Unconditional Contracts
As we saw in Section 6.4, capital gains are generally deemed to arise on the date of unconditional contract for CGT purposes. However, while that general rule continues for most other purposes, for the purposes of BADR, any attempt to artificially beat the increase in the applicable CGT rate on 6th April 2025 or 6th April 2026 by using unconditional contracts in anything other than an arms' length, commercial transaction will be thwarted by anti-forestalling rules with the result that the new, higher rate will apply.

Hence, if planning a sale or transfer in anything but a commercial, arms' length deal, it is important to *complete* the contract before 6th April 2026.

9.25 BUSINESS PREMISES OWNERS

Individuals who own the business premises of their own trading business are entitled to a number of reliefs not available to other property investors. Generally speaking, these benefits apply to sole traders, partners in a trading business, and trading company owners, and include BADR (Section 9.24), rollover relief (Section 9.26), and holdover relief (Section 5.7).

For sole traders, the position is relatively simple, but for business partners and trading company owners, who own their partnership or company's trading premises personally, there are a number of issues to be taken into account.

Firstly, if anything less than full market rent is charged, this will be a non-commercial letting, subject to the restrictions on capital allowances and loss relief detailed in Section 4.20.

On the other hand, where rent *is* charged, this may lead to a restriction in the BADR available on the sale of the property. Hence, there is an effective trade-off between BADR and other potential reliefs.

Associated Disposals

BADR may extend to property owned personally but used in the trade of a personal company (see below), or a partnership in which the owner is a partner. Such a disposal is referred to as an associated disposal. The relief is only available where the owner is also disposing of an interest in the company or partnership. The interest being disposed of must generally be either at least a 5% share, or their entire remaining share out of an earlier share of at least 5%.

The property must have been owned for at least three years at the date of disposal; and must also have been used in the company or partnership's business for at least two years immediately prior to the sale of the company or partnership share or, if earlier, cessation of the business. In the latter case, the disposal must take place within three years after cessation.

Relief is restricted where any payment has been received for the use of the property after 5th April 2008. Where the property was acquired after that date and a full market rent received throughout the period of use in the company or partnership trade, no relief will be available. Where the property was acquired earlier, or rent was charged at a lower rate, there will be a partial restriction in relief.

The BADR available on an associated disposal is also restricted to reflect any periods when the asset was not being used in a qualifying business carried on by the company or partnership.

Personal Companies

The definition of personal company for BADR purposes is broadly:

i) The individual holds at least 5% of the ordinary share capital
ii) The holding under (i) provides at least 5% of the voting rights
iii) The company is a trading company (see below)
iv) The individual is an officer or employee of the company (an officer includes a director or company secretary)
v) The individual must either:
   a) Have at least a 5% interest in both the distributable profits and net assets of the company by virtue of their holding under (i), or
   b) Be entitled to at least 5% of the sale proceeds arising on a disposal of the company's entire ordinary share capital

Each of these rules must be satisfied for at least two years immediately prior to the disposal in question or, where the company has ceased trading, for at least two years immediately prior to the cessation.

A company is a trading company provided any non-trading activities are not substantial. HMRC generally accepts this test is met where neither non-trading income nor non-trading assets exceed 20% of the totals for the company as a whole. However, this test is only a yardstick and is not conclusive.

In a recent tax case, it was held that non-trading activities would only be regarded as substantial where they were of material or real importance in the context of the company's activities as a whole.

Planning Implications for Business Premises Owners

If looking to secure additional BADR by putting the business premises of your trading company into joint names with another individual (e.g. your spouse), it is important that the company will qualify as the transferee's personal company (as defined above) in their own right. This means they must be an officer or employee of the company *and* own at least 5% of the share capital for at least two years. They will also need to own their share of the property for at least three years.

In the case of your partnership's trading premises, the transferee will need to be a partner for at least two years and, if the property is jointly owned personally by you and the transferee, they will need to own their share of the property for at least three years. (Note: it is possible to either hold partnership property personally, ***or*** for the property to be owned by the partnership, even when the owners/partners are the same people: see Section 9.33 for further details.)

See also Section 9.24 for further points to be considered re CGT and SDLT on business property transfers. The whole thing is quite complex, so do take professional advice.

Should You Charge Rent?

As explained above, there is effectively a trade-off between charging your trading company or partnership a market rent for business premises you own personally, and thus qualifying for capital allowances and loss relief; or not charging rent, and thus qualifying for BADR on an associated disposal. This complex area of tax planning is covered in detail in the Taxcafe guide *Putting it Through the Company*, but it is worth me making a few general points here:

- The maximum saving produced by BADR will be just £60,000 per person from 6th April 2026
- Some or all of this potential saving will be used on the disposal of your company shares, or partnership share
- There is no guarantee that an associated disposal of the property will happen
- You need to charge rent to obtain tax relief for mortgage interest and any other property costs you incur personally
- Capital allowances will generally produce Income Tax savings at 42% or 47%, and even up to 63%, from 2027/28 onwards
- Rent is a very tax-efficient form of profit extraction for company owners

So, while each case needs to be examined on its own merits, the odds are heavily in favour of charging a market rent.

9.26 ROLLOVER RELIEF

The capital gain arising on the sale of a property used in your own trading business may be rolled over into the purchase of a new trading property within the period beginning one year before, and ending three years after, the disposal of the original property. This defers any CGT liability on the original property until such time as the new property is sold. FHLs were treated as trading property for these purposes until 5th April 2025.

Full relief is available only if the old property was used exclusively for trading purposes throughout your ownership. It is the sale ***proceeds*** that must be reinvested, not just the capital gain. Any shortfall in the amount reinvested is deducted from the amount of gain eligible for rollover.

If there is less than full trading use of the property then an appropriate proportion of the gain arising may be rolled over.

Example: *Stavros sells an office building in March 2027 for £600,000, realising a capital gain of £240,000. He has owned the building since March 2017 and, until March 2022 he rented all of it out. From March 2022 until the date of sale he used two thirds of the building as his own premises from which he ran a property development business.*

Stavros is eligible to roll over £80,000 (£240,000 x 5/10 x 2/3) of his capital gain into the purchase of new trading premises. The eligible amount is restricted by reference to both the proportion used for trading purposes and the time for which it was so used.

In August 2028, Stavros buys a gift shop in Cornwall for £180,000 and begins using it as his trading premises. He can claim rollover relief of £60,000. He cannot claim the full £80,000 that was eligible, because he has only reinvested £180,000 out of the £200,000 qualifying proportion of his sale proceeds (£600,000 x 5/10 x 2/3 = £200,000). The amount reinvested fell £20,000 short, so £20,000 must be deducted from the amount eligible for rollover.

The new property does not need to be in the same trade or even the same kind of trade. For purchases before 6th April 2025, it could even be an FHL.

There is no minimum period for which the new property must be used for trading purposes, although it must be acquired with the intention of using it for trading purposes. In our example, Stavros could run the gift shop for, say, two years then convert it into residential property. His CGT rollover relief would not be clawed back, although he would have a reduced base cost for the property when he eventually came to sell it.

> **Tax Tip**
> Where you have a capital gain eligible for rollover relief, it is only necessary to use the replacement property for trading purposes for a limited period. This might include initially running the new property as a guest house before later converting to long-term letting or even adopting it as your home.

Rollover relief is not generally available to property investors, except as noted in Sections 9.23 and 9.25. A property where the landlord provides significant additional services, akin to a guest house, may also qualify. Gains on other rental properties will only be eligible for rollover relief in a few limited circumstances, such as a compulsory purchase of commercial property, or property purchased by a tenant under the Leasehold Reform Act 1967.

9.27 PART DISPOSALS

A part disposal of property can occur for a number of reasons, many of which we have seen elsewhere in this guide, including when:

- A property is physically divided into two or more new properties and one or more of these is disposed of (Section 9.14)
- Part of the garden or grounds of a property is sold off (Sections 9.15 and 9.16)
- A lease of two years or more is granted at a premium (Section 9.28)
- Insurance proceeds are not used to rectify the damage or loss that was the subject of the claim (Section 3.12)
- A dilapidation payment is treated as a capital receipt (Section 4.21)
- Compensation payments are received, e.g. due to a loss of access or a right to light claim (Section 4.21)
- Deposits are retained where a property sale is not completed

Special rules apply to premiums received for granting a lease of between two and fifty years' duration: we will return to these in Section 9.28.

In other cases, the proceeds of a part disposal become sale proceeds for CGT purposes (unless the property is trading stock, as discussed in Chapter 2, in which case the proceeds are trading income). The base cost to be used in the CGT calculation is based on the proportionate value of the proceeds of the part disposal compared with the value of the property retained and is derived using the formula: **A/(A+B)**

A is the proceeds of the part disposal. For the purposes of applying the formula, this is the total proceeds before deducting any incidental costs, rather than the net proceeds.

B is the market value of the property, or part of the property retained (where a physical disposal has occurred), after the part disposal.

On the grant of a lease, **B** is the market value of the superior interest retained by the grantor (the freehold or longer leasehold). This is termed the reversionary interest and its value is much less than the market value of the property itself because the property is now subject to the lease.

Example: *Llewellyn owns the freehold of a commercial property in Cardiff with a base cost of £600,000. He grants a 60-year lease to Brian, a businessman from Belfast moving into the area. Brian pays a premium of £900,000 for the lease. Llewellyn incurs legal fees and other incidental costs of £12,500 on the transaction. Although Llewellyn's net proceeds are £887,500, the amount for 'A' in the part disposal formula is £900,000.*

The value of Llewellyn's reversionary interest is established as £100,000. This is the amount for 'B' in the part disposal formula, making 'A + B' equal to £1m in this case. The base cost Llewellyn is able to deduct is therefore: £600,000 x £900,000/£1m = £540,000. This gives him a capital gain of £347,500 (£887,500 – £540,000).

Only the remaining, unused part of the base cost (£60,000 in Llewellyn's case) will be available to deduct from the proceeds on any future disposal.

The treatment of lease premiums is supported by legislation and is beyond dispute. In Section 4.21, however, we discussed the conflicting views over the treatment of dilapidation payments received where a property is damaged by a tenant but is not repaired (or not fully repaired). To illustrate the potential difference in the property owner's tax liability, let's look at an example.

Example: *Charles is a higher rate taxpayer with taxable income of £80,000. In 2026/27, he receives a dilapidation payment of £50,000 from a former tenant who damaged one of his rental properties. He decides not to repair the damage, as it relates to an old part of the building that is rarely used, and continues to rent the property out as it is. The base cost of the property is £240,000 and its market value in its current state is £350,000.*

If we follow HMRC's view and treat the dilapidation payment as rental income, it will give rise to additional Income Tax as follows (see Section 3.10 for the marginal tax rates used here and below):

£20,000 x 40%	*£8,000*
£25,140 x 60%	*£15,084*
£4,860 x 45%	*£2,187*
Total	*£25,271*

Alternatively, if we treat this as a part disposal (as argued by many experts), Charles will be able to deduct part of his base cost, as follows: £240,000 x £50,000/(£50,000 + £350,000) = £30,000. His capital gain is thus only £20,000 (£50,000 – £30,000). Deducting his annual exemption of £3,000 leaves a taxable gain of just £17,000 and a CGT bill of £4,080 (at 24%). Treating the payment as a part disposal will save Charles over £20,000!

If the dilapidation payment were received in 2027/28 and taxed as income, Charles would suffer Income Tax of £26,522, meaning arguing for part disposal treatment would save him almost £22,500.

9.28 LEASE PREMIUMS

Granting a lease for two years or more at a premium is a capital disposal chargeable to CGT, and is dealt with under the part disposal rules we looked at in Section 9.27. However, where the duration of the lease is no more than 50 years, part of the premium will be taxable as income. The part treated as capital disposal proceeds is then restricted to 2% of the premium for each complete year of the lease in excess of one year.

Example: *Alexandra owns the freehold to a property and grants a 12-year lease to Kenneth for a premium of £60,000. The lease exceeds one year by eleven years and hence 22% of this sum (£13,200) falls within the CGT regime. Alexandra is subject to Income Tax on £46,800 (£60,000 less 22%).*

Alexandra's base cost in the property is £250,000 and the value of her reversionary interest is established as £386,800.

Following the part disposal formula in Section 9.27, she is able to deduct a base cost of: £250,000 x £13,200/(£13,200 + £386,800) = £8,250. This gives her a chargeable gain of £4,950 (£13,200 – £8,250) in addition to her deemed rental income of £46,800 (less any incidental costs incurred on the transaction).

The remaining £241,750 of Alexandra's base cost is available to deduct against any future disposal proceeds.

In effect, as the example demonstrates, granting a lease at a premium is a good way to get an advance deduction for part of a property's base cost.

For those with rental losses brought forward, granting a short lease at a premium could be a good way to utilise those losses. Furthermore, for those who also have interest and finance costs on residential rental property, it may prevent those losses being converted into unrelieved interest, as we saw in Section 4.18.

If the tenant is running a business from the property (including sub-letting it as a landlord in their own right), the element of the premium taxed as income in the hands of the grantor is allowable as a deduction in the tenant's business.

The tenant must, however, claim the allowable element of the premium over the life of the lease. In Kenneth's case, he would be able to claim a deduction of £3,900 each year (£46,800/12 = £3,900). This deduction is not allowed where the tenant is using the cash basis.

Assigning a Lease

Assigning a lease with no less than 50 years' duration remaining is a straightforward capital disposal. The capital gain arising is calculated in more or less the same way as for a freehold property sale. Any applicable reliefs may be claimed in the usual way.

Leases with less than 50 years remaining are treated as wasting assets. When a leaseholder assigns such a lease, this is again a capital disposal, but they are required to reduce their base cost in accordance with the schedule at: *www.taxcafe.co.uk/shortleases.pdf*

For example, for a lease with 20 years remaining, and which had more than 50 years remaining when first acquired, the base cost must be reduced to 72.77% of the original premium paid for the lease (plus other applicable purchase costs).

Where the lease had less than 50 years remaining when originally acquired, the necessary reduction in base cost is achieved by multiplying the original cost by the factor applying at the time of sale and dividing by the factor applying at the time of purchase.

Furthermore, that original base cost (before reduction) also depends on whether the lease was originally assigned by the previous tenant, or granted by the freeholder (or holder of a superior leasehold interest). We'll look at each of these situations in turn.

Example: *Claudia pays a premium of £100,000 for the assignment of a lease with ten years remaining. Five years later, she assigns the lease to Nero at a premium of £60,000. When calculating her capital gain, the amount Claudia can claim as her base cost is: £100,000 x 26.722/46.695 = £57,227.*

Example Revisited: *Let's now assume the premium of £100,000 Claudia paid was for the grant of a ten-year lease, rather than an assignment by an existing tenant. This means Claudia's base cost is only £18,000 (18% or 9 x 2%) and the amount she can claim when calculating her capital gain is only: £18,000 x 26.722/46.695 = £10,301.*

Assuming Claudia was using the property in a qualifying business, she will have been able to claim £8,200 each year as a deduction against her taxable income in respect of the remaining 82% of the original premium. However, of the £100,000 Claudia paid for the lease, she will only have received relief for £51,301 (£10,301 as a deductible base cost and £41,000 in Income Tax deductions over five years).

In both versions of the example, we can see the leaseholder only obtained tax relief for a little over half of their original cost. Paying a premium for a short lease or a lease that will become short or expire before you dispose of it, can lead to significant amounts of unrelieved expenditure. Where possible, it may therefore make sense to pay a higher level of rent rather than a premium. This may also lead to SDLT savings (see Section 6.8).

On the other hand, as we have already seen, charging a lease premium can be advantageous for a grantor. Furthermore, from an assignor's point of view, it may be the only way to get some of their money back!

Short Leases and the Structures and Buildings Allowance (SBA)
Where the base cost is reduced on assignment of a lease with less than 50 years remaining, any SBA claim that must be added to sale proceeds (see Section 4.14) is also reduced in the same proportion.

9.29 THE BENEFITS AND PITFALLS OF RE-MORTGAGING

When a property has risen in value, you can realise the 'profit' by re-mortgaging and thus obtain the cash value of your equity. When you re-mortgage a property, you have not actually made a disposal. Hence, you cannot be charged CGT.

Where the funds generated by re-mortgaging are used to purchase investment properties, the interest on the new borrowings can be claimed against the income from the new properties. This applies even if the re-mortgaged property is the borrower's own home. The interest relief remains available as long as the funds are invested for business purposes. However, it is important to remember Income Tax relief for interest paid by residential landlords is now at basic rate only (Section 4.7).

Sometimes the borrower will re-mortgage a property for other reasons: perhaps simply to provide living expenses. While this will still produce the CGT benefit described above, only interest on borrowings against a rental property up to the value of the property when first rented out (plus other capital invested in the business) will be eligible for Income Tax relief under these circumstances (see Section 4.5 for further details). See also Section 4.22 for further restrictions applying under the cash basis.

Where, or to the extent that, interest relief is available, relief is also available for the costs associated with re-mortgaging, including loan arrangement fees and relevant professional costs (see Section 4.6): although the relief may have to be spread over a number of years and, for residential landlords, will again be at basic rate only.

When re-mortgaging, it is important to remember the mortgage balance will not be deductible for CGT purposes in the event of a sale. In effect, if your mortgage balance is too high, you may need to fund some of your CGT bill from other resources.

Example: *Jenny sells an investment property for £500,000. The property has an outstanding mortgage of £425,000 and a base cost of £150,000. Jenny's net proceeds after repaying the mortgage are only £75,000, but her CGT bill could be up to £84,000 (her £350,000 gain at 24%).*

See also Section 6.6 regarding the impact of mortgages for SDLT purposes on a property transfer.

9.30 USING YOUR BASIC RATE BAND TO SAVE CGT

The rate of CGT applying to most gains depends on the level of your taxable income. Savings may be achieved by ensuring capital gains fall into a tax year in which you have a lower level of income. The savings are generated by the difference between the rate of CGT applying to gains falling into your basic rate band and the rate applying once the basic rate band has been exhausted (see Section 5.2).

Applying this difference to the whole basic rate band of £37,700 creates the maximum potential saving of £2,262 at current CGT rates.

To utilise your basic rate band, you may need to defer disposals until a tax year in which your taxable income has reduced. One way to do this, where you are in employment or self-employment, is to wait until you retire.

Example: *Edwina has an investment property that will yield a capital gain of £60,000 when she sells it. She has a salary of £40,000 but is due to retire in March 2027. She is also currently making a rental profit of £1,000 per month.*

If Edwina was to sell her property before 6th April 2027, she would be subject to CGT at 24% on a gain of £57,000 (£60,000 less her annual exemption of £3,000), giving her a bill of £13,680. On the other hand, if she delays her sale until after 5th April 2027 (remember, the date of sale for CGT purposes is the date on which there is an unconditional sales contract: see Section 5.4), she will pay CGT at 18% on £37,700 of her gain, reducing her CGT bill to £11,418.

I have assumed Edwina's total income for 2027/28 will be less than her personal allowance. This may be the case when an individual retires if they have no pension provision beyond the state pension, or if they defer their pension entitlement. Even if Edwina had enough pension or investment income to use up part of her basic rate band, she might still make a saving by waiting until she retires to sell her property.

Whether it is worth deferring a property sale for the sake of such a modest saving is perhaps questionable, however. Furthermore, in addition to the commercial risks involved in a delay, there is also the possibility that Edwina's taxable income for 2027/28 may be higher than she expects.

These points aside, the example also demonstrates the fact that selling an investment property early in a tax year means there is less income from that property to use up your basic rate band, thus potentially producing a CGT saving.

There are many other situations where property investors may be able to reduce their CGT liability by selling property in a tax year in which their taxable income is at a lower level. Examples include:

- Landlords undertaking major refurbishment projects that qualify as repairs expenditure (see Section 4.8)
- Self-employed taxpayers or commercial property owners making large capital allowances claims
- Employed taxpayers on career breaks
- Company owners who are able to refrain from taking income out of their company that year
- Investors reducing their taxable income by making tax-advantaged investments, such as investment bonds

Remember, however, there is no guarantee that CGT rates will not be increased in the future: another critical risk to any delay!

Extending the Basic Rate Band

The basic rate band can be extended through the payment of pension contributions or gift aid donations. While it is generally more beneficial to use this as a means to save Income Tax, it can also be used to save CGT. Furthermore, where a property owner is unlikely to ever have taxable income in excess of the higher rate tax threshold, this may be their best opportunity to make tax savings through these payments.

Example Revisited: *In Section 5.2, we met Boudica who had a taxable gain of £38,000. She had taxable income of £35,270 for 2026/27, leaving £15,000 of her basic rate band available, which reduced her CGT bill to £8,220.*

Let us now assume Boudica makes a net pension contribution of £16,000 in March 2027. This is grossed up for basic rate tax relief given at source and treated as a gross contribution of £20,000, extending Boudica's basic rate band and giving her a higher rate tax threshold of £70,270 (£50,270 + £20,000). This means there is now £35,000 (£70,270 – £35,270) of Boudica's basic rate band available and her CGT calculation will be:

£35,000 x 18% *£6,300*
£3,000 x 24% *£720*
Total *£7,020*

As we can see, Boudica's pension contribution has saved her £1,200 in CGT. Combining this with the tax relief of £4,000 given at source gives her a total benefit of £5,200: increasing the value of her net pension contribution by 32.5%.

However, to obtain tax relief on a gross pension contribution of £20,000, Boudica would need qualifying earnings of at least this amount: namely employment income, or self-employment or partnership trading income.

Without qualifying earnings, the maximum gross pension contribution that will obtain tax relief is £3,600 (or £2,880 net). Those with earnings of more than £3,600 can generally obtain tax relief for gross contributions up to the lower of £60,000 or their total earnings for the year. See the Taxcafe guide *Pension Magic* for further details.

9.31 AVOIDING THE CHILD BENEFIT CHARGE

Many parents are suffering the draconian CBC on income between £60,000 and £80,000. This creates the truly horrendous marginal tax rates set out in the table in Section 3.3. Some property investor couples may, however, be able to avoid the CBC by redistributing their income.

Example: *Cherilyn and Salvatore are a married couple with a portfolio of rental properties yielding annual profits of £110,000 and no other taxable income. Cherilyn owns more properties than Salvatore, so she receives £80,000 of this profit while he only receives £30,000.*

The couple have three young children and are therefore eligible to claim £3,268 per year in child benefit (at 2026/27 rates). However, Cherilyn's profit share means she will have to repay the child benefit by way of an additional Income Tax charge.

The answer to this problem is simple. If the couple put all their properties into joint ownership, they will each have taxable income of £55,000 and hence neither of them will be subject to the CBC: thus saving £3,268 per year (at 2026/27 rates). Further annual savings of £4,054 will arise because there is an extra £20,270 (£50,270 – £30,000) of profit on which Salvatore is paying Income Tax at 20% instead of Cherilyn paying at 40%, bringing the total saving to £7,322 per year (at 2026/27 rates).

Remember, if one member of a married couple isn't comfortable with the idea of putting their properties into equal joint ownership, the method in Section 9.6 could be used and the optimum position for Income Tax purposes can often still be achieved.

As a result of the restrictions on Income Tax relief for interest paid by residential landlords, many property investor couples are likely to be caught by the CBC. The strategy set out above remains sound, but these couples need to reduce their taxable profit before interest to £60,000 per person, or less, to avoid the CBC.

Unmarried Couples
For unmarried couples, the solution may not be so simple, as a direct transfer of properties from one partner to the other, or into joint names, will generally lead to a CGT charge. This can often be avoided using the technique in Section 9.19.

Alternatively, a small share in a property could perhaps be transferred to an unmarried partner at little or no CGT cost. Once the property is held jointly, the couple's rental profit shares can be set in such a way that neither partner has taxable income over £60,000. See Section 9.9 for more information on this technique for optimising rental profit shares for unmarried joint owners.

Joint Income over £120,000
A couple with total joint taxable income over £120,000 may not be able to avoid the CBC altogether but, if your total joint taxable income is less than £160,000, you could still minimise the impact by equalising your income. Alternatively, you could avoid the CBC by transferring properties into a trust or company. These strategies have many further tax implications and require professional advice.

9.32 GETTING EXTRA TAX RELIEF FOR RENT ARREARS

The question with rent arrears is whether these will eventually be paid late, or not at all. Under traditional accruals basis accounting, the rent arrears remain part of the landlord's *receivable* income and, in principle, continue to be taxable: although the landlord can claim a bad debt expense in respect of the arrears when they are able to make a reasonable judgement that they are not likely to be paid (see Section 4.15).

Under the cash basis, of course, the landlord is only taxed on rent actually received, meaning tax relief for bad debts is automatic and rent paid late is only taxed when the cash actually comes in. From a cashflow perspective, therefore, the cash basis will probably be beneficial when the landlord has significant rent arrears.

Example, Part 1: *Belinda has a portfolio of residential rental properties producing total annual rent receivable of £80,000. At 5th April 2026, all her tenants were up to date with their rent.*

During 2026/27, several of her tenants run into financial difficulties. At 5th April 2027, Belinda has rent arrears totalling £30,000. In other words, the rent she actually received during 2026/27 was just £50,000. If she uses the cash basis, she will obviously only pay tax on this amount (subject to any adjustments required, as explained in Section 4.22).

By the time Belinda prepares her 2026/27 accounts and tax return, the position with the arrears outstanding at 5th April 2027 is as follows:

Received	*£16,000*
Arrangements in hand for payment to be made over an agreed period	*£10,000*
Tenant made redundant and unable to pay	*£4,000*

If Belinda uses traditional accruals basis accounting, she will have to include the £16,000 of arrears that have now been received in her taxable income for 2026/27. However, she may claim a bad debt expense for the £4,000 she is now unlikely to receive.

The £10,000 being paid over an agreed period is the most difficult part to assess under the accruals basis. Belinda will need to make a reasonable judgement regarding how much of this sum is likely to be recovered and include those recoverable elements within her taxable income for 2026/27. Depending on the circumstances, she is likely to have to include somewhere between 50% and 90% of this income.

In summary, under the cash basis, Belinda will be taxed on rent received of £50,000. Under traditional accruals basis accounting, she will be taxed on rent receivable of somewhere between £71,000 and £75,000. In other words, the cash basis will defer between £21,000 and £25,000 of Belinda's taxable income into a later tax year.

Assuming Belinda is a typical higher rate taxpayer, using the cash basis will give her a tax saving of between £8,400 and £10,000 for 2026/27. In cashflow terms this is obviously extremely beneficial. The only question is: will she have a significantly higher marginal tax rate when this timing difference reverses in later years?

She probably will have a higher marginal tax rate, of course. If she remains a typical higher rate taxpayer, her marginal tax rate on her rental profits will increase to 42% from 2027/28 onwards. But, if this is the only increase, the ultimate additional overall tax cost will be just 2% of the taxable income deferred (or between £420 and £500) and Belinda may feel this is worthwhile in view of the significant cashflow advantage.

If her annual taxable income rises above £100,000, however, and her marginal tax rate increases to 47% or 63% (Section 3.10), the ultimate overall tax cost will be significantly more, and that is a risk Belinda will need to consider.

Nonetheless, the impact of the reversal in Belinda's timing difference can be mitigated and possibly reduced if she reverts to traditional accruals basis accounting for 2027/28. As explained in Section 4.22, where adjustment income arises on leaving the cash basis, this can be spread over six years.

Furthermore, adjustment income can be accelerated into any of those years (except the last) when the landlord has a lower marginal tax rate.

Example, Part 2: *Belinda uses the cash basis for 2026/27 but reverts to traditional accruals basis accounting for 2027/28. She must now assess how much of the rent arrears outstanding at 5th April 2027 she would have needed to include in her 2026/27 accounts if she had used the accruals basis. Obviously, this will include the £16,000 she had actually received by the time she was preparing her 2026/27 accounts. Let's now assume it would also include £8,000 of the amounts being paid up in instalments.*

Hence, Belinda has adjustment income of £24,000 on leaving the cash basis (for the sake of illustration, we will assume there are no other adjustments required). In the first instance, this adjustment income will be taxed over six years.

This is done by adding an additional £4,000 (£24,000/6) to her taxable income each year from 2027/28 to 2032/33.

In 2028/29, Belinda undertakes a major refurbishment programme on her properties and, as most of her expenditure is tax deductible (Section 4.8), her taxable income (before adding adjustment income) is reduced to £36,270 (she is normally a higher rate taxpayer). She therefore elects to accelerate an additional £10,000 of adjustment income into 2028/29, bringing her total taxable income up to the higher rate tax threshold of £50,270 (£36,270 + £4,000 + £10,000).

This leaves her with £6,000 of adjustment income remaining (£24,000 less £4,000 taxed in 2027/28 and £14,000 taxed in 2028/29). This is now spread over the remaining four years of her original spreading period. Hence £1,500 (£6,000/4) will be added to her taxable income each year from 2029/30 to 2032/33 (although she could elect to accelerate some of it again if a suitable occasion arises once more).

Assuming Belinda is a higher rate taxpayer in every other tax year, accelerating an additional £10,000 of adjustment income into 2028/29 will have saved her an extra £2,000 in Income Tax (being taxed at 22% instead of 42%).

9.33 PARTNERSHIP PROBLEMS AND OPPORTUNITIES

Some of the legal background to property partnerships was covered in Section 2.9. Most of the rules outlined throughout this guide apply equally to partnerships, including individuals who are members of corporate or limited partnerships.

In many ways, a property partnership simply combines joint ownership with a more sophisticated profit-sharing agreement. However, a partnership is considerably more flexible as, subject to the terms of the partnership agreement, partners may join, leave, or change their profit share, at any time.

Each partner is generally taxed on his or her share of rental income, trading profits, or capital gains, as allocated according to the partnership agreement. [Under certain circumstances, profits attributed to a partner not subject to UK Income Tax (typically a company) may be allocated to individual members of the partnership for tax purposes, but this is rare.]

There are restrictions on non-active partners claiming relief for their share of partnership trading losses. Broadly speaking, a partner is classed as non-active if they spend an average of less than ten hours per week engaged in the partnership's trading activities. See the Taxcafe guide *Small Business Tax Saving Tactics* for further details.

A partner's share of partnership rental losses can only be set against their share of future rental profits from the same partnership.

Interest Relief

Partnerships investing in residential rental property are subject to the same restrictions on relief for interest and finance costs as individuals. A partner who borrows funds to invest in the partnership is entitled to tax relief for interest on those borrowings, but this is subject to the restrictions in Section 4.7 (to the extent the partnership is investing in residential rental property) and the tax relief cap covered in Section 3.19. Relief is not permitted on borrowings to invest in a partnership using the cash basis for landlords (Section 4.22), except funds borrowed to purchase a partnership share. See also Section 9.34 regarding LLPs.

Treatment of Partnership Property

For both CGT and SDLT, each partner is effectively treated as if they individually own a share of the partnership properties. This means tax may be charged whenever a partner introduces property into a partnership; takes property out; or changes their share in the partnership properties. Additional SDLT may be charged where a partner withdraws capital from a partnership within three years of introducing property.

For CGT purposes, a partner's share in partnership properties is determined according to the first item on this list the partners have entered into:

i) An agreement as to how capital assets are allocated
ii) An agreement as to how capital profits are shared
iii) An agreement as to how income profits are shared

If there is no agreement falling under any of (i) to (iii) above, the partners' shares are deemed to be equal. By having a fixed agreement as to how capital assets or capital profits are allocated, partners can change their income profit shares without giving rise to any CGT. Sadly, the same cannot be said for SDLT.

Stamp Duty Land Tax

For SDLT purposes, a partner's share in partnership properties is based on their share of income profits. Furthermore, the deemed consideration for SDLT on transactions between business partners and the partnership is based on market value. This makes any changes in profit shares a potentially costly exercise (but see below for family partnerships).

Example: *Dave is in a property investment partnership with Dozy, Beaky, Mick, and Tich. Each partner has a 20% profit share. Dave would like to retire and leave the partnership. As consideration for giving up his partnership share, Dave takes Dee Towers, an office building worth £1m, with him.*

Dave already had a 20% share in Dee Towers through the partnership, so he is treated as acquiring an 80% share, worth £800,000, when he leaves. He will therefore face a SDLT charge of £29,500 (see Section 6.5).

As a result of Dave's departure, each of the continuing partners increases their profit share from 20% to 25%. After Dee Towers is transferred to Dave, the partnership is left with a commercial property portfolio with a total gross value of £15m and borrowings of £11m. While the partnership's net assets are only £4m, each of the continuing partners is treated as having acquired an additional 5% interest in property worth £15m. Worse still, as these are linked transactions (Section 6.7) the SDLT arising is calculated on a total value of £3m (£15m x 5% x 4) and amounts to £139,500 (see Section 6.5), giving Dozy, Beaky, Mick, and Tich a charge of £34,875 each!

The transfer of one property worth £1m has given rise to SDLT charges totalling £169,000 (£29,500 + £139,500), or 16.9% of the property's value.

If the continuing partners had paid Dave in cash instead, he would have had no SDLT to pay, but they would each have acquired a 5% interest in commercial property worth a total of £16m, giving rise to SDLT based on deemed consideration of £3.2m (£16m x 5% x 4), resulting in a total charge of £149,500, or £37,375 each. The cash route is better overall, but we're still looking at a charge equal to almost 15% of the actual transaction value.

By and large, anyone using a property investment partnership should try to get their profit shares right in the first place and do their utmost to avoid changing them later. If you and your colleagues are likely to change profit shares, a company may be a better route (see further below).

It is striking that neither the net asset value of the partnership, nor the amount actually paid to purchase a partner's profit share, has any bearing on the SDLT payable. This is based on the gross value of the partnership's property portfolio. Note, a straightforward cash investment into the partnership will not incur any SDLT if there is no change in profit shares.

The SDLT rules for partnerships apply not only to property held by the partnership, but also property held by one or more partners for the purposes of the partnership business.

Family Partnerships

The proportion of the property deemed to be transferred for SDLT purposes is reduced not only by the partnership share held by the transferor, but also by any partnership shares held by connected persons, such as spouses and other close relatives (as per Appendix B, but with heading (vi) disregarded).

Hence, the SDLT charges on changes of profit share, or on introduction of property into a partnership, will be far less, and possibly nil, in the case of a family partnership. A married couple, or parents and their adult children, in partnership together, for instance, will face no such SDLT charges (assuming there are no other, unconnected partners).

Example Revisited: *Taking the same facts as before, let's now assume Dave, Dozy, and Beaky are brothers (Mick and Tich are cousins). Dave is now deemed to have had a 60% share in Dee Towers through the partnership, so he is only treated as acquiring a 40% share, worth £400,000, when he leaves. He will therefore face a SDLT charge of just £9,500 (see Section 6.5).*

Dozy and Beaky are each deemed to have had a 60% share of the remaining portfolio before Dave's departure, but only 50% afterwards, so they aren't treated as acquiring any profit share and have no SDLT to pay.

As before, Mick and Tich have each increased their profit share from 20% to 25%. Assuming they are not connected with each other, the SDLT arising is now calculated on a total value of £1.5m (£15m x 5% x 2), and amounts to £64,500 (see Section 6.5), giving Mick and Tich a charge of £32,550 each. What can I say: blood is thicker than tax!

If all five partners had been brothers (or other connected persons), there would have been no SDLT to pay at all.

Profit Shares in Trading Partnerships

There is no SDLT charge on the purchase of profit share in most trading partnerships. Sadly, this relaxation does not apply to property investment, development, or dealing partnerships.

Land and Buildings Transaction Tax/Land Transaction Tax

Partnerships investing in property in Scotland or Wales will be subject to LBTT or LTT on those properties rather than SDLT. Most of the principles outlined above continue to apply, although the rates are different (see Sections 6.10 and 6.13).

Other Partnership Restrictions

The trading income allowance (Section 8.1) is not available on partnership trading income. The annual investment allowance (Section 4.11) is not available to a partnership where one or more members of the partnership is a company, and nor is the cash basis of accounting.

Partnership Benefits

Property can generally be transferred into a partnership free from both CGT and SDLT if the partnership shares in the property following the transfer match the individual partners' shares in the property prior to the transfer. Partnership shares in property for this purpose are determined under the rules outlined earlier in this section, which are different for each tax.

Furthermore, as discussed above, the proportion of a property deemed to be transferred for SDLT purposes is reduced not only by the partnership share held by the transferor, but also by partnership shares held by connected persons. The transferor must be one of the partners for this to apply.

Hence, a transfer of property into a partnership made up of yourself and your spouse or other close relatives (as per headings (ii) to (v) in Appendix B), will be completely exempt from SDLT. This could be a good way to avoid the problems described in Section 6.6 regarding property subject to an outstanding mortgage.

Property transferred into a partnership made up of yourself and your spouse will also be exempt from CGT.

Transfers of property from a partnership to a company controlled by the same individuals are usually exempt from SDLT, and may also be exempt from CGT. For further details of the tax position on both transfers into a partnership, and from a partnership to a company, see the Taxcafe guide *Using a Property Company to Save Tax*.

9.34 LIMITED LIABILITY PARTNERSHIPS

Like a Scottish partnership, an LLP is a legal person and may own property directly. The rules described in the previous section apply equally to LLPs, subject to the following additional points:

- Interest on funds borrowed to invest in, or lend to, a property investment LLP is not eligible for Income Tax relief.
- Members of an LLP whose profit share is mostly fixed without reference to the overall performance of the business may, under certain circumstances, be treated as employees for Income Tax and NI purposes.
- Where the LLP makes a trading loss, the members of the LLP cannot generally set any part of their share of that loss in excess of their capital contribution to the LLP against other income or capital gains.
- LLPs cannot use the cash basis of accounting.

9.35 EMIGRATING TO SAVE CAPITAL GAINS TAX

Emigration to save UK CGT is a strategy that is generally only worth contemplating when the stakes are high, so professional advice is essential. Furthermore, as explained in Section 2.10, non-UK residents are now liable to UK CGT on all UK property. Despite this, there are still opportunities for long-term investors to make significant CGT savings.

In this section, I will provide an overview of what is required to successfully achieve non-UK resident status for CGT purposes and the benefits arising. The main points worth noting are:

- Emigration must generally be permanent or long-term (a period that covers at least five complete UK tax years is usually required)
- Disposals should be deferred until you are non-UK resident. In most cases, you will need to wait until the next tax year after you have left the UK
- Limited return visits to the UK are permitted (see below)
- Resuming UK residence before the expiry of the required period may result in additional CGT liabilities

It is also important to avoid becoming liable for higher rates of tax elsewhere. There's no point jumping out of the frying pan into the fire!

Example: *Eleanor has been a successful property investor for decades. By April 2015, she had a UK residential property portfolio worth £12m, with total base costs of just £4m (i.e. existing gains of £8m). By April 2019, she also had a portfolio of UK commercial property worth £15m, with total base costs of £10m (i.e. existing gains of £5m). Eleanor decides to emigrate and on 3rd April 2026 flies to Utopia to start a new life. During the 2026/27 UK tax year, she sells all her UK properties.*

Her UK residential property portfolio sells for a total of £18m. As a non-UK resident, she is only liable for UK CGT on the portfolio's increase in value after 5th April 2015: £6m. Her UK commercial property portfolio sells for a total of £17.5m. As a non-UK resident, she is liable for UK CGT on the increase in value after 5th April 2019: £2.5m.

Eleanor is a higher rate taxpayer for UK tax purposes. Hence, she has a CGT bill of £2.04m (£8.5m x 24%).

Eventually, Eleanor decides to return home and, in May 2031, she comes back to the UK to live. As she was non-UK resident for over five years, she remains exempt from UK CGT on the remaining part of the gains realised in 2026/27.

Emigrating has saved Eleanor £3.12m in UK CGT (£8m + £5m = £13m x 24%): the tax she has avoided on her pre-April 2015 residential property gains and her pre-April 2019 commercial property gains.

In fact, she can probably save even more, since a non-UK resident subject to CGT on UK property can compute their taxable gain in one of three ways, and may choose the best option on a *property by property basis*:

i) The gain arising using the property's market value in April 2015 (plus any subsequent improvement expenditure) as the base cost
ii) The gain arising using the property's actual base cost and time apportioning that gain so that only the proportion arising after 5th April 2015 is taxable
iii) The whole gain arising as computed under normal principles

For non-residential property, simply substitute 2019 for 2015 in (i) and (ii). Option (iii) will rarely be the most beneficial, so it is usually a choice between options (i) and (ii).

Example Continued: *Let's assume one of Eleanor's residential properties was purchased in April 1987 for £100,000, was worth £600,000 in April 2015, and was sold for £900,000 in April 2027.*

The taxable gain under option (i) is £300,000 (£900,000 – £600,000). Using option (ii), it would be £240,000 (£900,000 – £100,000 = £800,000 x 12/40).

By using option (ii), Eleanor can reduce her taxable gain on this property by £60,000, saving her a further £14,400 in CGT: and she can make this choice on a property by property basis across her entire portfolio (including her commercial property).

But Remember: Utopia does not exist! Real countries have their own tax systems and may tax immigrants like Eleanor on their UK capital gains. It is therefore essential to take professional advice in your destination country.

Becoming Non-UK Resident

Special rules apply to individuals working full-time overseas and individuals who maintain a home in the UK without having a home overseas. Individuals working full-time in the UK for even part of the year may also be deemed UK resident.

Apart from individuals working full-time overseas, you will usually remain UK resident for the whole of the tax year in which you depart and become UK resident again for the whole of the tax year in which you return.

Subject to these points, to achieve, or maintain, non-UK resident status, you simply need to limit your visits to the UK. The maximum number of days a non-UK resident may spend in the UK is determined by the number of 'ties' they have. The ties for this purpose are:

i) **The Family Tie**: The individual has a spouse, common-law partner, or minor child resident in the UK. A minor child need only be counted if the individual sees them on more than 60 days in the tax year. Separated spouses do not need to be counted.
ii) **The Accommodation Tie**: The individual has a home or other accommodation available to them in the UK for at least 91 consecutive days during the tax year and spends at least one night there during the tax year (or spends at least 16 nights there if the available accommodation is the home of a close relative).
iii) **The Work Tie**: The individual works in the UK for more than three hours on at least 40 days during the tax year.
iv) **The 90-Day Tie**: The individual spent more than 90 days in the UK in either of the two previous tax years.
v) **The Country Tie**: There is no other country where the individual was present at midnight on more days during the tax year than in the UK.

The maximum permitted visits to the UK depend on whether the individual was UK resident in any of the three previous tax years. The middle column below applies if they **were** UK resident in **any** of those years. The right-hand column applies if they were **not** UK resident in any of those years and, in this case, the country tie is disregarded.

Maximum Return Visits to UK

No. of Ties	**Res in last 3 Years**	**Not Res last 3 Years**
0	182 Days	182 Days
1	120 Days	182 Days
2	90 Days	120 Days
3	45 Days	90 Days
4 or 5	15 Days	45 Days

The general rule is any day on which you are present in the UK at midnight is counted for the purpose of these tests. In other words, we actually count nights rather than days!

9.36 NEW ARRIVALS

In Section 9.35, we looked at those leaving the UK. The opposite side of the coin is, of course, new arrivals becoming UK resident (the same statutory residence test applies… broadly speaking). Here again, there are tax planning opportunities.

From 2025/26 onwards, individuals resident in the UK for no more than four UK tax years after having been non-UK resident for at least ten consecutive UK tax years prior to becoming UK resident, are able to claim exemption from: UK Income Tax on overseas income, including overseas property income; and UK CGT on disposals of overseas assets, including foreign property.

Qualifying individuals can opt whether to claim the exemption on a year by year basis, but there is a cost: if the exemption is claimed, the individual loses entitlement to their Income Tax personal allowance and CGT annual exemption. Nonetheless, the exemption will generally be worthwhile for an individual with any of the following:

- Foreign income of at least £12,570, or £16,170 if they have any UK capital gains
- Total taxable income (if they had not claimed the exemption) of at least £125,140, or £126,740 if they have any UK capital gains
- Foreign capital gains of at least £26,569 (£27,616 from 2027/28 onwards)
- No UK income or gains

The exemption will still be worthwhile in many other cases, but you will need to do the number crunching.

Short-term residents remain UK residents for most other UK tax purposes, although individuals becoming UK resident after being non-UK resident for at least ten consecutive UK tax years may be exempt from UK IHT on overseas property and certain other assets for up to nine years. See the Taxcafe guide *How to Save Inheritance Tax* for more information.

Appendix A

UK Tax Rates and Allowances: 2025/26 to 2027/28

	2025/26	2026/27	2027/28
Income Tax (1)			
Personal allowance	£12,570	£12,570	£12,570
Basic rate band	£37,700	£37,700	£37,700
Main basic rate	20%	20%	20%
Property/savings (2)	20%	20%	22%
Dividends	8.75%	10.75%	10.75%
Higher rate threshold	£50,270	£50,270	£50,270
Main higher rate	40%	40%	40%
Property/savings (3)	40%	40%	42%
Dividends	33.75%	35.75%	35.75%
Personal allowance withdrawal	£100,000	£100,000	£100,000
Additional rate threshold	£125,140	£125,140	£125,140
Main additional rate	45%	45%	45%
Property/savings	45%	45%	47%
Dividends	39.35%	39.35%	39.35%
Starting rate band (2)	£5,000	£5,000	£5,000
Dividend allowance	£500	£500	£500
Marriage allowance (4)	£1,260	£1,260	£1,260
National Insurance			
Primary Threshold	£12,570	£12,570	£12,570
Rate: Directors (Class 1)	8%	8%	8%
Self-Employed (Class 4)	6%	6%	6%
Upper earnings limit (UEL)	£50,270	£50,270	£50,270
Additional rate above UEL	2%	2%	2%
Secondary Threshold	£5,000	£5,000	£5,000
Rate: Employers	15%	15%	15%
Employment allowance	£10,500	£10,500	£10,500

Notes

1. Different rates and thresholds apply to Scottish taxpayers (except on savings income and dividends)
2. Savings income falling into the starting rate band, or covered by a personal savings allowance of £1,000 is exempt
3. Savings income covered by a personal savings allowance of £500 is exempt
4. Available where neither spouse/civil partner pays higher rate tax

Appendix B

Connected Persons

The definition of connected persons differs slightly from one area of UK tax law to another. The definition applying for CGT, SDLT, and Corporation Tax purposes is set out below, and also forms a reasonable guide to the definition for other purposes.

An individual's connected persons include:

i) Their husband, wife, or civil partner
ii) The following relatives:
    - Mother, father or remoter ancestor
    - Son, daughter or remoter descendant
    - Brother or sister
iii) Relatives under (ii) of the individual's spouse or civil partner
iv) Spouses or civil partners of the individual's relatives under (ii)
v) Spouses or civil partners of an individual under (iii)
vi) The individual's business partners and their:
    - Spouses or civil partners
    - Relatives (as defined under (ii) above)
vii) Trusts where the individual is:
    - The settlor (the person who set up the trust or transferred property, other assets, or funds into it), or
    - A person connected (as defined in this appendix) with the settlor
viii) Companies under the control of the individual, either alone, or together with persons under (i) to (vii) above
ix) Companies under the control of the individual acting together with one or more other persons

Appendix C

Abbreviations Used in this Guide

ADS	Additional Dwelling Supplement
AIA	Annual Investment Allowance
API	Application Programming Interface
BADR	Business Asset Disposal Relief
CBC	Child Benefit Charge
CGT	Capital Gains Tax
CIS	Construction Industry Scheme
CO2	Carbon Dioxide
CPI	Consumer Price Index
EEA	European Economic Area
EIS	Enterprise Investment Scheme
FHL	Furnished Holiday Let or Letting
HMO	House in Multiple Occupation
HMRC	HM Revenue and Customs
ICAEW	Institute of Chartered Accountants in England and Wales
IHT	Inheritance Tax
LBTT	Land and Buildings Transaction Tax
LLP	Limited Liability Partnership
LTT	Land Transaction Tax
MIRAS	Mortgage Interest Relief At Source
MTD	Making Tax Digital
NI	National Insurance
PAT	Portable Appliance Testing
PAYE	Pay As You Earn
PLR	Private Letting Relief
PRR	Private Residence Relief
SBA	Structures and Buildings Allowance
SDLT	Stamp Duty Land Tax
SPA	State Pension Age
SPV	Special Purpose Vehicle
TV	Television
UK	United Kingdom of Great Britain and Northern Ireland
USA	United States of America
UTR	Unique Taxpayer Reference
VAT	Value Added Tax

www.ingramcontent.com/pod-product-compliance
Lightning Source LLC
LaVergne TN
LVHW022156200926
848481LV00006B/1770